THE ART OF RAILWAY PHO
—a pictorial manu

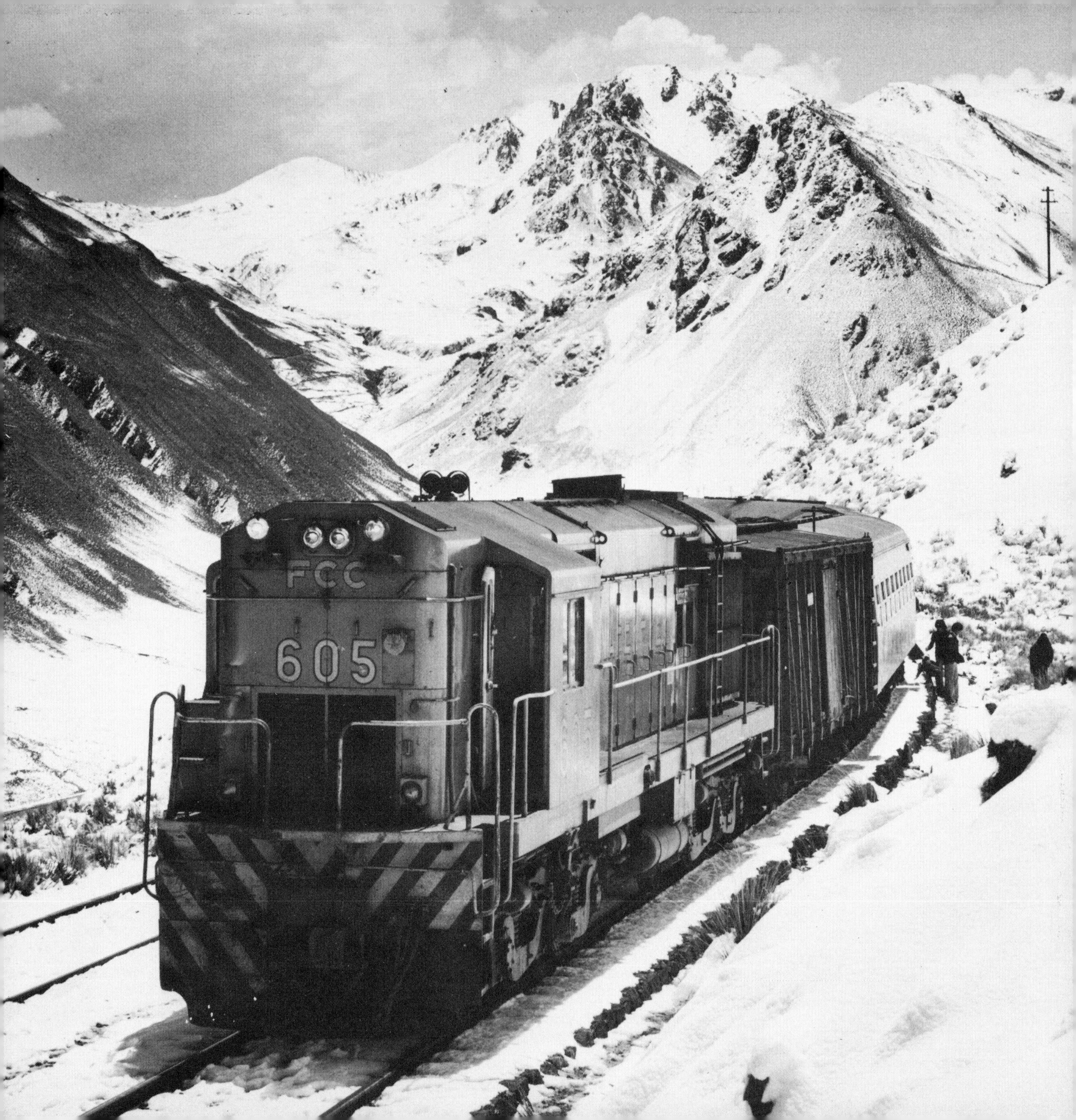
FCC
605

THE ART OF RAILWAY PHOTOGRAPHY

a pictorial manual of photo-technique

L.A. NIXON

D. BRADFORD BARTON LTD

Frontispiece:
Central Railway of Peru diesel electric No.606 pauses at Meiggs, 14,000 feet above sea level, with a Lima to Huancayo train in August 1976.

Pentax 6 × 7 105mm Takumar FP4 D76 (1:1) 1/500th second f 6.3, exposure meter reading 1/500th second f 11.

9805/3LB *ISBN 0 85153 367 1*

printed in Great Britain by H. E. Warne Ltd, London and St. Austell for the publishers

D. BRADFORD BARTON LTD · Trethellan House · Truro · Cornwall · England

CONTENTS

FOREWORD

In recent years railway photography as a hobby has enjoyed a tremendous increase in popularity. Further, the demise of the steam engine and a general upsurge in the interest in railways has meant that more and more cameras are being trained upon railborne subjects.

Railway photography of a high standard is far from easy, and few over the years have achieved consistent outstanding standards which will stand the test of time. The work of the traditional school, for example, F. R. Hebron, T. G. Hepburn and Bishop Eric Treacy, to name but a few, will be long remembered; perhaps not for originality of approach but certainly for technical excellence as well as the outstanding overall quality of their work. A renaissance occurred in the mid-1960s. Standard lenses were apparently consigned to limbo; long focal length lenses became the order of the day, and concepts which had remained unchallenged for years were abandoned almost overnight. It became the fashion to shoot on dull murky days in winter, to point the camera into the sun and to actively encourage grain. Predictably this reaction was extreme and fortunately attitudes have since mellowed and matured; both schools of thought now enjoy a peaceful, if at times uneasy, co-existence. A recognition that there are many ways of expression through the photographic medium is essential if maximum enjoyment from the hobby is to be realised. An awareness and an appreciation of other photographers' work may be realised in a number of ways; the regular perusal of magazines and books, membership of a photographic society, or active participation in one of the numerous railway photographic postal portfolios are but a few.

The question of what constitutes a good photograph is, however, rather subjective, indeed, to quote a well-known phrase 'one man's meat is another man's poison'. However, a really good photograph is instantly recognised for its real worth by both photographers and non-photographers alike. In this volume are brought together a collection of photographs which I personally find satisfying. They have been chosen to illustrate the wide ranging possibilities open to the serious railway photographer while, at the same time, identifying some of the fundamental aspects of equipment, technique, composition and presentation. It is my hope that both beginners and more advanced workers will find something both of interest and of value in the following pages. If the reader is further inspired to venture forth with a renewed interest and enthusiasm for railway photography then I shall feel well satisfied.

TECHNICAL ASPECTS

My very earliest photographs were taken with an elderly pre-war box camera costing, at the time, less than £1. This very modest instrument boasted a single shutter speed, 1/25th second, and an aperture which could be varied by moving a strip of metal drilled with three different-sized holes behind the single element meniscus lens. Surprisingly, central definition of the 6 × 9cm negatives was quite good, as this photograph of 'Castle' Class No.5075 *Wellington* at Chester shed in May 1951 shows.
I vividly recall wasting yards of film in fruitless attempts to obtain reasonable pictures of trains on the move.

Brownie Box 6 × 9cm   120 Verichrome film   exposure and process details not recorded.

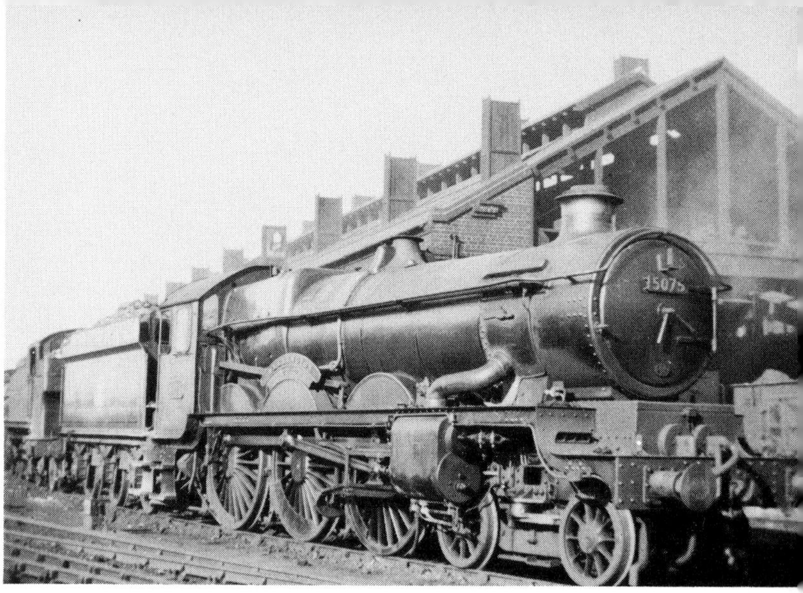

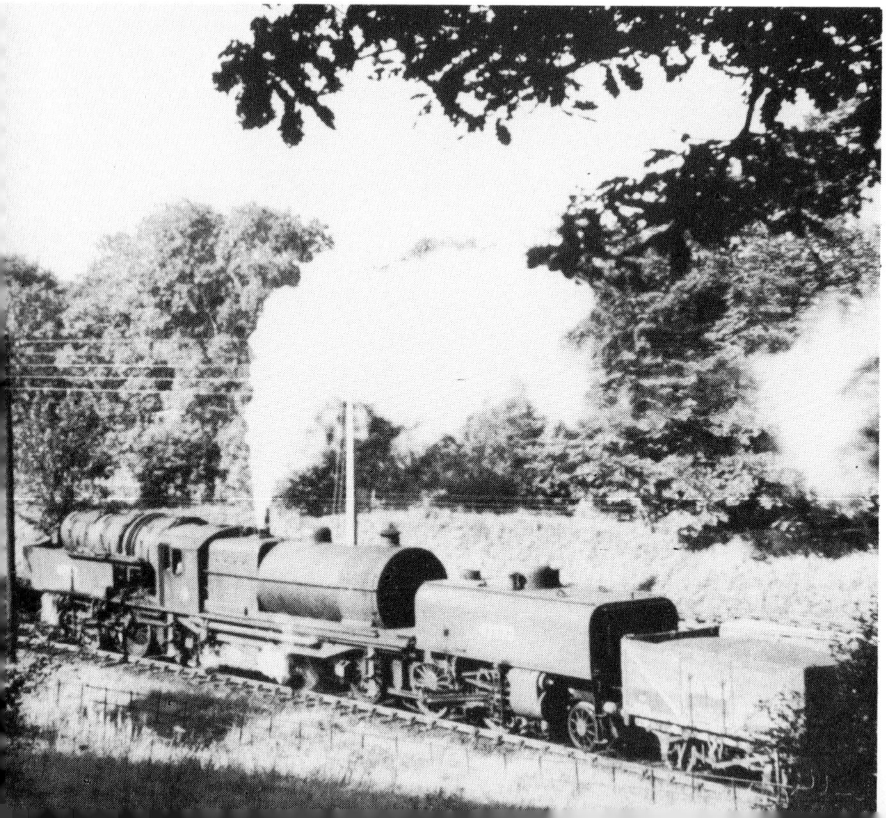

Virtually all cameras on the market today will produce at least the equal in quality of this study of ex-L M S Garratt No.47972 rounding the curve at Totley towards the Hope Valley in the summer of 1952. Close inspection reveals that none of the photograph is critically sharp, indicative of a very modest lens performance. The fact that the camera, a Boots Bencini Comet, had a maximum shutter speed of only 1/100th second also meant that camera shake was, more often than not, present—particularly if one had to rush to the location at the last moment to catch a passing locomotive. [T. Dodgson]

Boots Bencini Comet   Selochrome   exposure and process details not recorded.

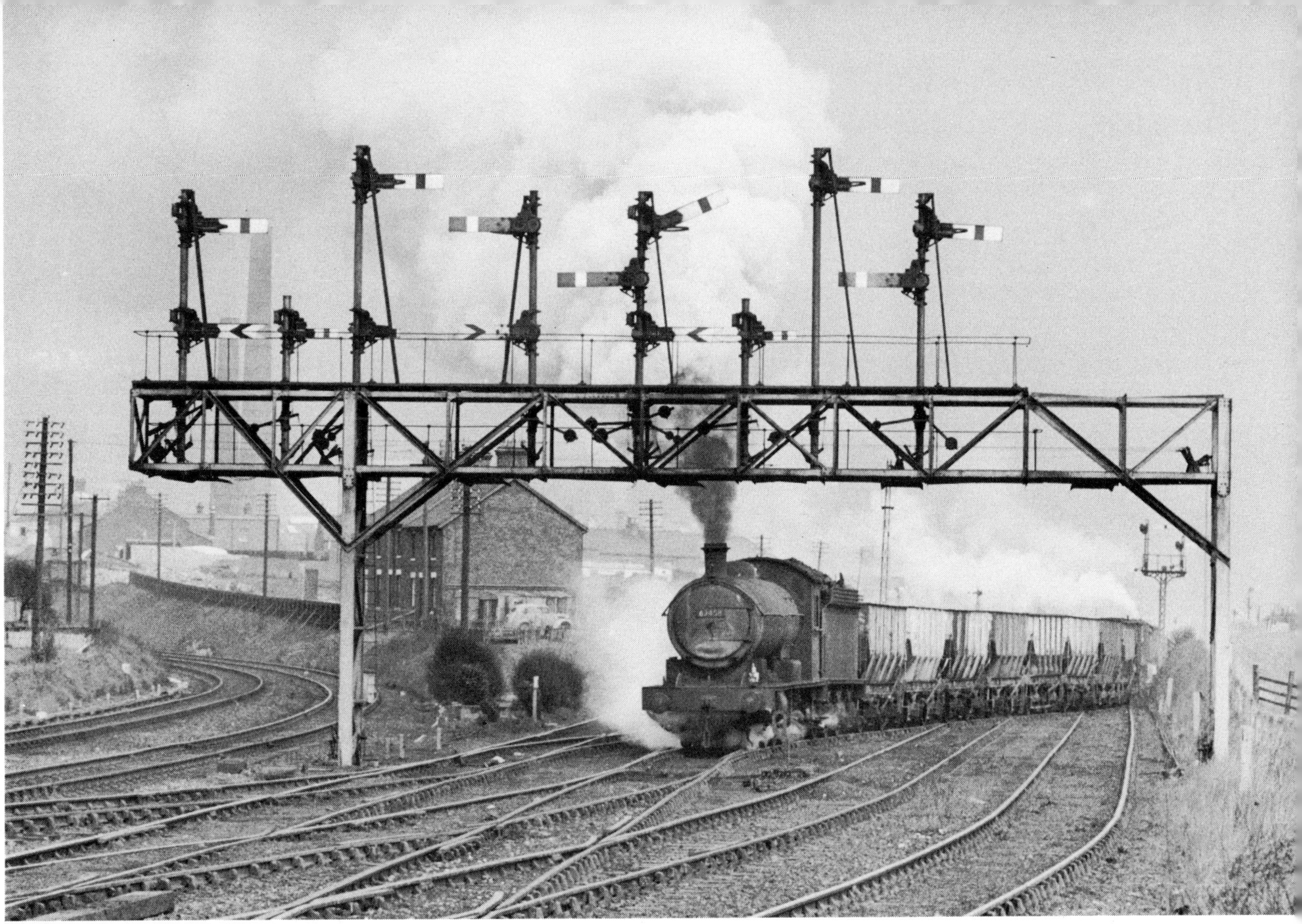

Most amateur photographers use 35mm cameras for both black-and-white as well as colour photography. The advantages of this format are numerous; small compact size, a wide variety of cameras, both as regards make and price, the generous depth of field given by even medium focal length lenses and the relatively low cost of film are but a few. Even modestly priced 35mm cameras of the present generation are capable of producing technically first class results, but the attainment of *consistent* quality is far from easy. The slightest imperfection in a 24 × 36mm negative will appear as a very obvious defect in a whole plate (21.5 × 16.5cm print), whereas in a 6 × 7cm negative it would be barely noticeable. For a given print size, the degree of enlargement from the smaller 35mm negative is almost four times that required from the 6 × 7cm format. In 35mm work the careful control of exposure and development (to minimise grain and to optimise tonal qualities), along with the meticulous exclusion of dust, grit and hairs from the jaws of the cassette and the negative are essential if the best results are to be obtained. The photograph above was taken with an Exakta Varex IIa camera fitted with an 80mm Zeiss Biometer lens; the technical quality is adequate, but imperfections are becoming apparent even at this modest degree of enlargement. Note the indifferent definition, poor tonal quality and the blemishes in the sky.

Class Q6 0-8-0 No. 63458 approaching Ryhope Junction near Sunderland in August 1966.

Exakta Varex IIa 80mm Biometer FP4 Acutol 1/250th second f 6.3.

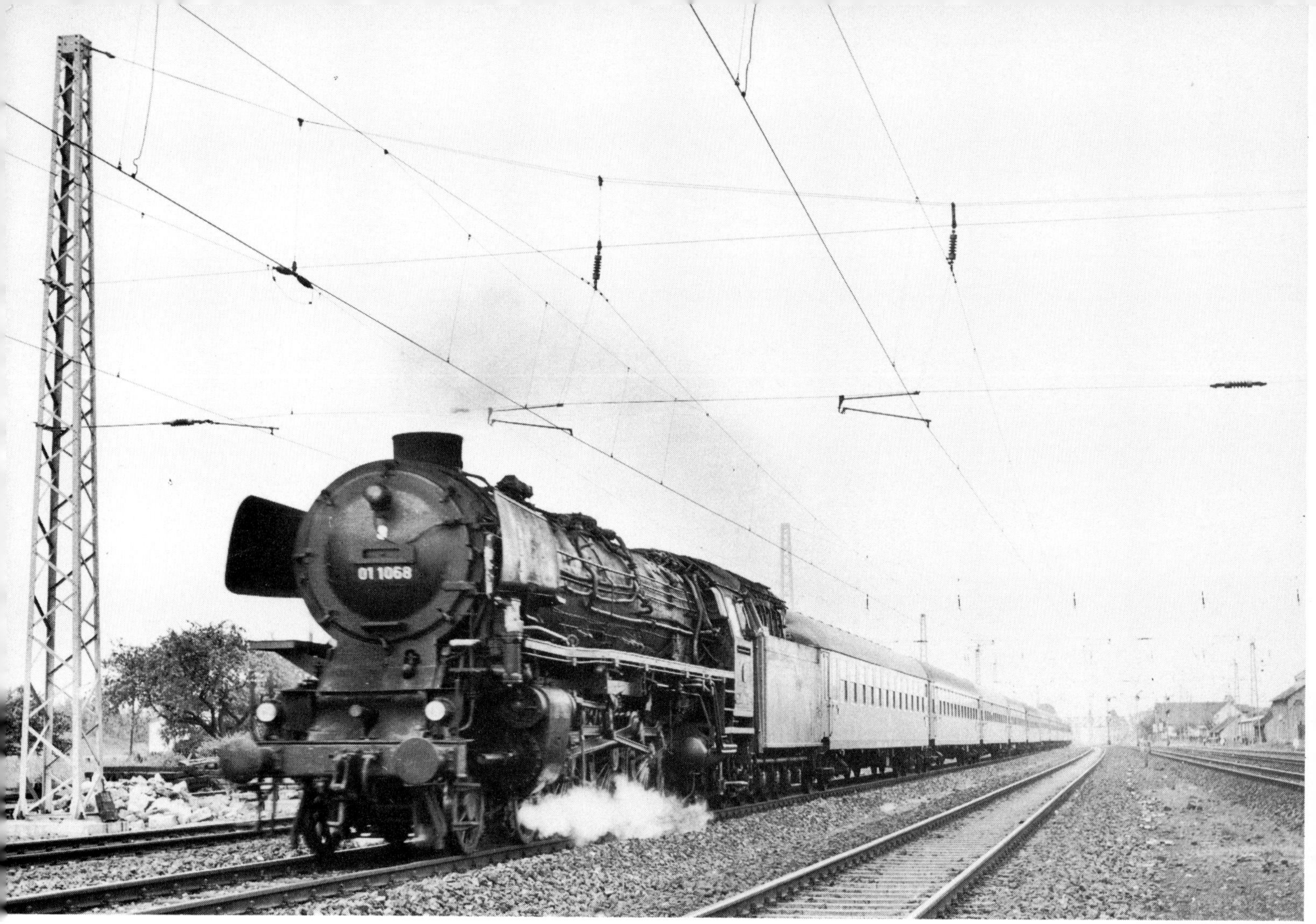

The less expensive medium format cameras, such as the Minolta Autocord or Yashicamat twin lens reflex, are usually fitted with an in-between-the-lens iris type shutter. In operation the iris is fully opened and then closed by a complicated spring mechanism, variable effective shutter speeds being obtained by altering the spring tensions. This arrangement has quite severe limitations as far as the minimum realisable shutter speed is concerned. Simply, whatever the applied spring tension, a minimum time is required to complete the shutter cycle and this is usually found to be in the region of 1/400th second; this in spite of the fact that the camera may boast a 1/500th second on the speed selection dial. Obviously with older cameras shutter springs may have gradually become less efficient, with the result that the fastest shutter speed available may only be of the order of 1/250th second. Not that this is of any great concern if one is attempting to photograph subjects which are moving at less than about 35 m.p.h., but it is a totally different story with fast-moving expresses. A train travelling at 60 m.p.h.—a modest speed by today's standards—will travel no less than four inches in 1/250th second and speed blur becomes almost inevitable, as in this photograph of West German Railways (D.B.) Class 01 Pacific No.01 1068, travelling at about 65 m.p.h. near Bohmte on 2 June 1968. The effect can be minimised by altering the camera to subject angle. Blur will be most pronounced when subjects move across the field of view and at a minimum when the camera faces the subject in an almost head-on position. With a train travelling at 60 m.p.h., the former situation would require a shutter speed of at least 1/1000th second and the latter 1/250th second to completely arrest movement.

Minolta Autocord 6 × 6 75mm Rokkor Tri-X D76 (1:1) 1/500th second f 6.3.

The classic three quarter front study of a steam locomotive at work depends heavily upon technical excellence for success. Undoubtedly the user of a modern medium/large format camera, fitted with a focal plane shutter rated at 1/1000th second, has a distinct advantage over a less well-equipped colleague. A fast film may be used without fear of excessive grain since only relatively small enlargements will be required. On the debit side problems may be experienced with limited depth of field even when a standard lens is used. In this study of Royal Scot No.6115 *Scots Guardsman* at speed near Burton Salmon the exposure, on Tri-X film developed in D76 (1:1), was 1/1000th second at f 4.5. Although the definition of the locomotive is beyond reproach the rear half of the train is far from sharp. Note the selection of a vantage point to show the train on a curve with a weak hazy sun in a three quarter rear position.

Pentax 6 × 7 105mm Takumar Tri-X D76 (1:1)
1/1000th second f 4.5.

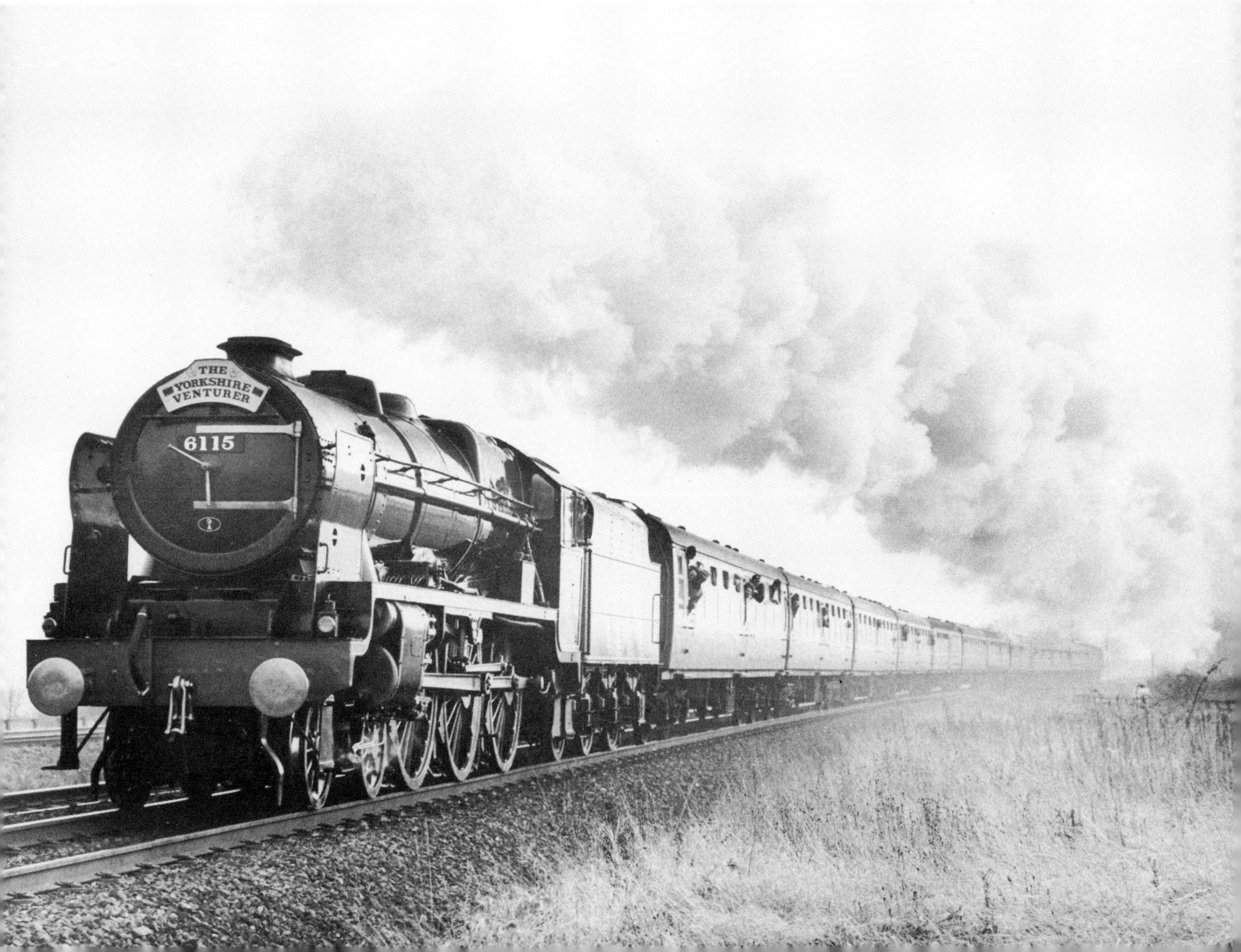

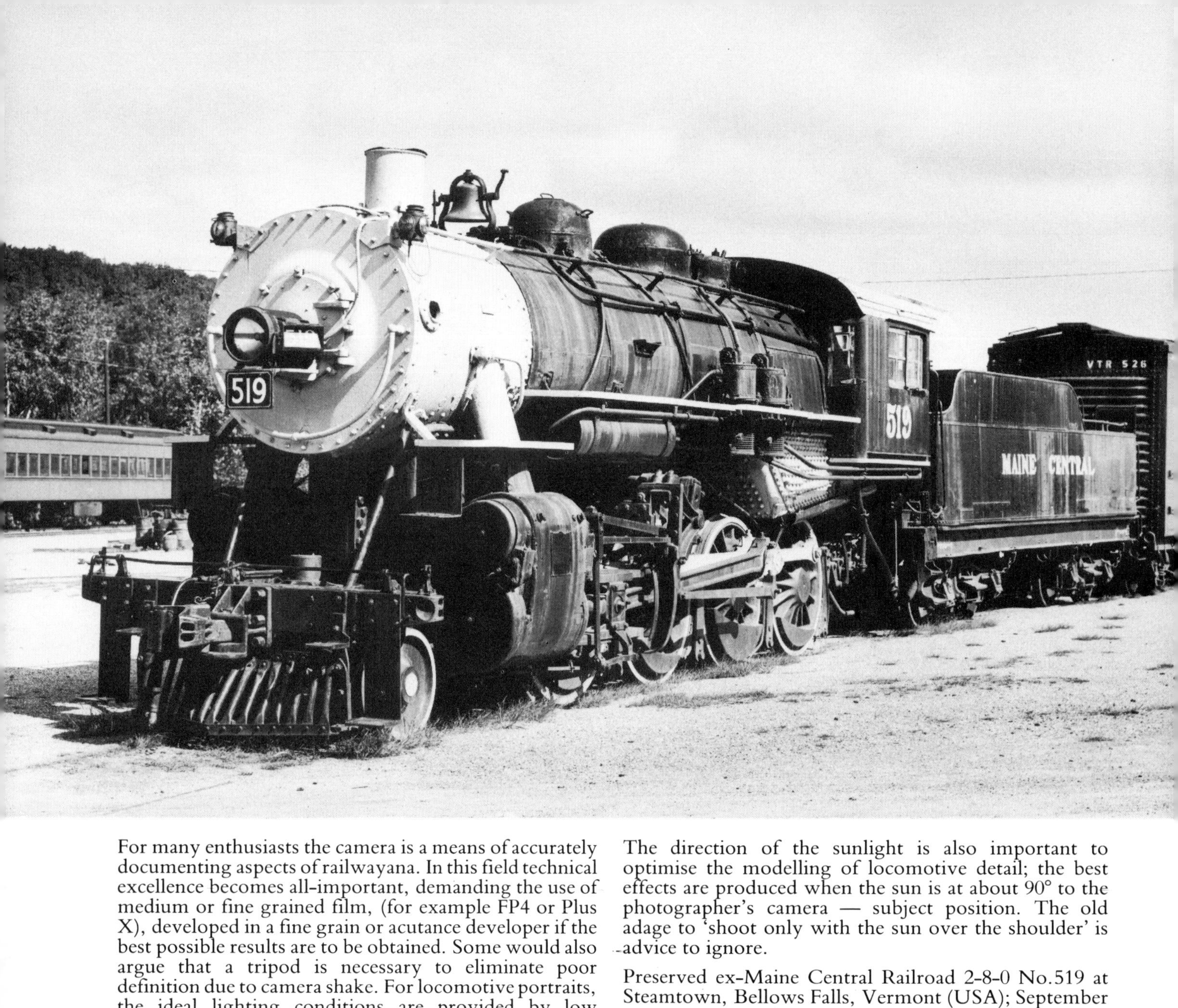

For many enthusiasts the camera is a means of accurately documenting aspects of railwayana. In this field technical excellence becomes all-important, demanding the use of medium or fine grained film, (for example FP4 or Plus X), developed in a fine grain or acutance developer if the best possible results are to be obtained. Some would also argue that a tripod is necessary to eliminate poor definition due to camera shake. For locomotive portraits, the ideal lighting conditions are provided by low sunlight either early in the morning or late in the afternoon when obscure parts of the valve gear, wheels, etc. are nicely illuminated. The direction of the sunlight is also important to optimise the modelling of locomotive detail; the best effects are produced when the sun is at about 90° to the photographer's camera — subject position. The old adage to 'shoot only with the sun over the shoulder' is advice to ignore.

Preserved ex-Maine Central Railroad 2-8-0 No.519 at Steamtown, Bellows Falls, Vermont (USA); September 1976.

Pentax 6 × 7 105mm Takumar FP4 D76 (1:1)
1/250th second f 8.

To produce a quality action photograph of a train on a dull but dry day requires an appreciation and complete mastery of the technical aspects of the hobby. Inevitably a fast film such as Kodak Tri-X would be selected and preferably used in a camera producing larger format negatives. Exposure would be just enough to give adequate shadow detail when the film was developed in a genuine fine grain developer such as Microdol X, or Perceptol. Careful printing of the rather thin negative on a hard grade of paper should then afford a first class result. The excellent tonal qualities of this photograph, depicting Class 4F 0-6-0 No.43924 at work on the Keighley & Worth Valley Railway during enthusiasts' weekend in 1977, are clearly evident. Microdol X or Perceptol developers will give negatives of moderately fine grain but at the expense of film speed. As a rule of thumb, one extra stop of exposure should be allowed: with for example, normal 400 ASA film, an effective speed of about 200 ASA would be appropriate.

Pentax 6 × 7 Tri-X Perceptol (1:1) 1/250th second f 4.5.

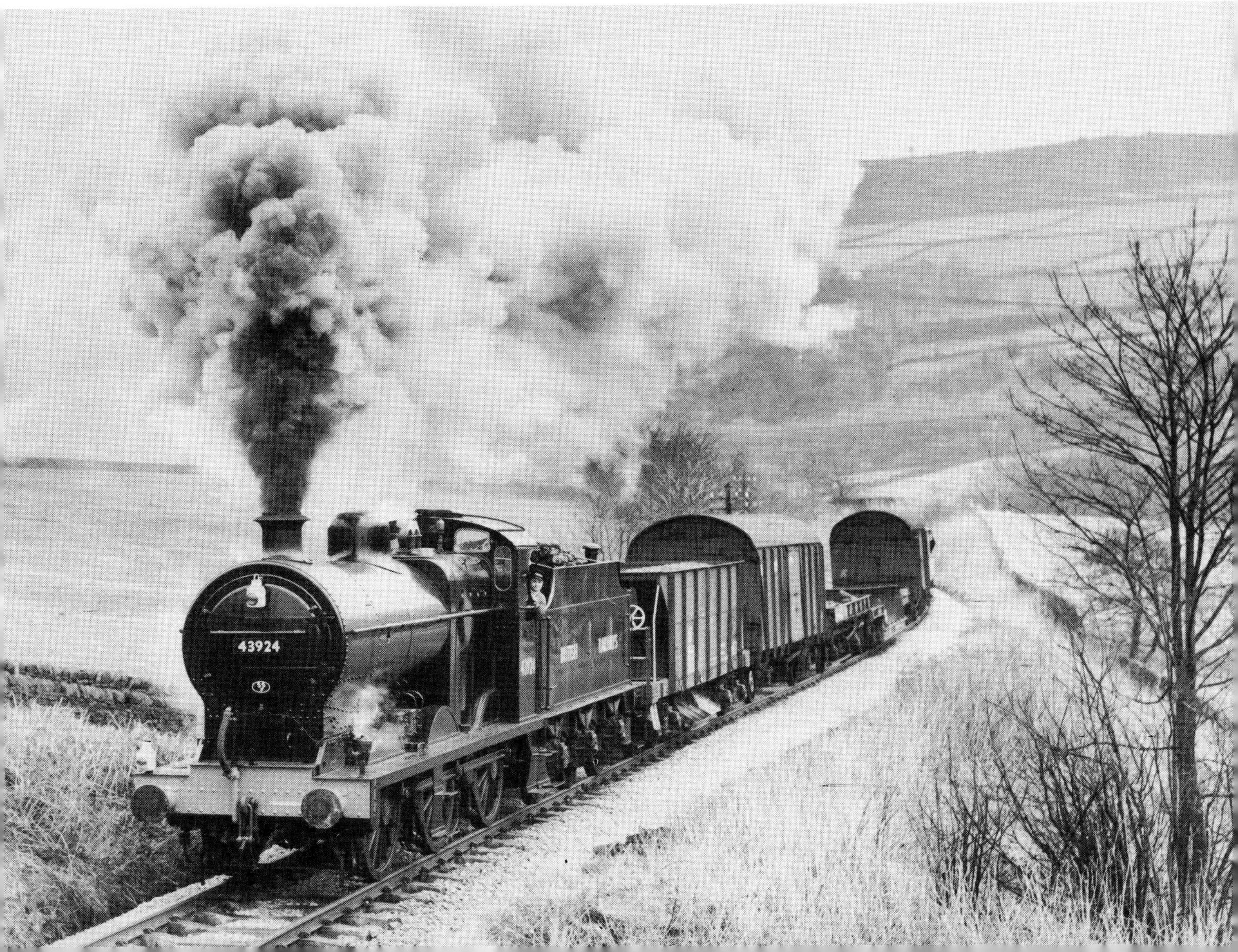

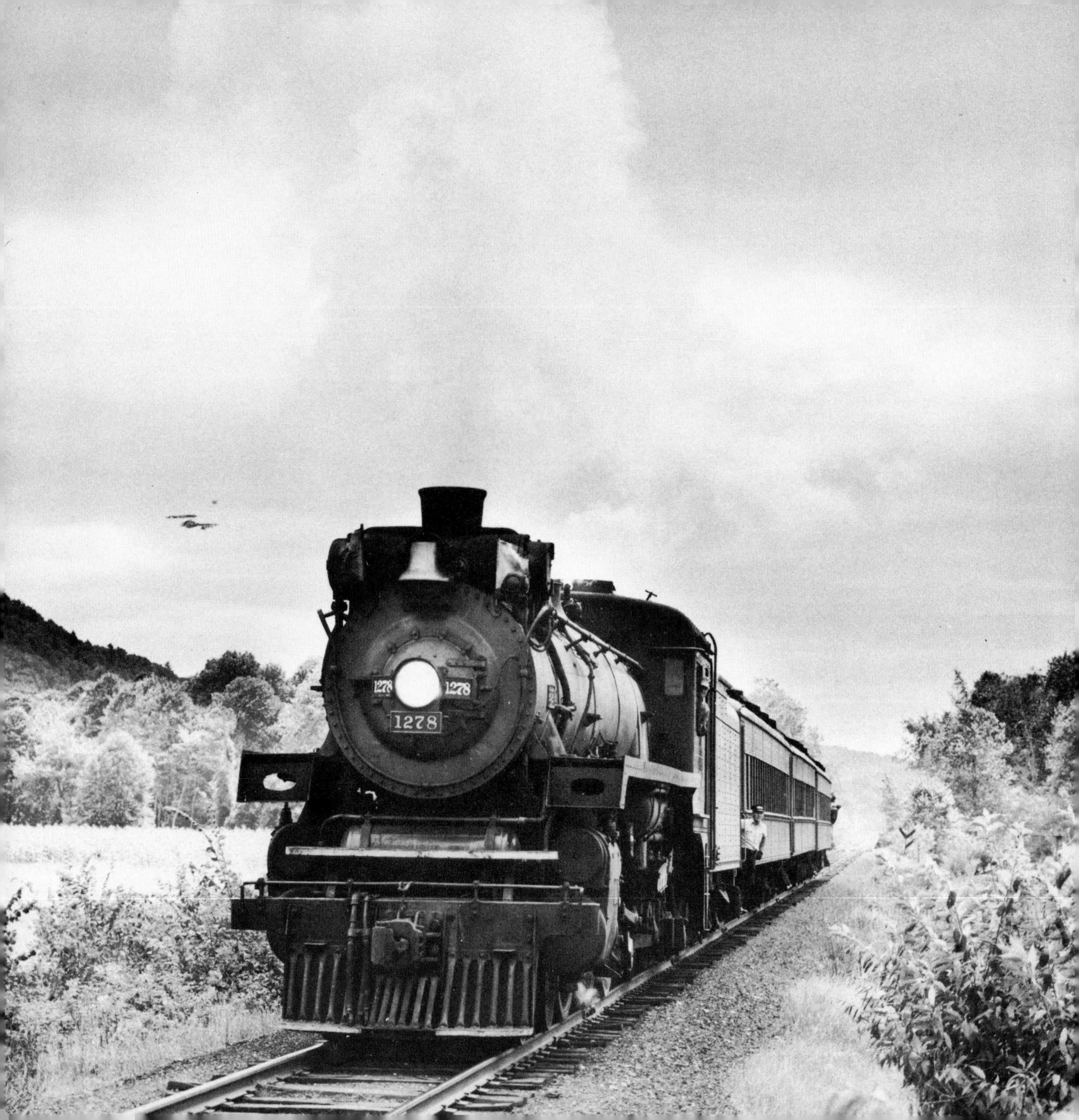
1278
1278
1278

So often excellent work with the camera is ruined at the printing stage. It is quite pointless to have the results of an expensive camera negated by the use of an optically indifferent enlarger; a good instrument should give even illumination over the whole negative area and crisp edge-to-edge definition. Technically, printing is the most demanding aspect of black and white photography and a number of skills need to be acquired. First an ability to match a grade of printing paper to a negative such that the brightest highlight is recorded as almost pure white, the darkest shadow as a true black along with — and this is most important — a full range of intermediate tones. Secondly it must be recognised that a printing paper cannot deal with the same contrast range as a negative and consequently, during exposure of the printing paper, shadow areas may need minimal exposure compared with the highlight regions. The usual procedure is to give extra exposure to the highlights by a process known as 'burning in'. Selected areas, such as the sky tones, may often require more than double the exposure of the rest of the negative to give satisfactory tones. Dextrous use of the hands is probably the best way to achieve this selective additional exposure; the hands being continually on the move so that tones will merge smoothly one into the other. This has not been optimised in the photograph opposite where the extra exposure has been, inadvertently, extended to include the trees on the skyline to the left of the locomotive. Additionally note the presence of a slight halo around the engine and train. Finally, the appearance of a black-and-white print is enhanced considerably by careful attention to detail. Even with meticulous darkroom work specks of dust and small hairs may find their way on to the negative during enlargement, particularly when glass negative carriers are used. The negative may also collect dust and dirt during the drying stage and it may well be found that the particles adhere very tenaciously to the emulsion surface and defy all attempts of removal. Here prevention is better than cure; processed films should be dried, if at all possible, in a calm, warm and dust free atmosphere. Perfect images of any intrusion will, of course, show on the print as white blemishes but they are easily obscured by spotting with a print dye such as those marketed by Winsor & Newton Ltd. The dyes are available in two colours, blue/black or brown/black; the former gives the best colour match for bromide papers. This technique may also be used for deleting other unwanted highlight areas from a print as shown on page 58.

It is much less common to find negative imperfections which lead to unwanted black spots in a print; these usually arise from imperfections in the emulsion or from mechanical damage during processing. Providing the spots are quite small they can be removed by careful treatment with a sharp retouching knife. This simply involves removal of part of the surface of the print in the region of the spot using the knife with a delicate stabbing movement. The damage to the print surface may be apparent, particularly with glossy prints, if the print is viewed critically from certain angles.

Both types of defect are present in this photograph of preserved Canadian Pacific Class G5d 4-6-2 at work at Steamtown (Vermont, USA) in August 1976.

Pentax 6 × 7 105mm Takumar Tri-X D76 (1:1) 1/500th second f 8.

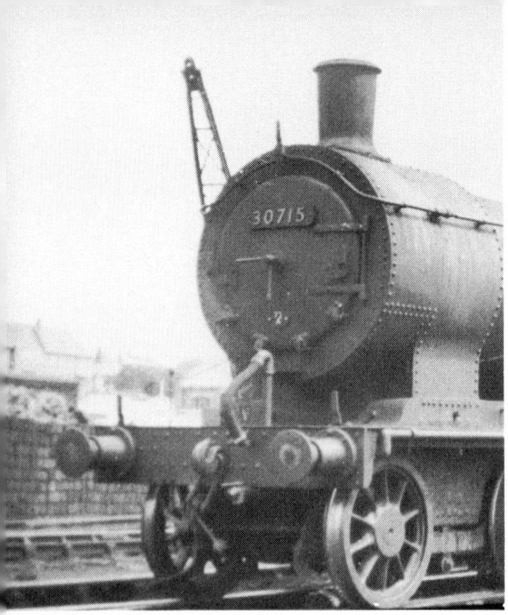

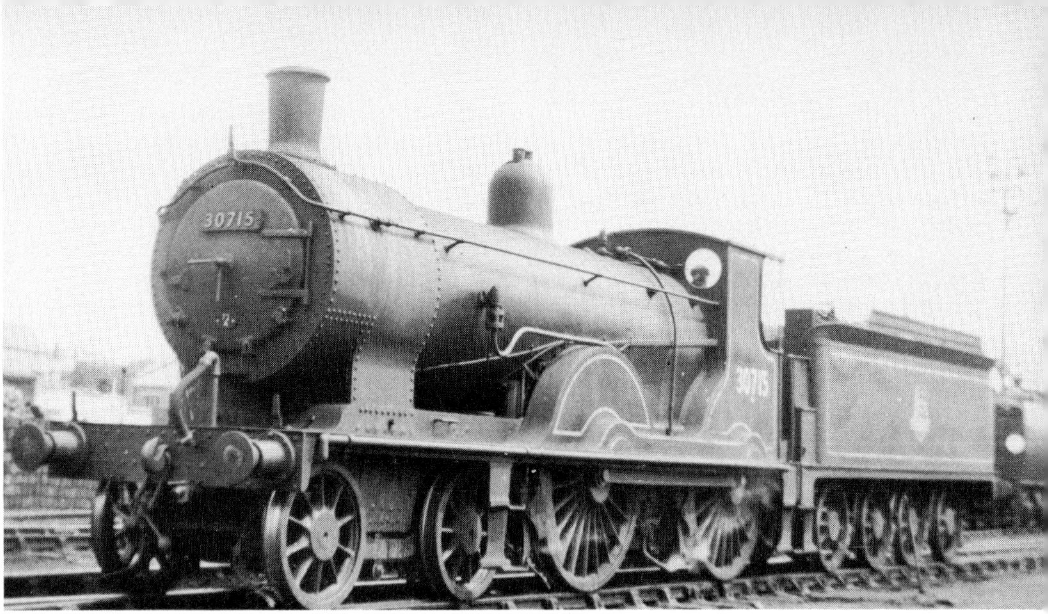

One of the advantages of black-and-white photography is the way in which technical improvements may be attempted after the vital moment the shutter is pressed. For example, developers and development times may be varied to suit the occasion but more importantly, perhaps, negatives may be modified to good effect. The pure record photographer may, predictably, throw up his hands in horror at the very thought of modifying the faithful image in any way. However, there are occasions when improvements may be readily effected without detriment to the record aspect. Illustrated here is an indifferent locomotive portrait of the ex-L S W R Class T9 4-4-0 No.30715 at Exmouth Junction shed in 1952. Most enthusiasts would condemn the appearance of the crane jib apparently emerging from the smokebox of the T9. To delete the offending ironmongery three methods are available. The first would be to paint out the problem on the negative with photographic opaque — an irreversible process, but one which was used universally in days gone by in the production of 'official' photographs of locomotives. Secondly, one could bleach out the image from the final print with suitable chemicals. Alternatively, the printing paper could be covered at the appropriate place with a carefully shaped piece of card during exposure. The third alternative was used in this case. Note that, whichever of the methods is used, all sky tones will, of necessity, be lost.

Box Brownie 6 × 9cm Selochrome exposure and process details not recorded.

Facing page:

A rather more frequent modification to a photograph is to add some particular feature. Three examples immediately come to mind: the addition of a good exhaust pattern; the inclusion of overhanging branches of a tree to frame a picture; or the addition of clouds. Since the objective is to deceive a viewer into thinking that he is looking at a 'straight' picture, considerable thought and expertise is required. Ingredients must be very carefully matched. For example, a negative might portray a steam locomotive approaching the camera with steam from the safety valves drifting towards the photographer but with no visible exhaust from the chimney. It is entirely possible to 'print in' a smoke effect from another negative but obviously the fall of the smoke should not be in a direction contrary to that of the safety valve steam. Similarly, summer clouds should not be matched with a mid-winter scene; otherwise artistic licence will soon be noticed.

Noting that the technique will only work convincingly with subjects where the locomotive chimney is surrounded by sky tones, the modus operandi for printing in an exhaust is as follows. First make a straightforward exposure of the printing paper using the negative featuring the train. Cover the whole of the printing paper with a thin card, turn on the enlarger lamp, and, without disturbing the position of the card, draw the outline of the smokebox, chimney and boiler. Replace the original negative by the negative featuring the exhaust to be printed in. Alter the degree of enlargement and the position of the paper easel, until the source of the exhaust, when in sharp focus, matches the size of the chimney of the locomotive. Remove the card from the easel, cover the enlarger lens with one hand and turn on the enlarger lamp. Moving both hands continually, expose *only* the exhaust of the second negative for the requisite time. This stage does require some considerable skill if the final result is to be entirely convincing, so be prepared for a few failures before the technique is mastered. This photograph features preserved Class A4 No.4498 *Sir Nigel Gresley* sporting the exhaust of a Taiwan Railways 2-8-2.

Pentax 6 × 7 105mm Takumar Tri-X Perceptol (1:1) 1/500th second f 5.6.

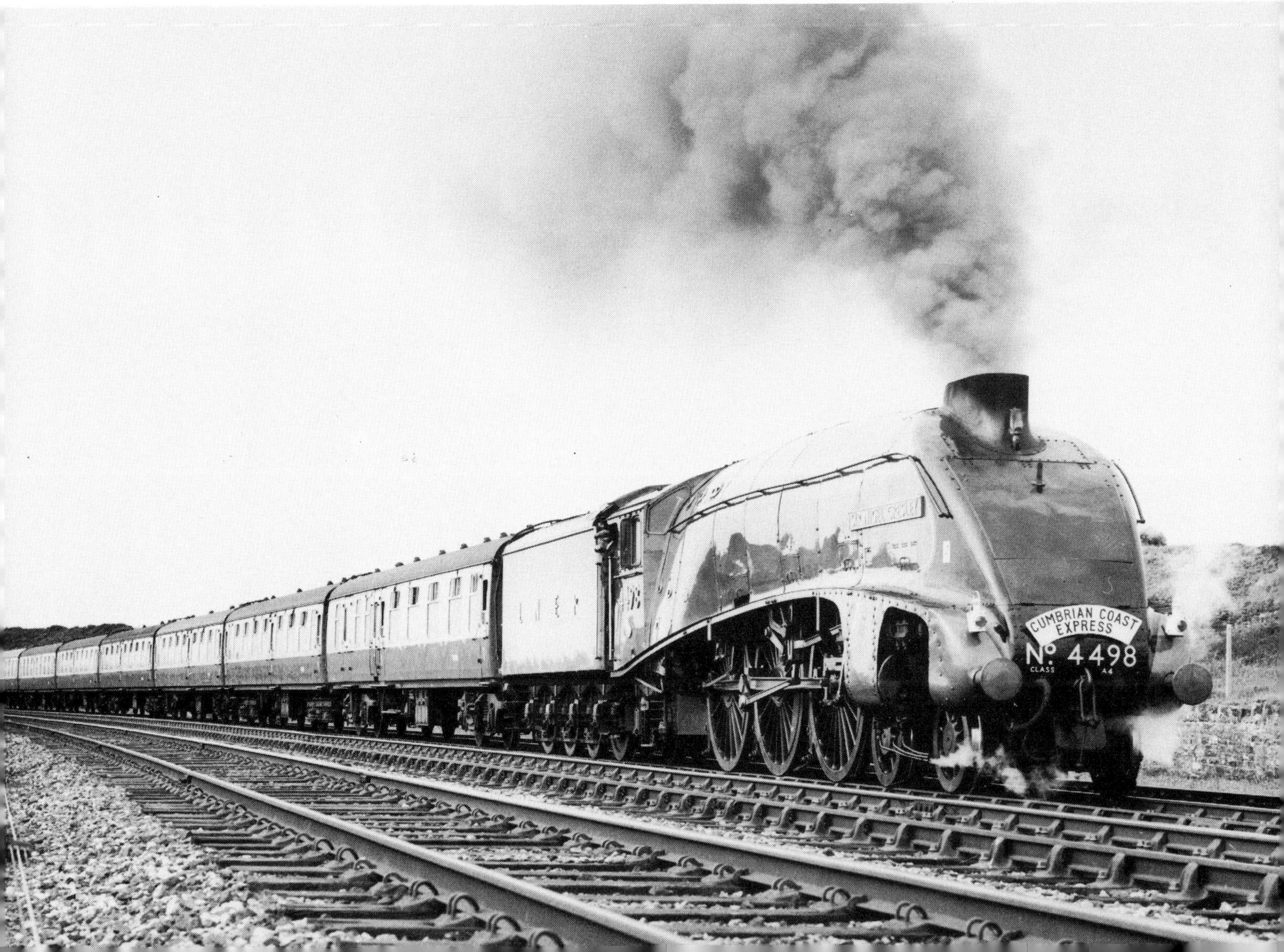

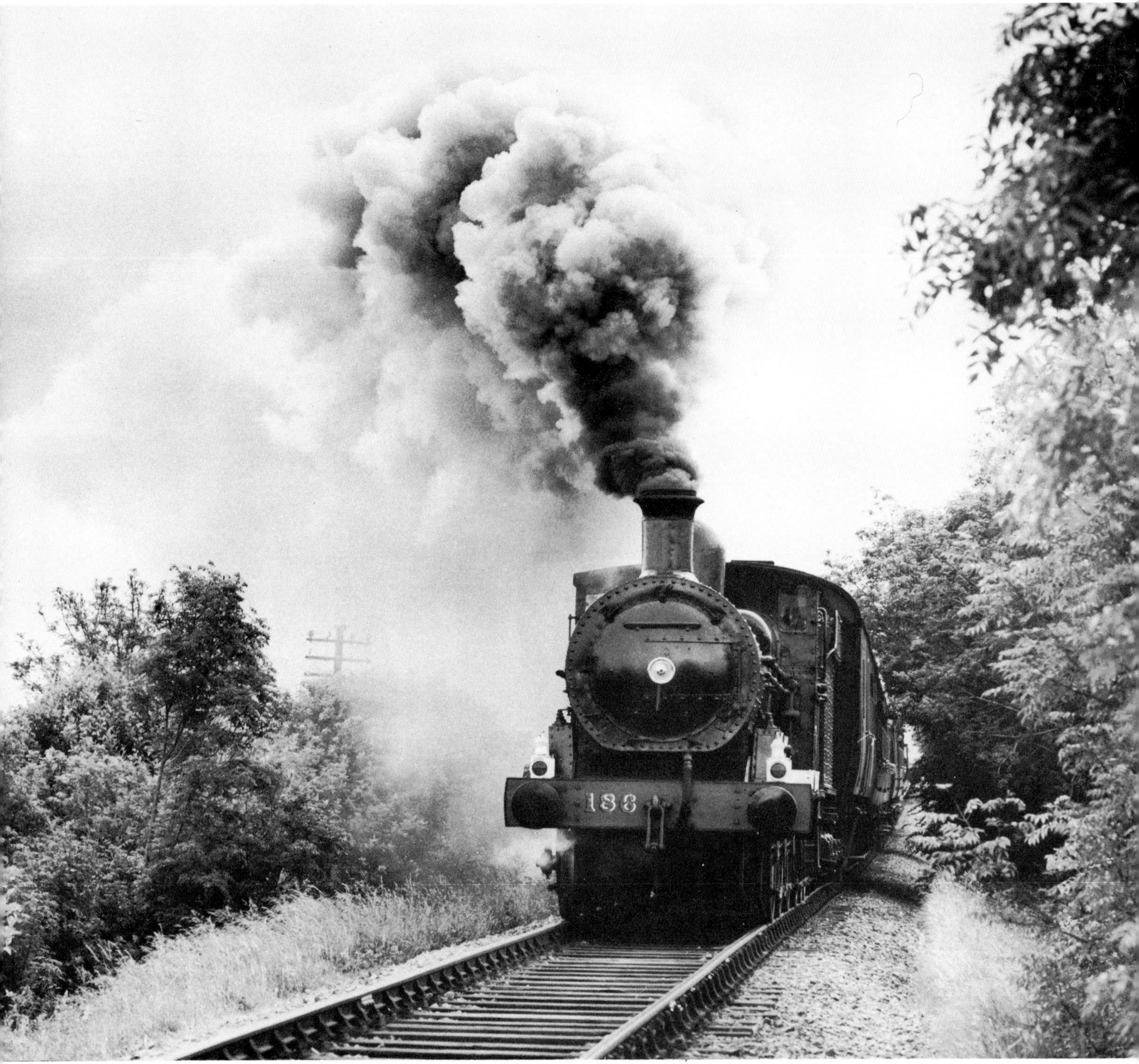
186

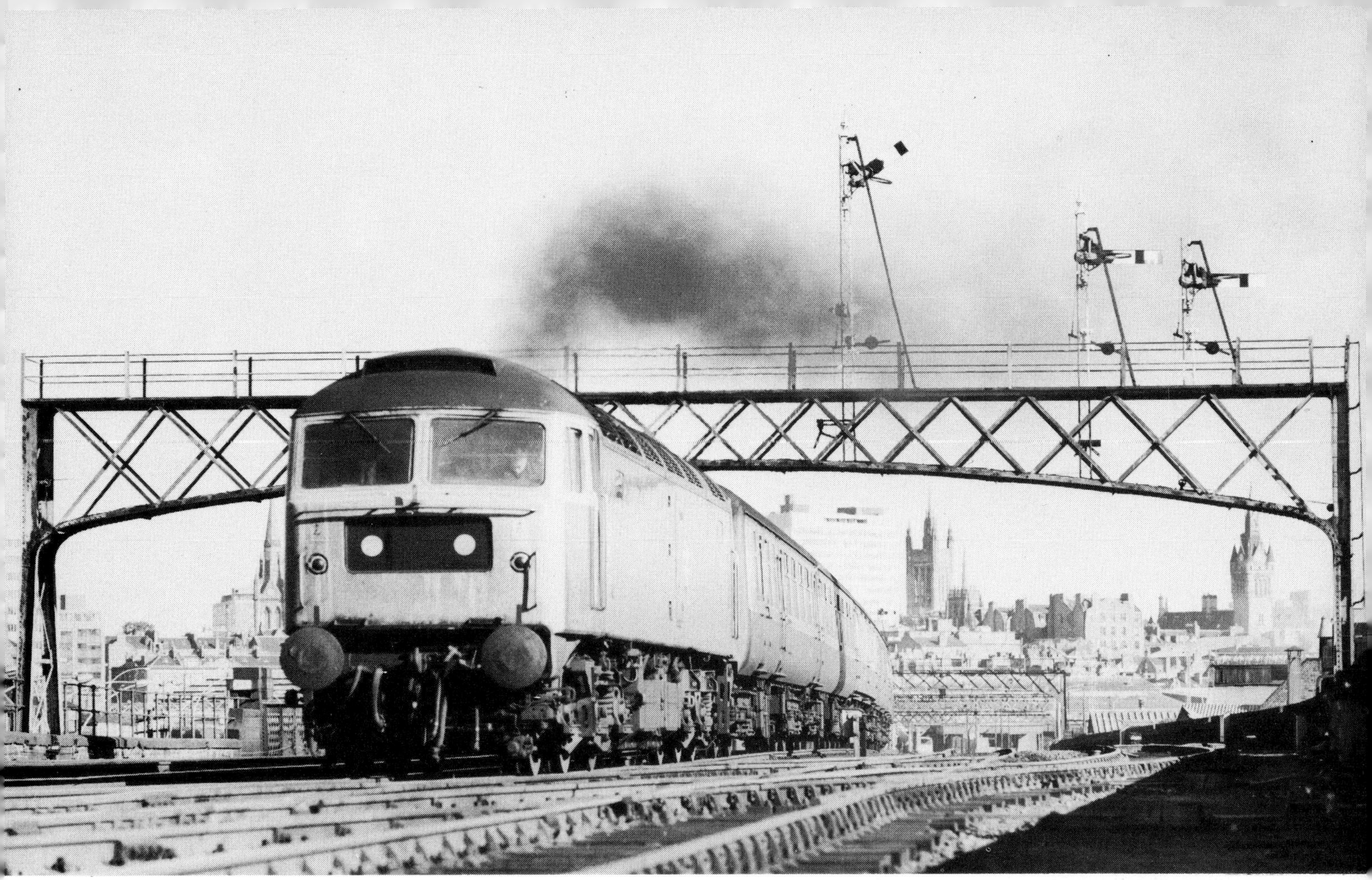

Inspiring locations are difficult to find in East Anglia or in the flat featureless bogs of central Ireland. Contrast the number of published photographs taken in the vicinity of Shap, for example, with those depicting trains at work on the L S W R main line to Basingstoke. The intelligent use of a telephoto lens can, however, produce an imposing result in even the most mundane environment, but a photographer should recognise that this technique is no panacea for all occasions, such as was the fashion of the late 1960s. The potential is well illustrated in this scene, with ex-G S W R 0-6-0 No.186 heading a Railway Preservation Society of Ireland excursion north of Athenry on 12 June 1977. Note the selection of a low camera viewpoint to emphasise the interesting shape of the front of the locomotive and the anticipation (from careful observation of the prevailing wind direction) that the exhaust would fill the top left hand corner of the scene. Unfortunately this is a formula which does not often work with modern subjects. An exception is the photograph above of Class 47 No.47 141 leaving Aberdeen with a morning train for Glasgow (Queen Street) on 3 September 1977. Once again, note the low camera angle and the way in which the prominent exhaust pattern brings the picture to life. Luck plays an important part in obtaining a good exhaust in photographs of diesel locomotives at work but a photographer can, up to a point, plan for a good smoke effect. Take the case of No.47 141. In the course of the day's photography this locomotive had already been noted smoking profusely as she worked her down train towards Aberdeen, and it seemed certain that she would oblige on her rostered return working up the steep bank from Aberdeen to Ferryhill.

(Above) Pentax 6 × 7 200mm Takumar FP4 D76 (1:1) 1/500th second f 6.3.

(Opposite) Pentax 6 × 7 200mm Takumar FP4 D76 (1:1) 1/500th second f 6.3.

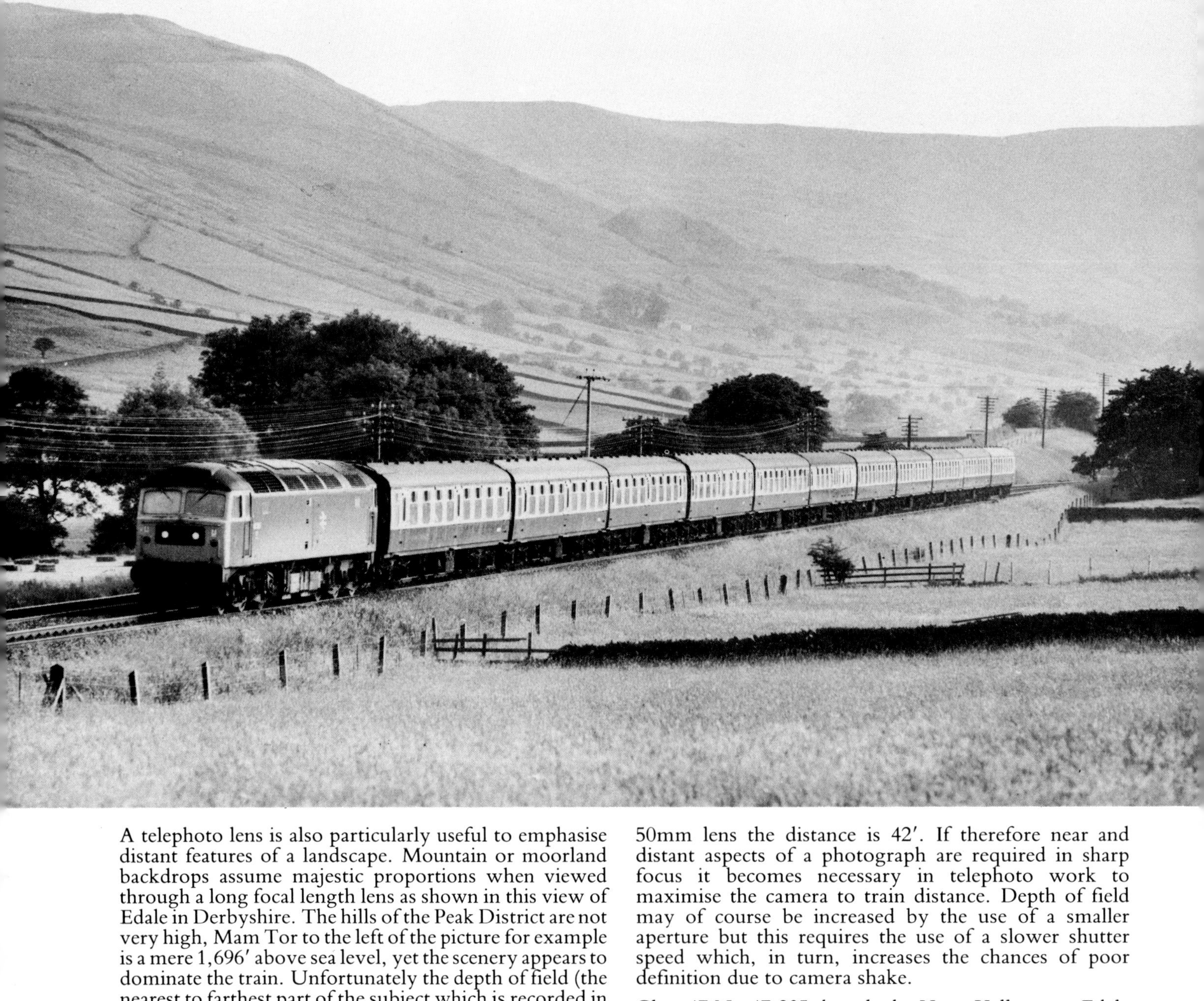

A telephoto lens is also particularly useful to emphasise distant features of a landscape. Mountain or moorland backdrops assume majestic proportions when viewed through a long focal length lens as shown in this view of Edale in Derbyshire. The hills of the Peak District are not very high, Mam Tor to the left of the picture for example is a mere 1,696′ above sea level, yet the scenery appears to dominate the train. Unfortunately the depth of field (the nearest to farthest part of the subject which is recorded in sharp focus) becomes progressively less as the focal length of a lens increases. The nearest object a lens of 135mm focal length, at an aperture of f 4 and focused at infinity, will render sharply is 103′ away whereas for a 50mm lens the distance is 42′. If therefore near and distant aspects of a photograph are required in sharp focus it becomes necessary in telephoto work to maximise the camera to train distance. Depth of field may of course be increased by the use of a smaller aperture but this requires the use of a slower shutter speed which, in turn, increases the chances of poor definition due to camera shake.

Class 47 No.47 235 threads the Hope Valley near Edale with an eastbound excursion in July 1978.

Pentax 6 × 7 135mm Takumar FP4 D76 (1:1)
1/250th second f 6.3.

There are a few occasions when the obvious presence of grain in the final print can be a distinct advantage. The mood and atmosphere of an industrial railway setting on a foggy or rainy winter's day readily lends itself to this sort of treatment. All the ingredients are present in this photograph of an unidentified Stanier Class 5 approaching Engine Shed Junction, Holbeck, Leeds in November 1965. Note the deliberate inclusion of the colour light signal in the immediate foreground; this gives the picture a feeling of depth which accentuates the misty atmosphere.

Exakta Varex IIa 50mm Pancolar FP4 Acutol exposure not recorded.

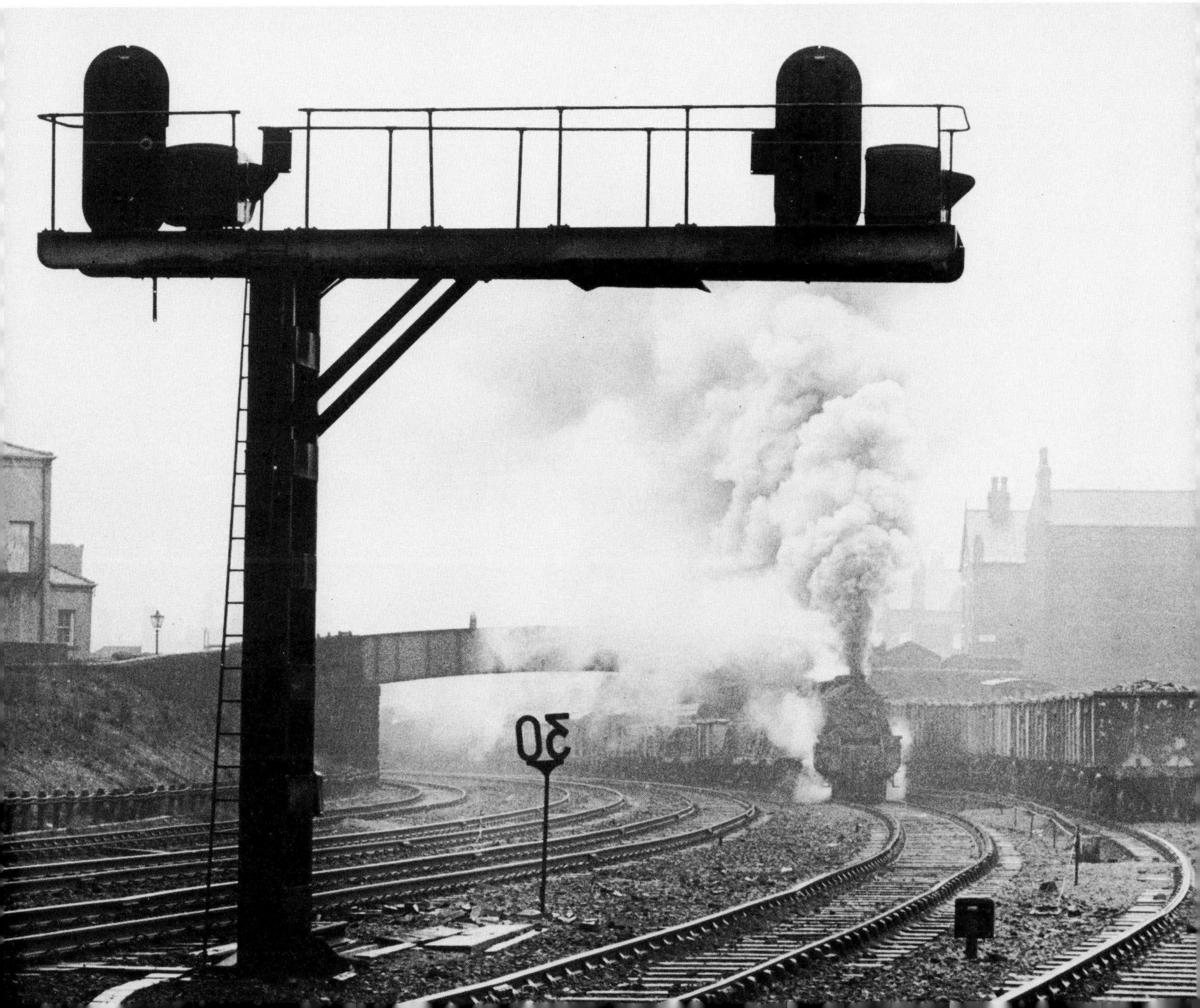

WEATHER

Blizzard conditions are rarely conducive to excellent railway photography. Personal discomfort is likely to be extreme which will certainly tend to inhibit a logical and critical approach. The traditional objective of a first rate print showing the detail of the engine and train to perfection, will of course be impossible to achieve. The best effects are probably obtained when a train is recorded almost in silhouette providing a suitable dark backdrop for falling snow. The more prominent the train the greater will be the impact as in this photograph where the locomotive and the leading two coaches predominate. The choice of a viewpoint which included a few trees to impart a feeling of reality was deliberate but the splendid black smoke effect, absolutely ideal for the conditions, was simply good fortune.

Turkish Railways (T.C.D.D.) three cylinder 2-10-0 nears Ulakisla in the Taurus mountains with an Adana to Ankara express in March 1975.

Pentax 6 × 7 105mm Takumar Tri-X D76 (1:1) 1/250th second f 4.5.

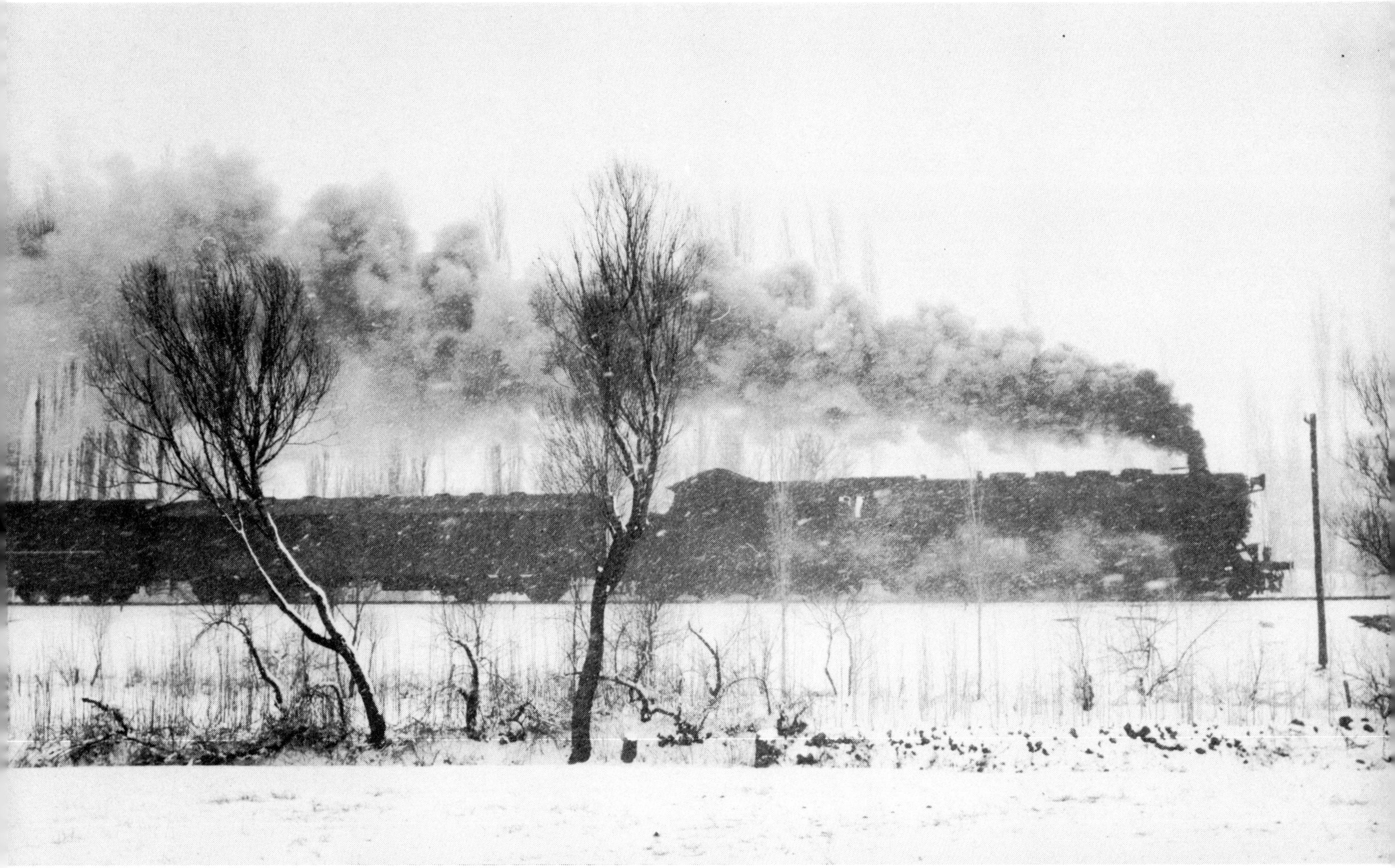

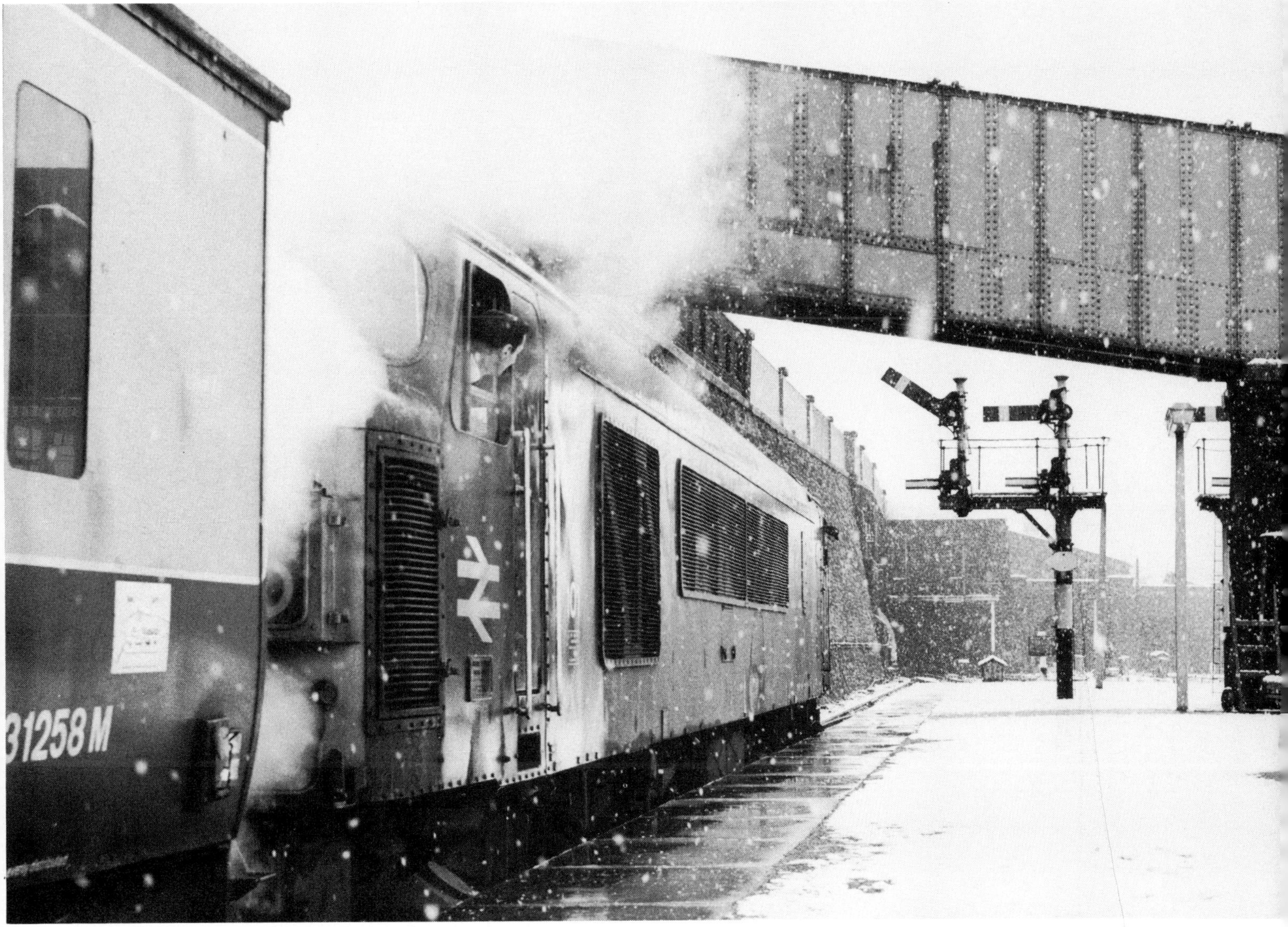

This is another situation where a dark background emphasises the individual snowflakes. However, a photographer should beware of optimistic light meter readings; slight over-exposure usually affords the best negatives. Incidentally, on occasions such as this, the use of a lens hood becomes almost mandatory if the camera lens surface is to be kept dry.

'Peak' Class 45 No.D101 prepares to leave Sheffield (Midland) with an extra express for St. Pancras on Christmas Eve 1971.

Minolta Autocord 6 × 6 75mm Rokkor Tri-X D76 (1:1) 1/250th second f 5.6.

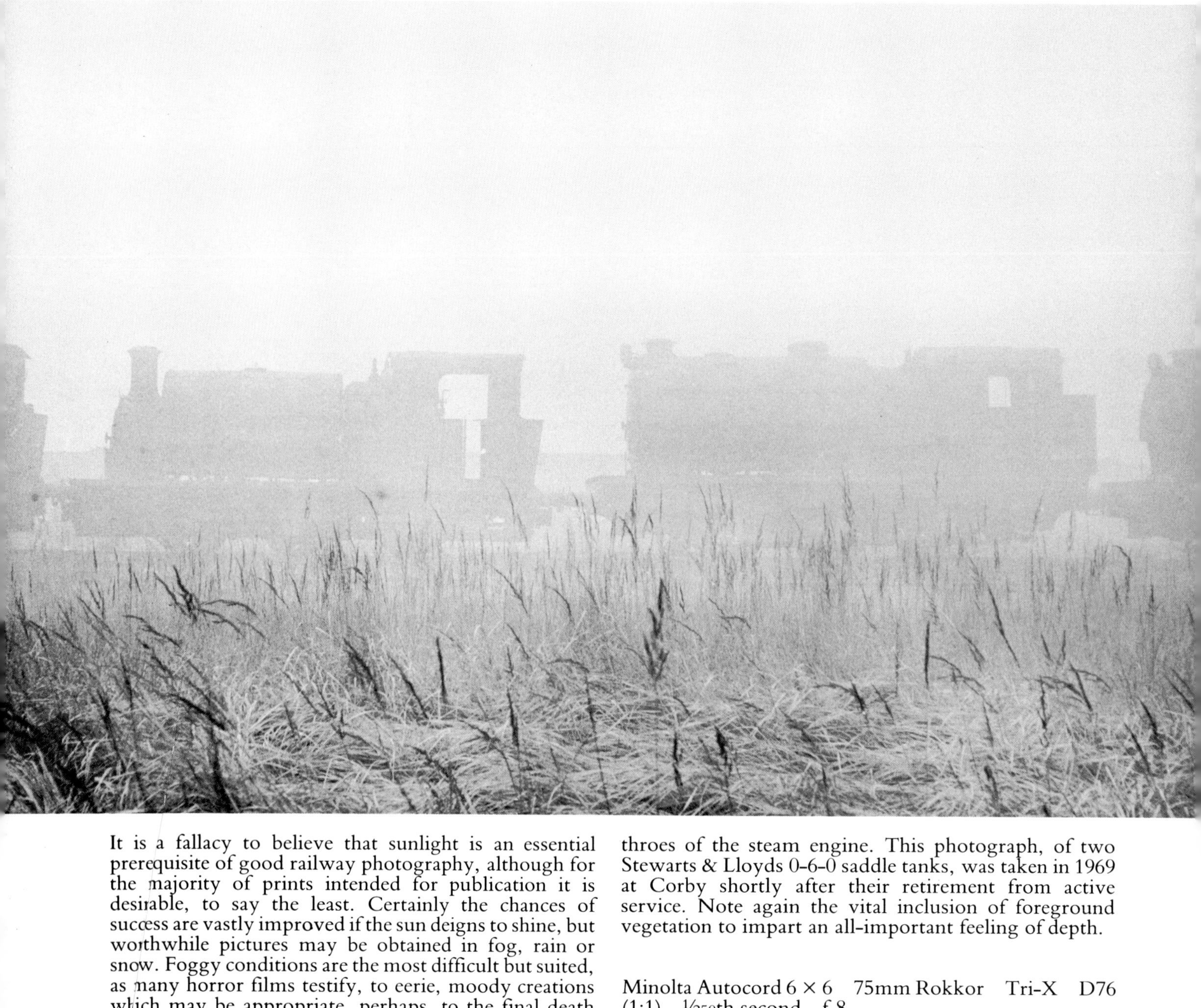

It is a fallacy to believe that sunlight is an essential prerequisite of good railway photography, although for the majority of prints intended for publication it is desirable, to say the least. Certainly the chances of success are vastly improved if the sun deigns to shine, but worthwhile pictures may be obtained in fog, rain or snow. Foggy conditions are the most difficult but suited, as many horror films testify, to eerie, moody creations which may be appropriate, perhaps, to the final death throes of the steam engine. This photograph, of two Stewarts & Lloyds 0-6-0 saddle tanks, was taken in 1969 at Corby shortly after their retirement from active service. Note again the vital inclusion of foreground vegetation to impart an all-important feeling of depth.

Minolta Autocord 6 × 6   75mm Rokkor   Tri-X   D76 (1:1)   1/250th second   f 8.

Even using Tri-X black-and-white film rated at 400 ASA the available light on this occasion was so weak that an exposure of 1/60th second at an aperture of f 3.5 was required to yield a negative with reasonable shadow detail. The camera was supported on a nearby bollard to minimise camera shake and the focus carefully centred on the track midway between the signal and the leading locomotive. An exposure of 1/60th second was selected in preference to 1/125th since the latter would need the larger aperture of f 2.2 with consequent problems of limited depth of field. Fortunately the train was moving at a sufficiently slow speed to allow this, attempts to photograph trains travelling at speeds in excess of 10 m.p.h. using a shutter speed of 1/60th second are doomed to failure.

Class 5 4-6-0s Nos. 44871 and 45407 leave Leeds for Carnforth with an enthusiasts' excursion, 24 September 1977.

Pentax 6 × 7 105mm Takumar Tri-X D76 (1:1)
1/60th second f 3.5.

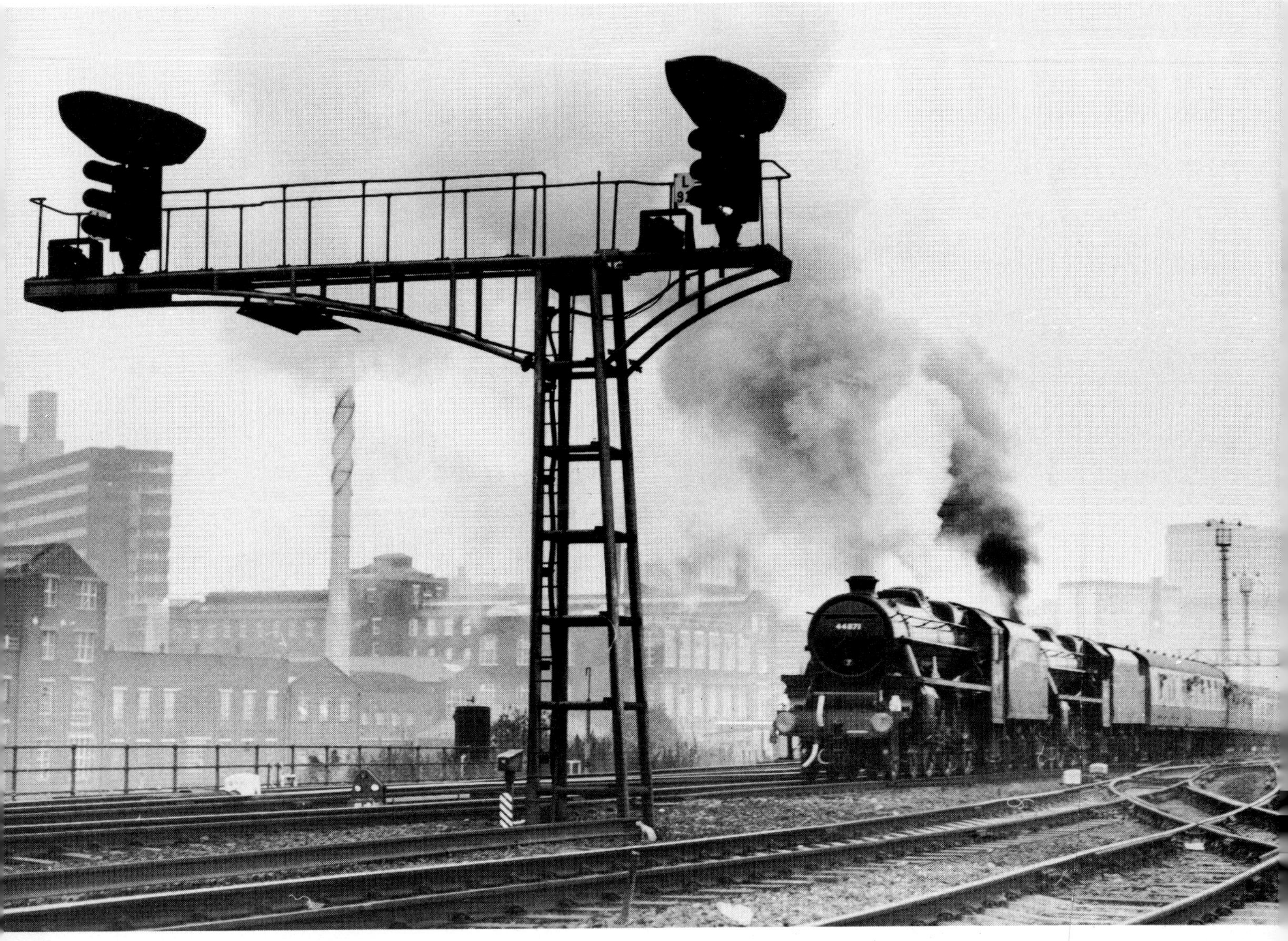

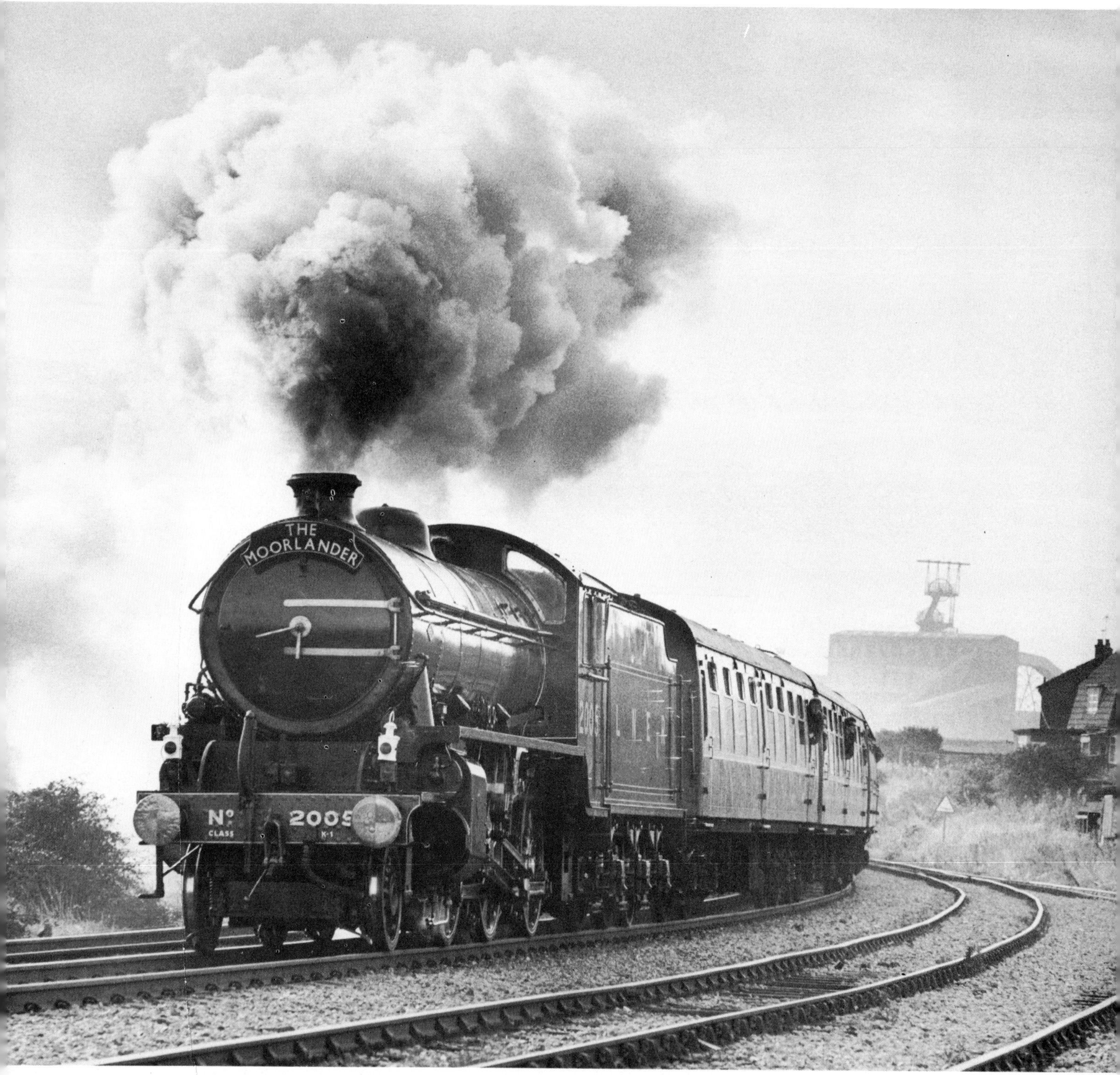
THE MOORLANDER
No 2005
CLASS K-1

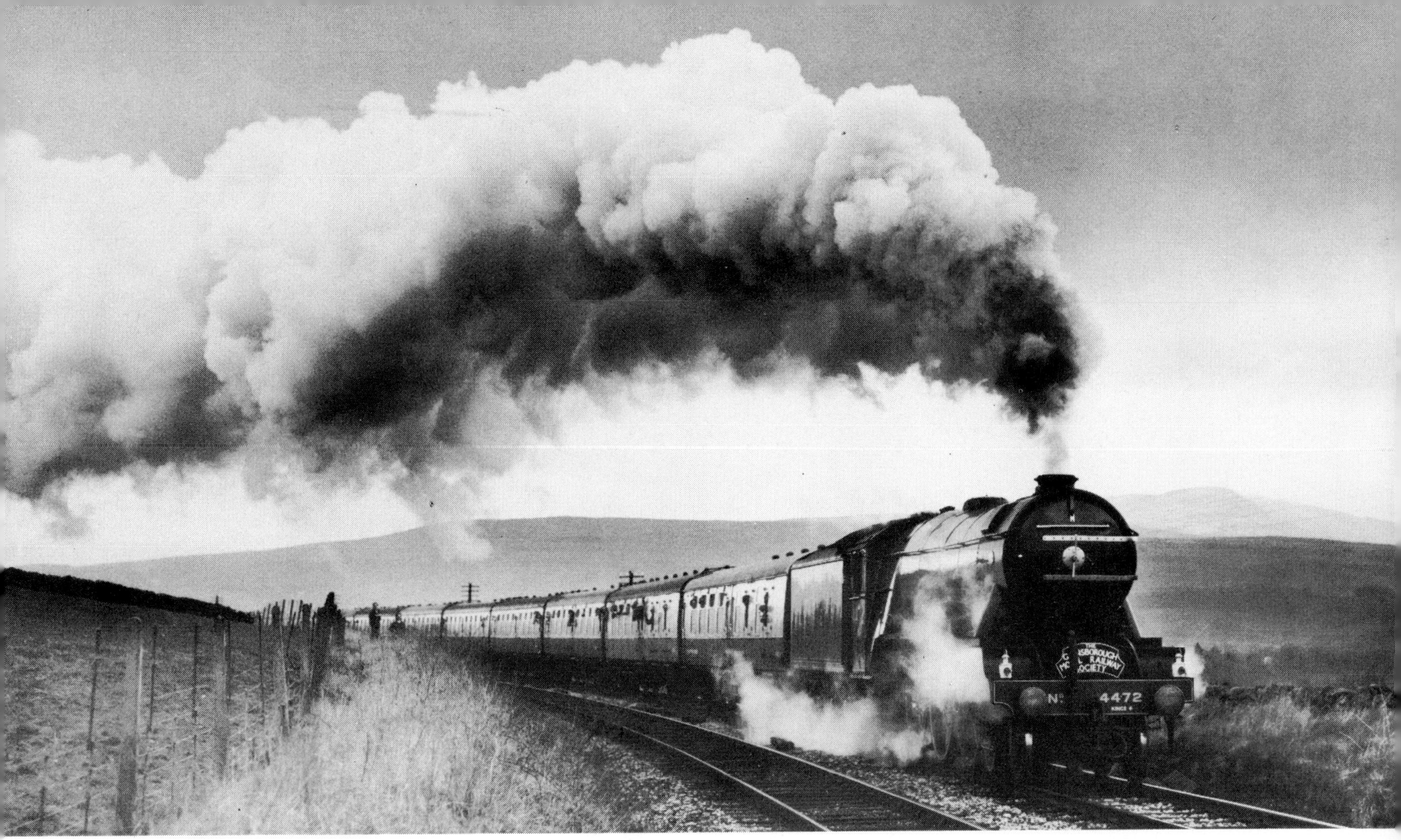

◀ In the photography of steam-hauled trains the strength and direction of the wind is often the prime meteorological consideration. So much so that a location will often be selected almost solely upon the appropriateness of the prevailing wind direction. Faced with the proposition of photographing K1 2-6-0 No. 2005 travelling north on the Durham coast route on the morning of 22 October 1978 the immediate reaction of most would be assessment of locations on the easterly side of the line since this would mean that both locomotive and train would be illuminated by the low morning sun. In the event a spot on the opposite westerly side was chosen because of a correctly anticipated problem of smoke from the engine blowing down to obscure part, if not all, of the train. The photographic emulsion is expected here to effectively deal with a wide contrast range. The ideal exposure for the exhaust and sky highlights would be insufficient to give adequate shadow detail. Under these conditions an accurately assessed compromise, with very little latitude for error, is required if an optimum negative is to be obtained.

Pentax 6 × 7 200mm Takumar Tri-X D76 (1:1)
1/500th second f 8.

The mood and excitement of thundery weather is not easy to portray convincingly in photography; particularly if the principal item of interest is a moving object. Under these conditions the level of available light will again be very low which in turn will require a large aperture and/or a slow shutter speed. Immediately a photographer should dismiss thoughts of technical perfection in favour of artistic impressionism. This location was chosen with two thoughts uppermost in the photographer's mind; firstly to include in the field of view the darkest clouds and secondly to ensure, by reference to the ever useful book of gradient profiles, that the locomotive would be working hard on an uphill stretch of line.

Preserved Class A3 Pacific *Flying Scotsman* climbs away from Clapham towards the summit at Eldroth with a special excursion from Carnforth on 24 April 1976.

Pentax 6 × 7 105mm Takumar Tri-X D76 (1:1)
1/250th second f 4.

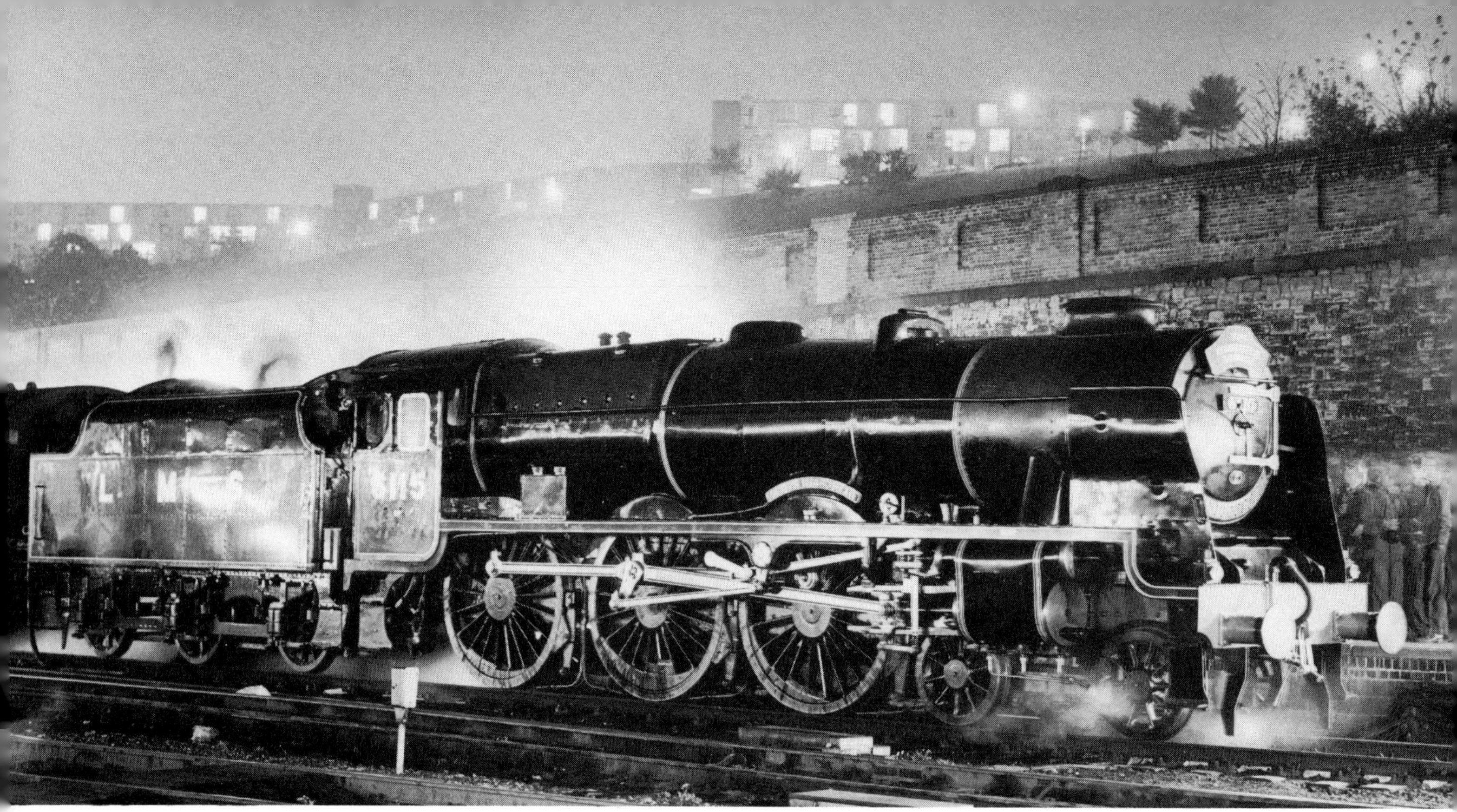

Photography after dark presents rather specialised problems. Obviously the lack of light is the major difficulty and hence photography is restricted to static subjects unless the photographer has the use of exceptionally powerful flashguns. The accurate assessment of exposure is of paramount importance; guesses are likely to introduce quite large margins of error. The use of a cadmium sulphide-battery exposure meter rather than the photo-electric variety, which generate a small electric current on exposure to light (for example the Weston series), will permit the accurate measurement of exposures of as long as one hour at f 2.8. The use of a tripod is almost mandatory and the best, in terms of stability if not portability, are those with a minimum number of telescopic extensions: three per leg represents a reasonable compromise. However even the best exposure meter will not take account of reciprocity failure. A photographer presumes that a simple relationship exists between shutter speed and aperture which determines the amount of light falling upon the emulsion. This is the case over a limited range of camera settings, thus 1/250th second at f 5.6 will pass the same amount of light as 1/125th second at f 8. As the exposure becomes longer it is found that this simple relationship becomes, progressively, in error and increased exposures are required to yield adequately exposed negatives or transparencies. As a rough guide, exposures of between two and three minutes require about double the indicated meter value whereas those of about seven minutes duration may need a threefold increase.

Long exposures are obtained with the shutter speed dial of the camera set on the B position and the shutter released and closed by means of a long cable release. Frequently the level of available light is such that there will be large unlit areas of the subject but this may be overcome by either 'painting' the area with light from a powerful torch or by the selective use of a number of flashes from an electronic flash gun. In this photograph of 'Royal Scot' No.6115 *Scots Guardsman* at Sheffield Midland station on 11 November 1978 an exposure of three minutes at f 4 was used. Other photographers who were present provided fill-in flash which has effectively highlighted the wheels and motion of the locomotive. Note the ghost figures on the tender caused by the crew moving coal forward during part of the period of exposure. A figure which is present in the field of view for just a few seconds will not usually be recorded.

Pentax 6 × 7 105mm Takumar Tri-X D76 (1:1)

In night photography, excessively contrasty negatives are to be expected. The exposure of highlights over a prolonged period of time will produce, on development, localised very high density deposits of silver while, inevitably, other areas will be almost completely devoid of shadow detail. Overexposure and underdevelopment of an inherently low contrast fast emulsion, such as Tri-X, will give the best results. Nevertheless the negatives may be rather difficult to print; most will be of rather uneven density and hence require extensive burning-in of the highlight regions during exposure of the printing paper. In this print the tender and cab of the locomotive required almost three times the exposure of the remainder to produce an acceptable result.
French Railways (S.N.C.F.) Class 140C 2-8-0 No. 140-C-146 at Verdun shed in March 1971.

Minolta Autocord 6 × 6 75mm Rokkor Tri-X D76 (1:1) 4 minutes f 5.6.

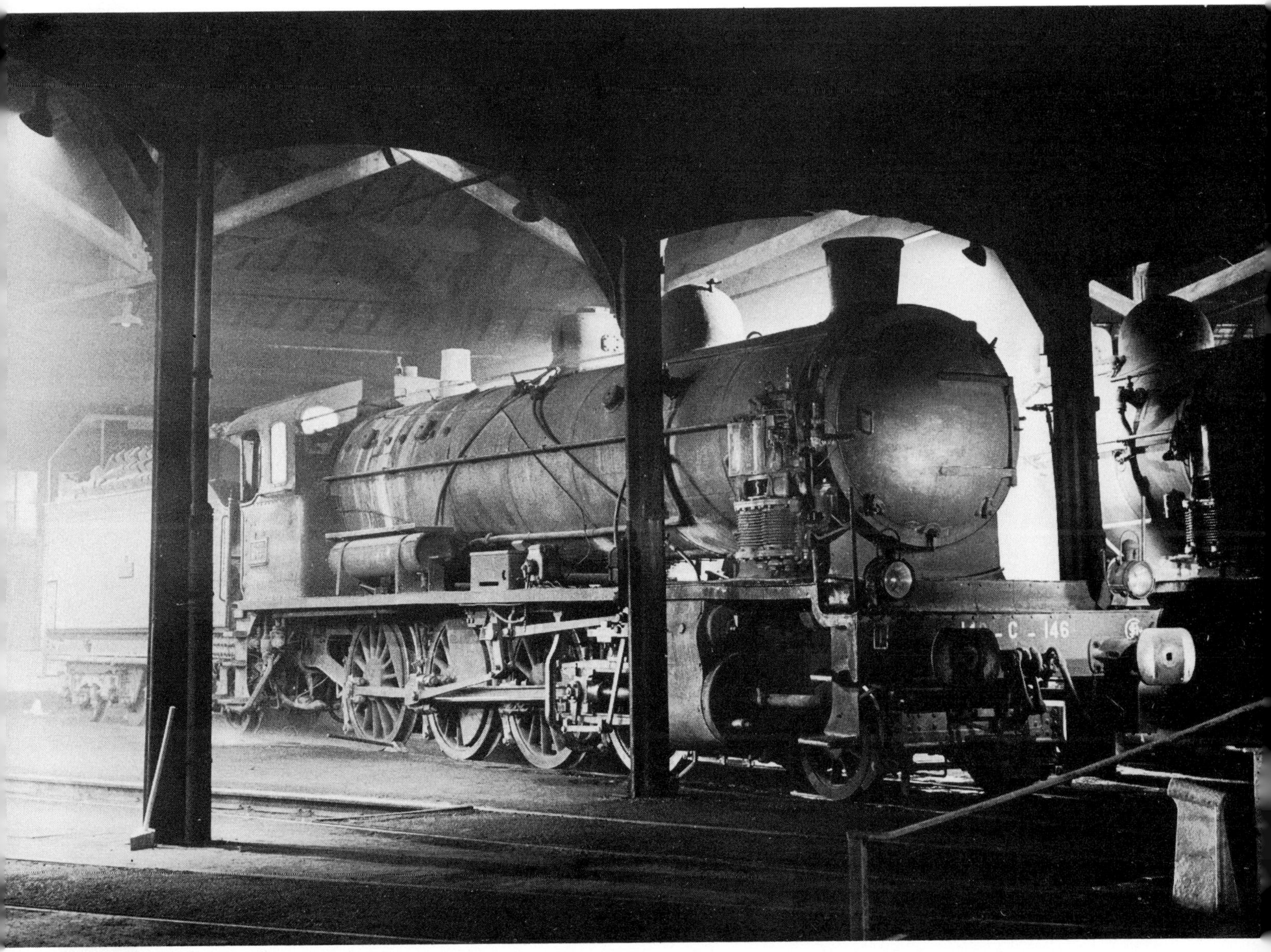

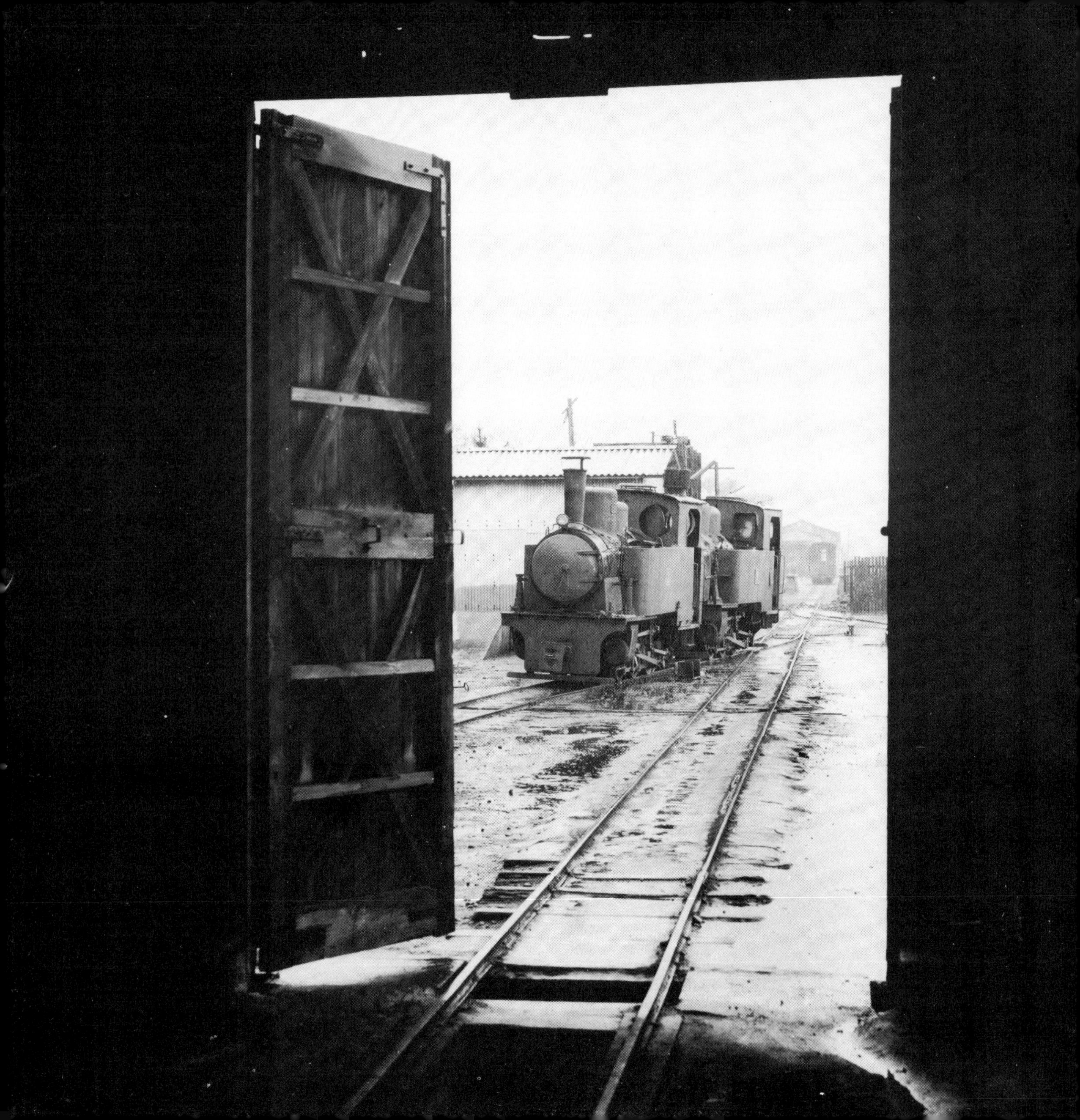

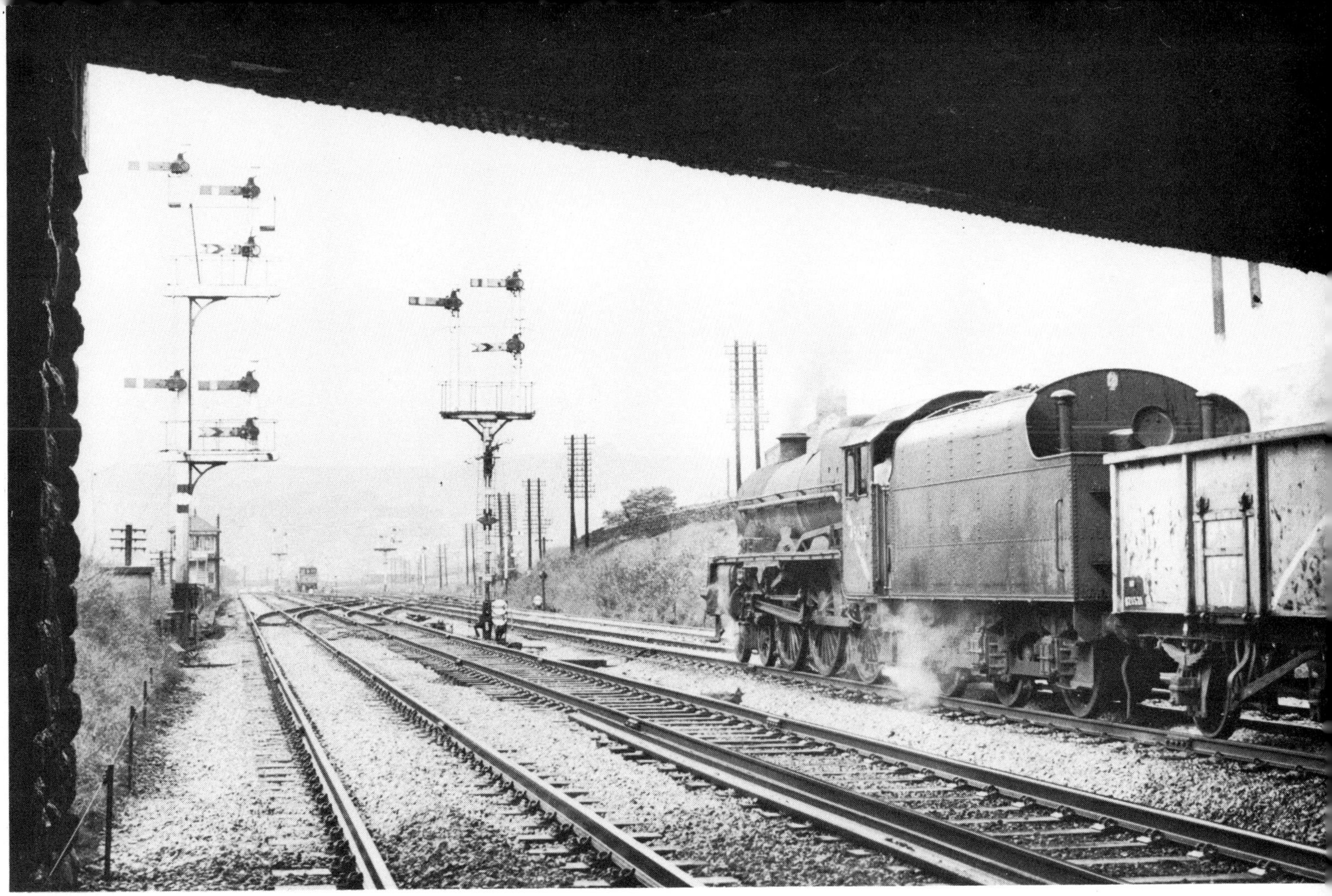

'Jubilee' No.45632 at New Mills South junction on 9 September 1965.

Exakta Varex IIa FP4 Acutol 1/250th second f 4.5.

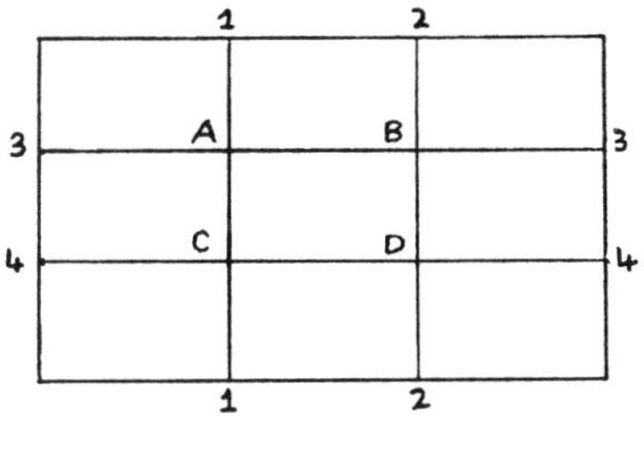

◀ 2′6″ gauge 0-6-0T locomotives Nos.2 and 9 of the Lotung - Tu Chang forestry railway, Taiwan, stand outside the shed at Lotung on 23 March 1978.

Pentax 6 × 7 105mm Takumar Tri-X Perceptol (1:1) 1/125th second f 6.3.

COMPOSITION

The composition of a picture, or the principles of arrangement of subjects with respect to each other, is of tremendous importance particularly in pictorial photography. Although it is impossible to lay down hard and fast rules of composition, certain guidelines are worthy of note. Imagine a photograph divided into nine units each of equal area as shown in the accompanying figure. Generally a leading object of interest should lie somewhere on the lines 1, 2, 3 or 4 but never in the exact centre of the picture. The intersections, i.e. A, B, C and D are particularly important; an object placed at one of these points obtains considerable emphasis. In the photograph above, at New Mills South junction, 'Jubilee' No.45632 *Tonga* is centred at position D. If the reader cares to check it will be found that these concepts hold good for the majority of the illustrations presented in this volume.
Another compositional dodge used by photographers to lead the eye directly into the picture is the inclusion of an

arch of a bridge or perhaps a doorway in shadow, with little or no detail. The photographs on pages 28 and 29 illustrate this and the effect is further enhanced in the photograph (page 28) by the track which takes the eye from the foreground directly to the main point of interest, the two 0-6-0 tank engines. Usually however the theme is presented in a rather more subtle way, often so much so that the viewer may be totally unaware of the photographer's guile.

In the Javan scene below, the eye is taken directly to the locomotive since it is effectively framed by a combination of the tree trunk to the left, the overhanging branches, the black column of smoke and telegraph pole on the right and, last but not least, the shadow of the tree in the foreground.

Narrow gauge 0-8-0T locomotive No. 1 of the Pagottan sugar mill near Maduin, Java, raises steam on 30 July 1977.

Pentax 6 × 7 105mm Takumar FP4 D76 (1:1)
1/250th second f 8.

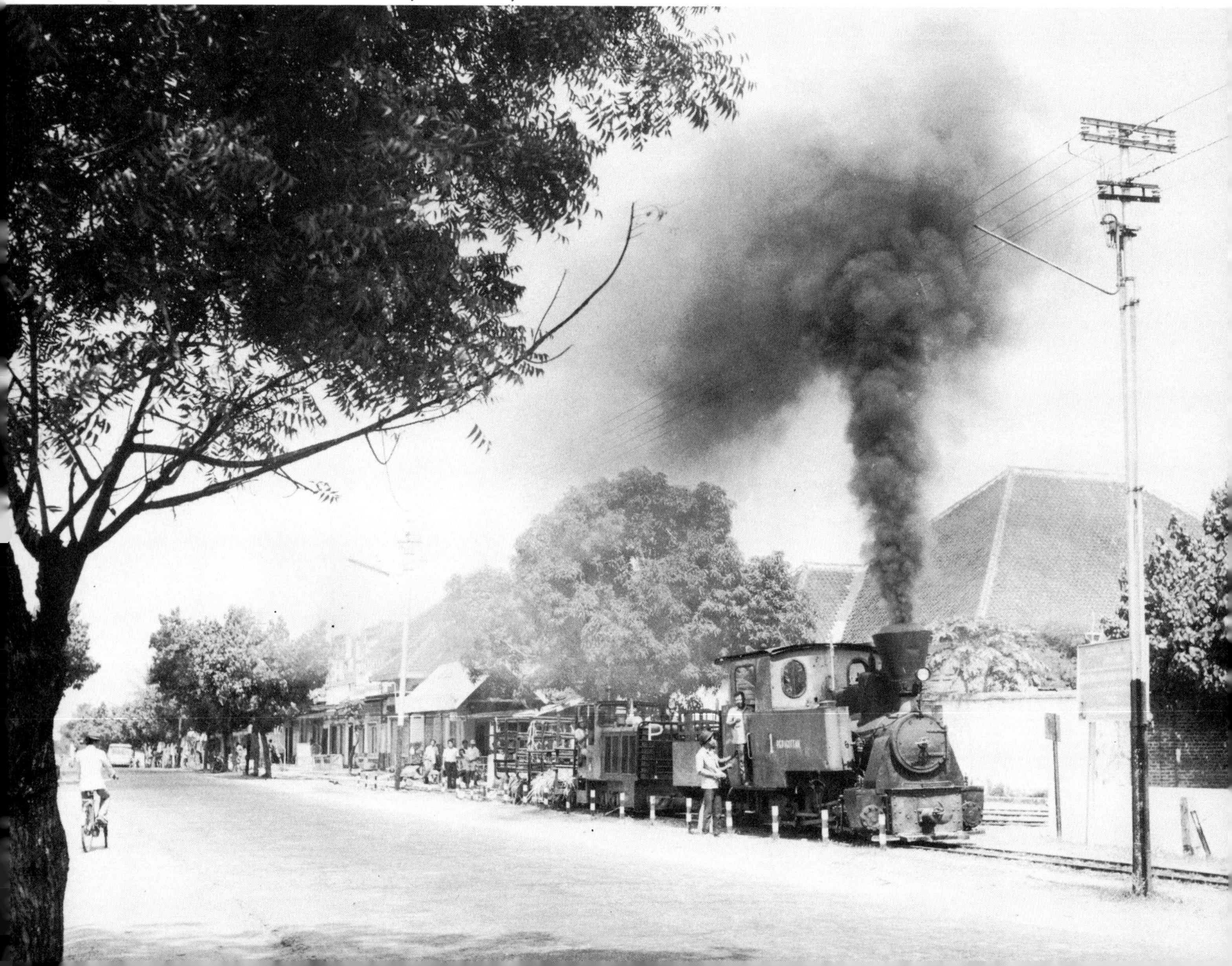

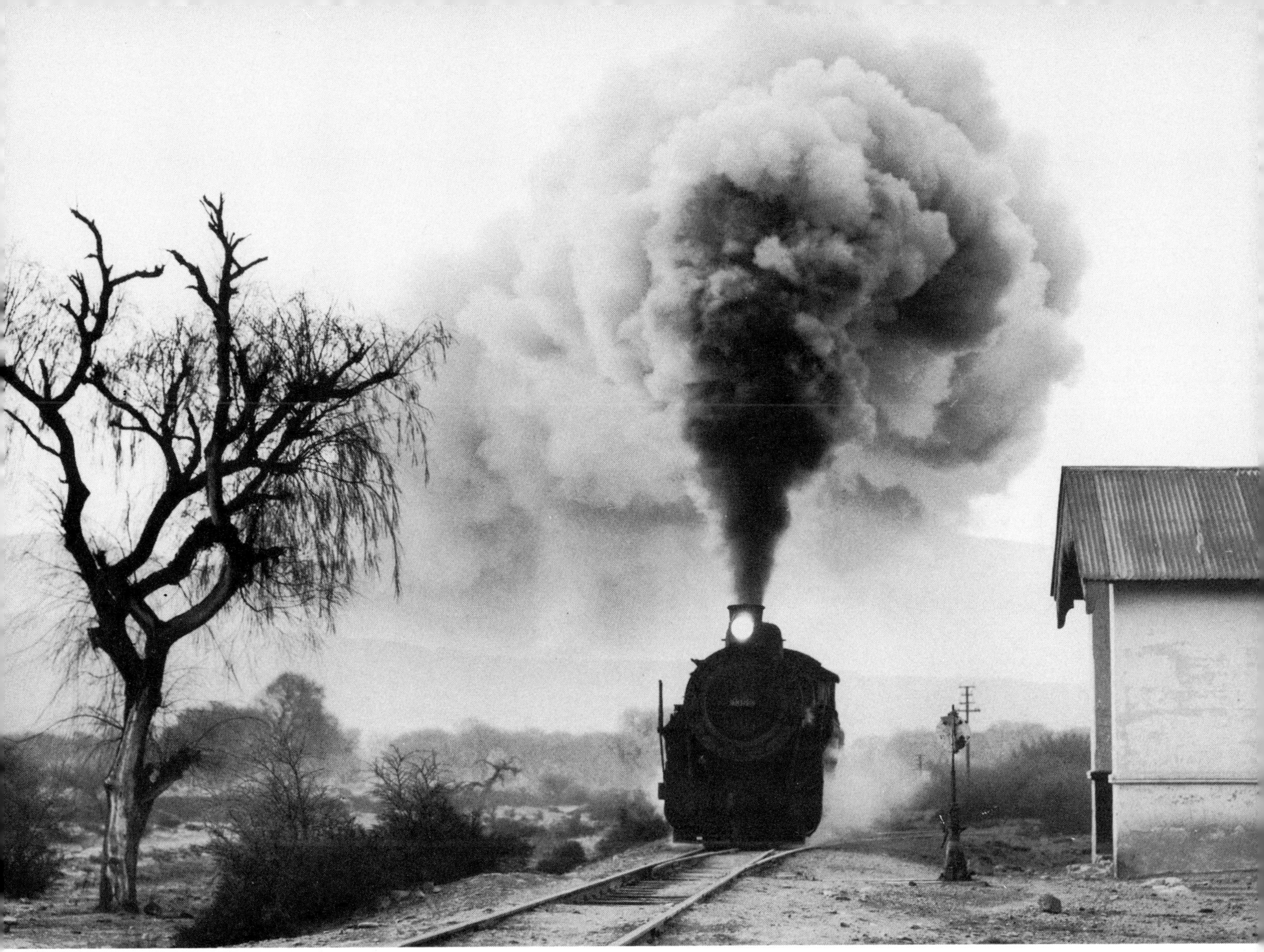

Another important aspect of composition is the 'balance' of a picture. The eye normally moves across the scene from a point of interest through the centre until it finds a co-related point on the other side. In this photograph the mass of the building on the right is balanced by the gaunt tree on the left. The idea of balance applies not only to the placing of the parts within the picture area, but to the relationships between objects situated in the various planes. This concept is best shown in the illustration on page 88 where the river and the railway in the foreground draw the interest through a series of curves back into the picture.

Argentina Railways 2-10-2 No.1359 storms away from Humahuaca at daybreak with a train for Bolivia which started its long journey some 40 hours earlier in Buenos Aires.

Pentax 6 × 7 105mm Takumar FP4 D76 (1:1) 1/250th second f 5.6.

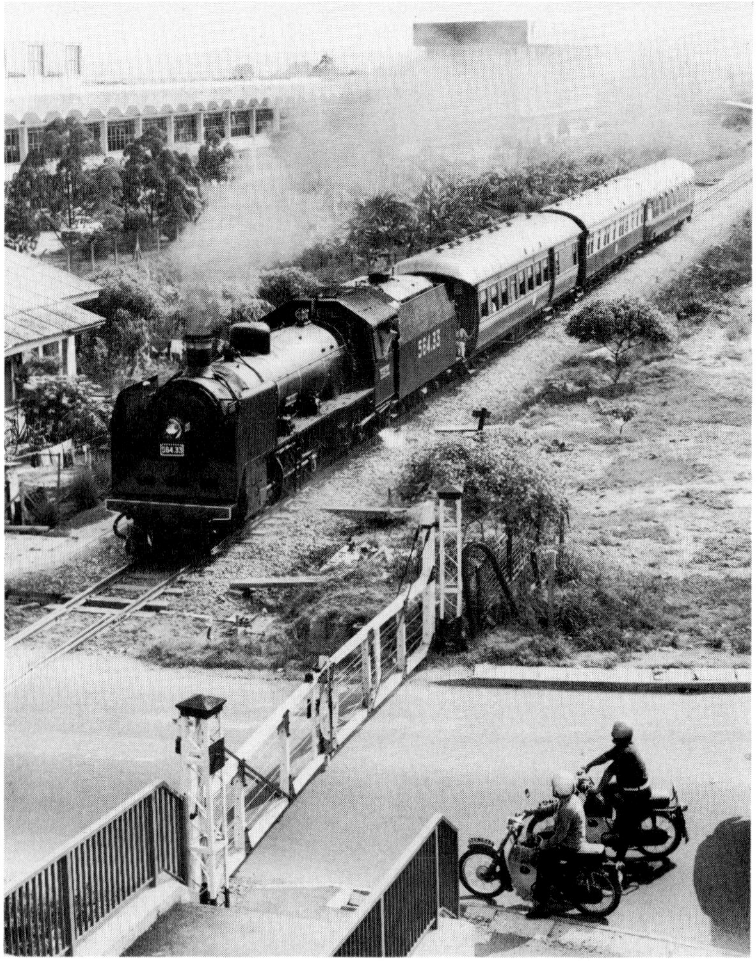

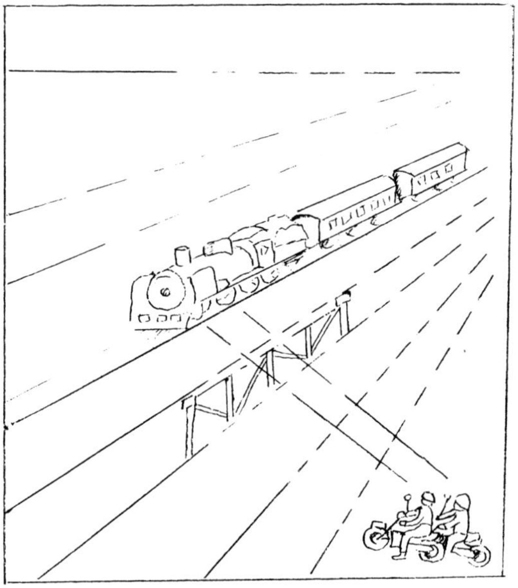

The composition of this photograph is rather complex but the most obvious feature is the sequence of straight lines originating at the left and bottom which tend to focus attention at a point in the top right hand corner of the photograph. However, this is nicely countered by the two motorcyclists who establish a contrasting line of interest with the locomotive. Again on the subject of balance notice how the motor cyclists are vitally important to the overall composition of the photograph; without them a most unattractive top heavy format would result.

Preserved Malayan Railways 4-6-2 No.564 33 *Jelebu* approaches Kuala Lumpur with a special excursion from Port Klang on 14 August 1977.

Pentax 6 × 7   105mm Takumar   FP4   D76 (1:1)
1/500th second   f 6.3.

Railway photography in the tropics is much more demanding than in the more temperate regions of the world. For most of the day the sun is almost directly overhead and the overall contrast of the subject is usually very high. Black-and-white films, particularly the inherently high contrast low and medium speed varieties, need to be exposed and developed with extreme care; underexposure and overdevelopment must be avoided at all costs. This unusual combination of 4-6-0s of the Ceylon Government Railways was photographed at about midday in the worst possible lighting conditions; the shadows on the sides of the tenders and the smoke box door clearly indicate the position of the sun. The best advice of course is to avoid midday photography unless some highly unusual subject is encountered. Note how the location is exactly appropriate to the length of the train. The chimney and boiler of the leading locomotive conveniently coincide with the gap in the trees while the tree on the right provides all-important balance.

C.G.R. Class B1 4-6-0 No.284 *James Mackenzie* and Class B3 tender tank 4-6-0 No.22 hurry a featherweight Matale to Kandy local train away from Katugastota in September 1974.

Pentax 6 × 7   105mm Takumar   FP4   D76 (1:1)
1/500th second   f 4.5.

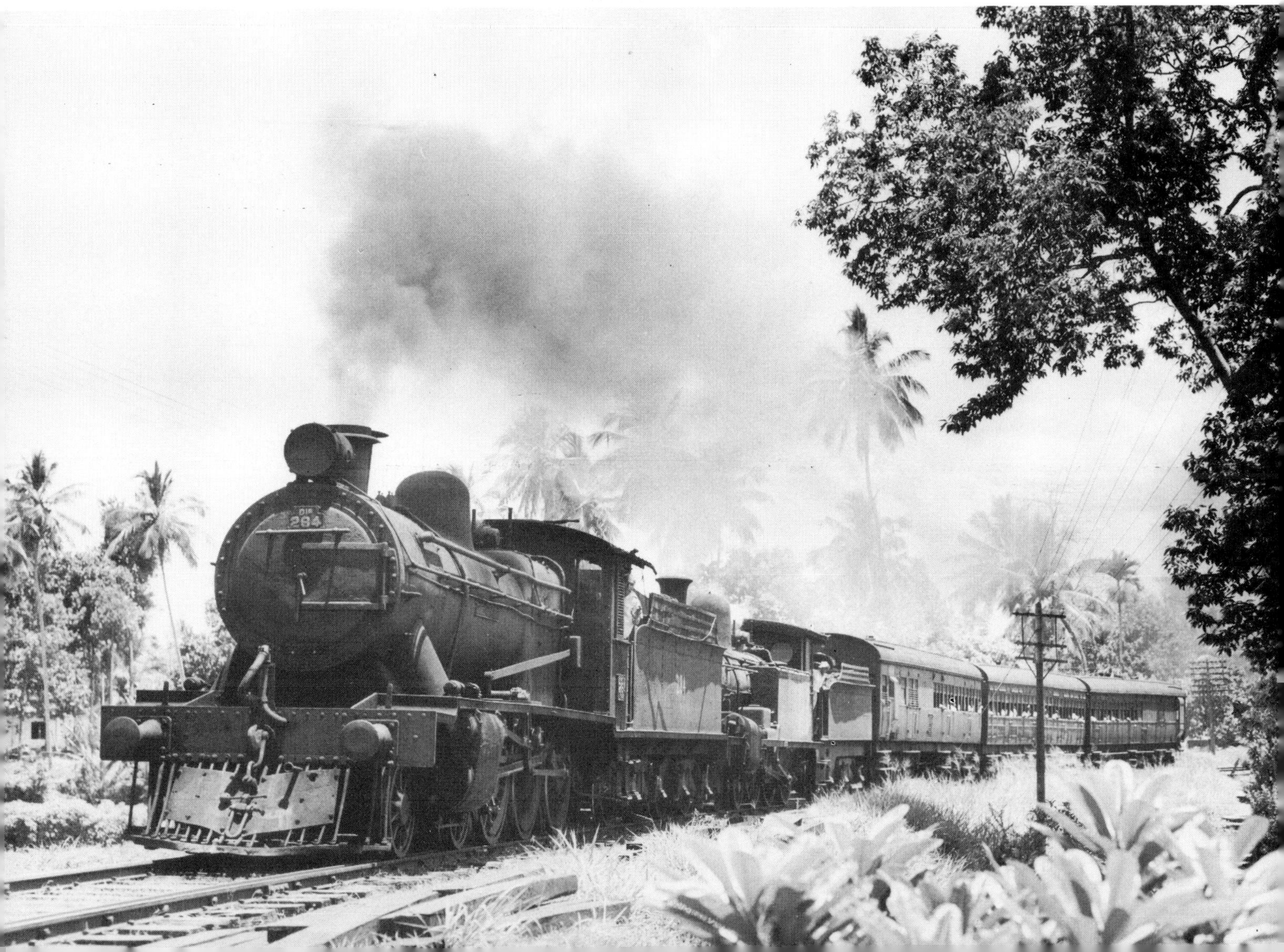

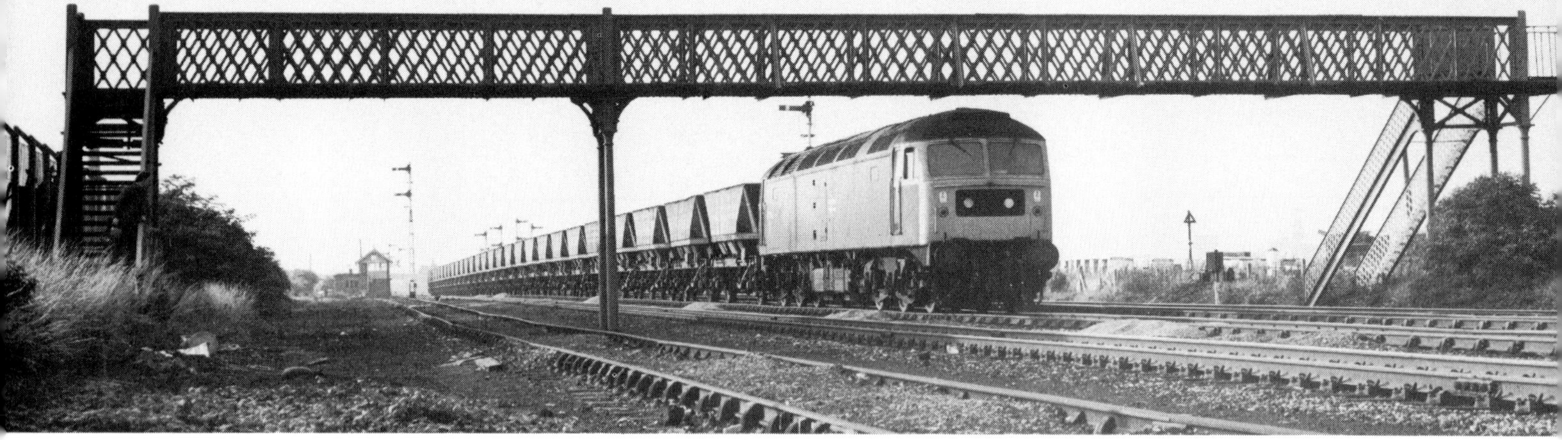

It is rare to find that the best composition exactly fits the negative size being used; this is particularly true of cameras producing the square 6 × 6cm format. A valid criticism of this size is that for most subjects some 40 per cent of the negative area is likely to remain unused at the printing stage, and consequently one of the prime advantages of the medium sized format is partially lost. By comparison a 6 × 4.5 or 6 × 7cm sized negative is much more useful for railway photography. The question then arises as to which part(s) of a negative should be excluded from the final print. In this context a great deal can be learned about composition by taking two L-shaped pieces of card and moving them about a photograph until the most satisfying result is obtained. It will soon be found that a manufacturer's printing paper size is rarely of exactly the required proportions. Indeed the slavish adherence to postcard or whole plate, for example, will tend in itself to lead to an appearance of monotony in a collection. In each of these three scenes, composition has been considerably improved by the use of less than 50 per cent of both negative and printing paper areas. In the photograph below, a skyline composed of high rise buildings, lamp posts and double deck buses has been excluded, as have the featureless sky plus uninteresting foreground in the scene above.

Above; Class 47 No.47 276 leaves Wath with an eastbound 'merry-go-round' train 14 October 1978.

Pentax 6 × 7 105mm Takumar FP4 D76 (1:1)
1/250th second f 4.5

Below; Class 45 No.45 117 hurries a down express from St. Pancras through the tunnels near Kentish Town on 21 May 1977.

Pentax 6 × 7 200mm Takumar FP4 D76 (1:1)
1/250th second f 5.6

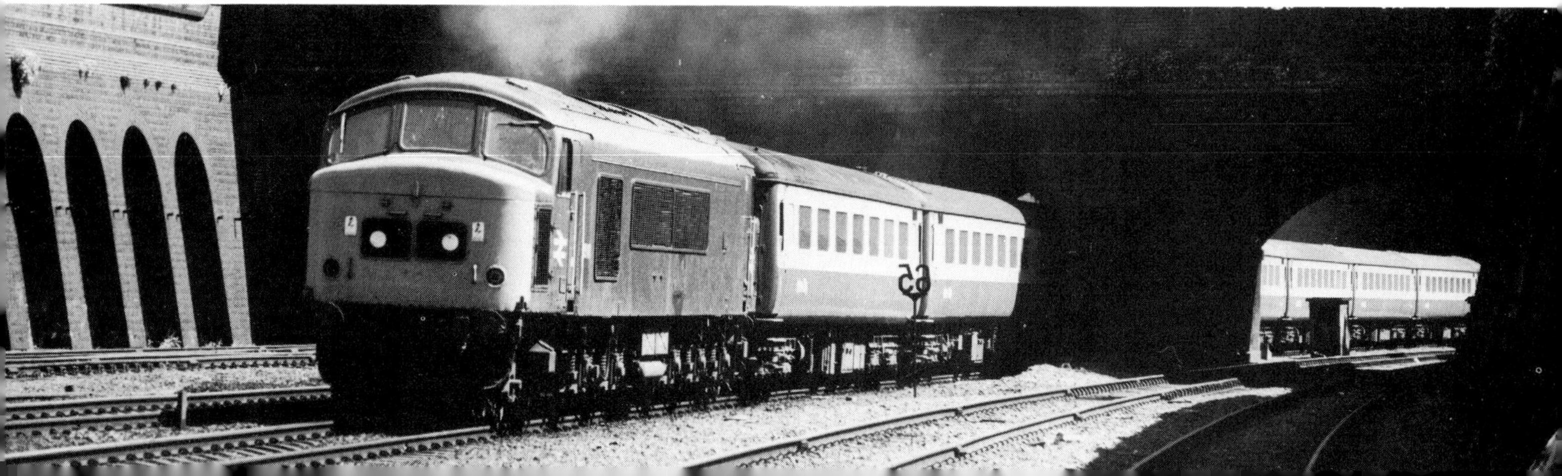

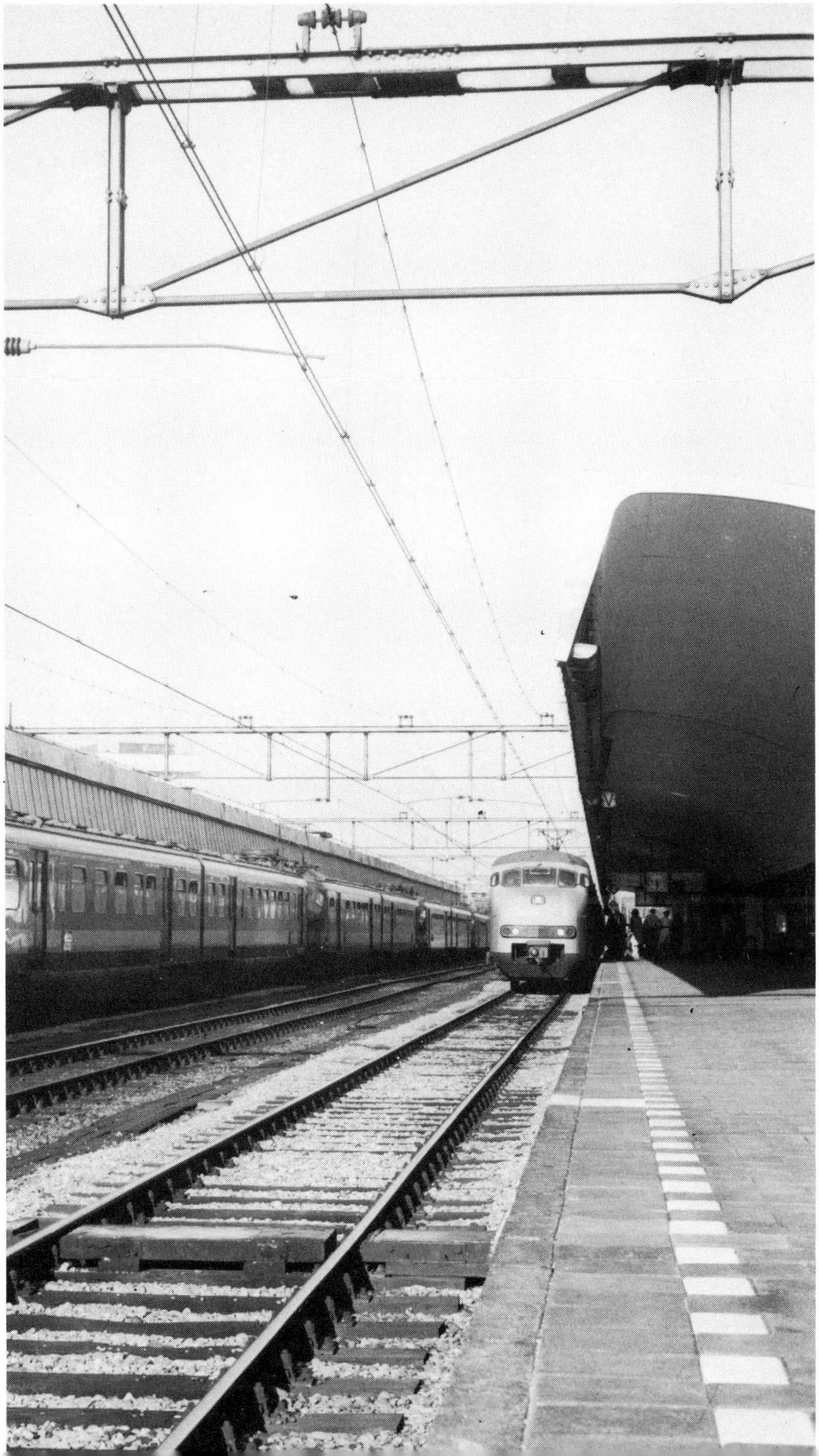

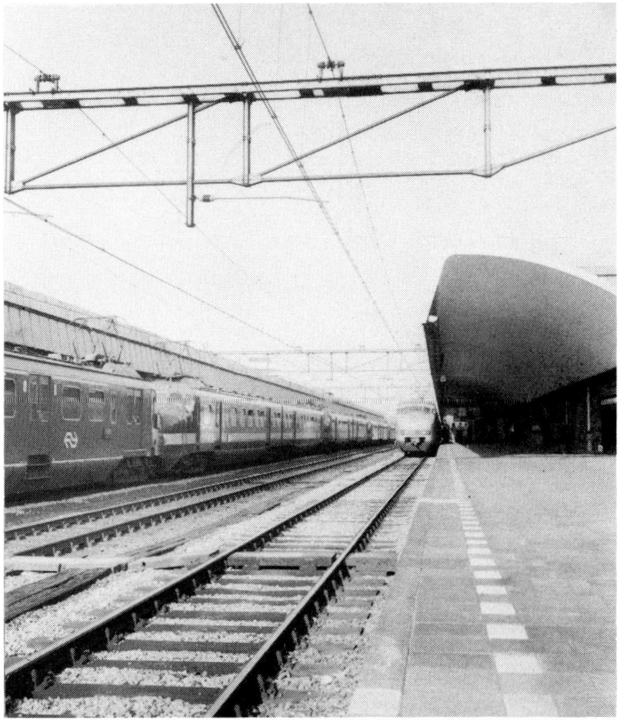

The compositional advantages of selective enlargement or of severe cropping of the print are clearly evident in these 'before and after' illustrations. Note how attention is focused upon the train through the numerous converging visual lines.

An emu of the Dutch Railways prepares to leave Rotterdam Central station in August 1975.

Minolta Autocord 6 × 6 75mm Rokkor FP4 D76 (1:1) 1/250th second f 6.3

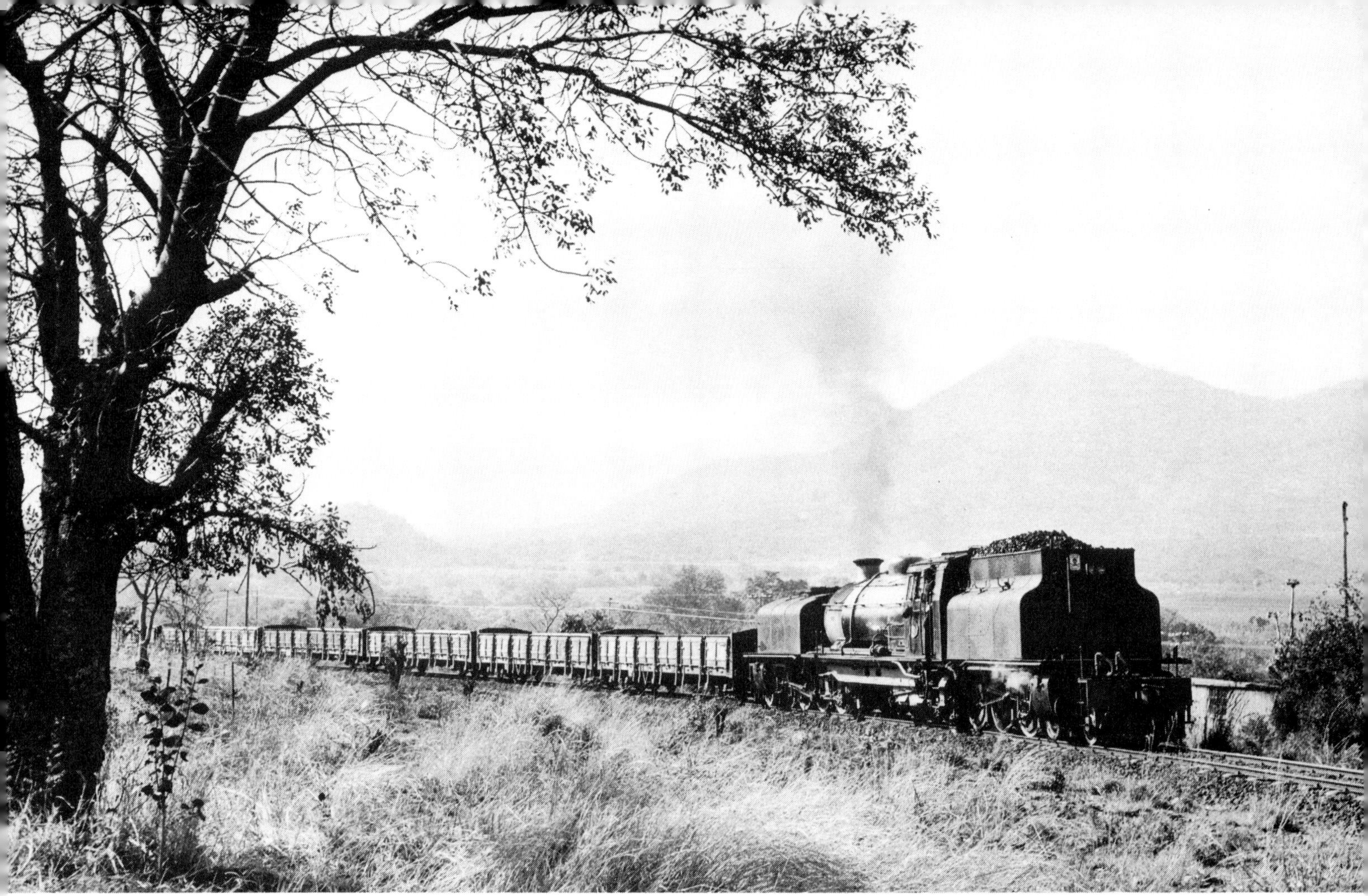

Trees are a particularly useful prop to lineside railway photography. The variety of shape, size and appearance at different times of the year is legion, while for the more agile enthusiast mature specimens may even provide grandstand vantage points. Trees may be used to frame a subject, to impart a feeling of depth or simply to emphasize a rural, sylvan setting. Simplicity is the password to success; one or two trees or bushes, carefully positioned relative to the subject, will often give the most satisfying results. Occasionally even part of a tree will provide a strong composition as in this illustration of a Class GF Garratt 4-6-2 + 2-6-4 negotiating a tight curve on the Barberton branch in South Africa. The inclusion of part of the trunk of the tree to support the overhanging branches is particularly important. Trees have also been used to good effect in the adjacent photograph of a vintage Class B51 4-4-0 at work on the Labuin branch in the jungles of Java. The luxuriant vegetation totally precluded a photograph of the complete bridge and a spot was chosen where palm trees would frame the locomotive as it crossed part of the viaduct. The relatively simple composition, arising from the inclusion of as few trees as possible, is appealing but note how the limited angle of view of a standard lens made it necessary to exclude the tops and the bases of the trees. The 'hole' in the centre of the photograph, above the locomotive, is a compositional weakness; a more prominent exhaust or a partially clouded sky would have improved matters considerably.

Deciding whether a restricted space, such as this, is sufficient to 'accommodate' a locomotive is not the easiest of tasks; luck was with me on this occasion.

Minolta Autocord 6 × 6 75mm Rokkor FP4 D76 (1:1) 1/500th second f 6.3.

Pentax 6 × 7 105mm Takumar Tri-X Perceptol (1:1) 1/250th second f 5.6.

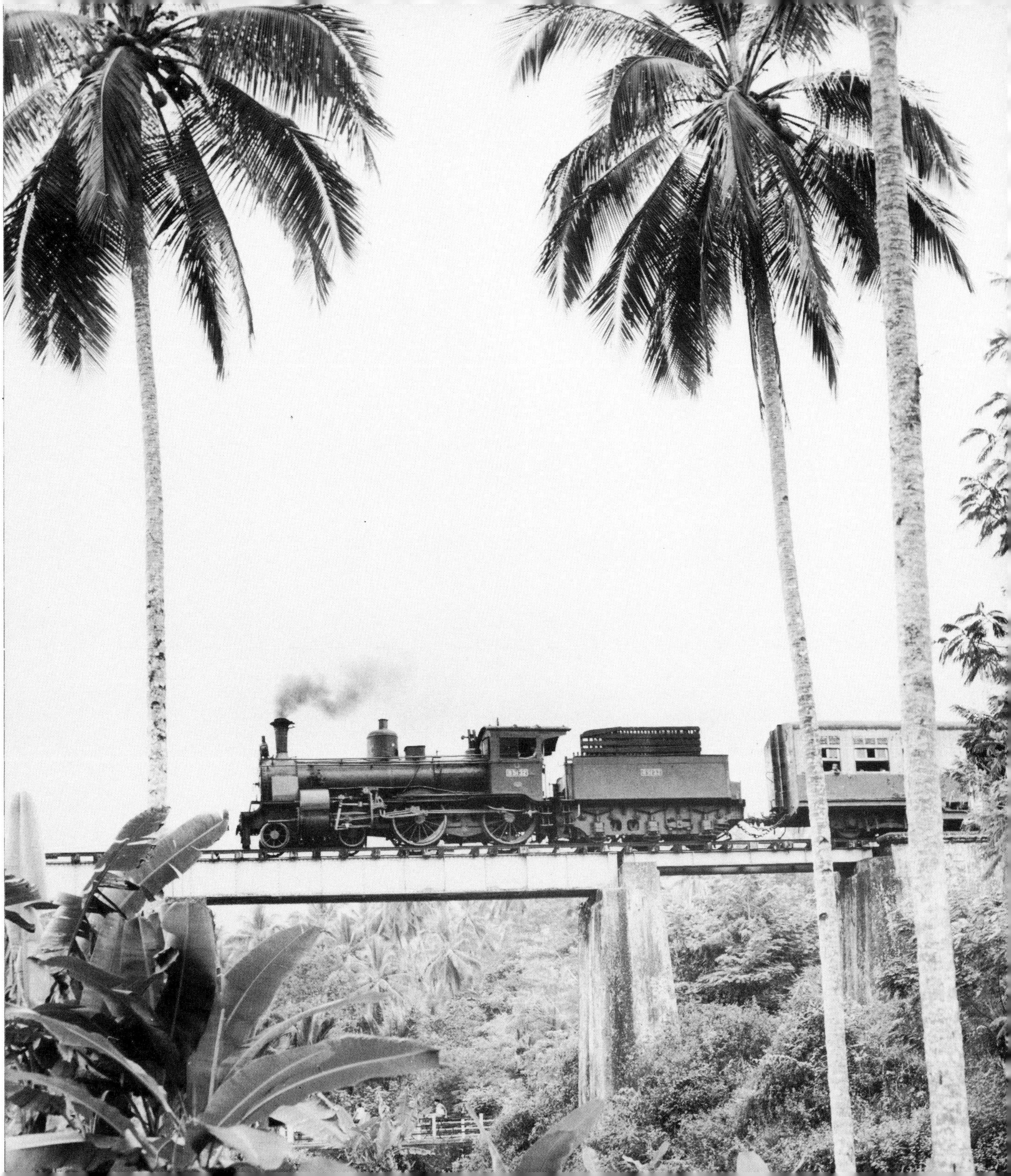

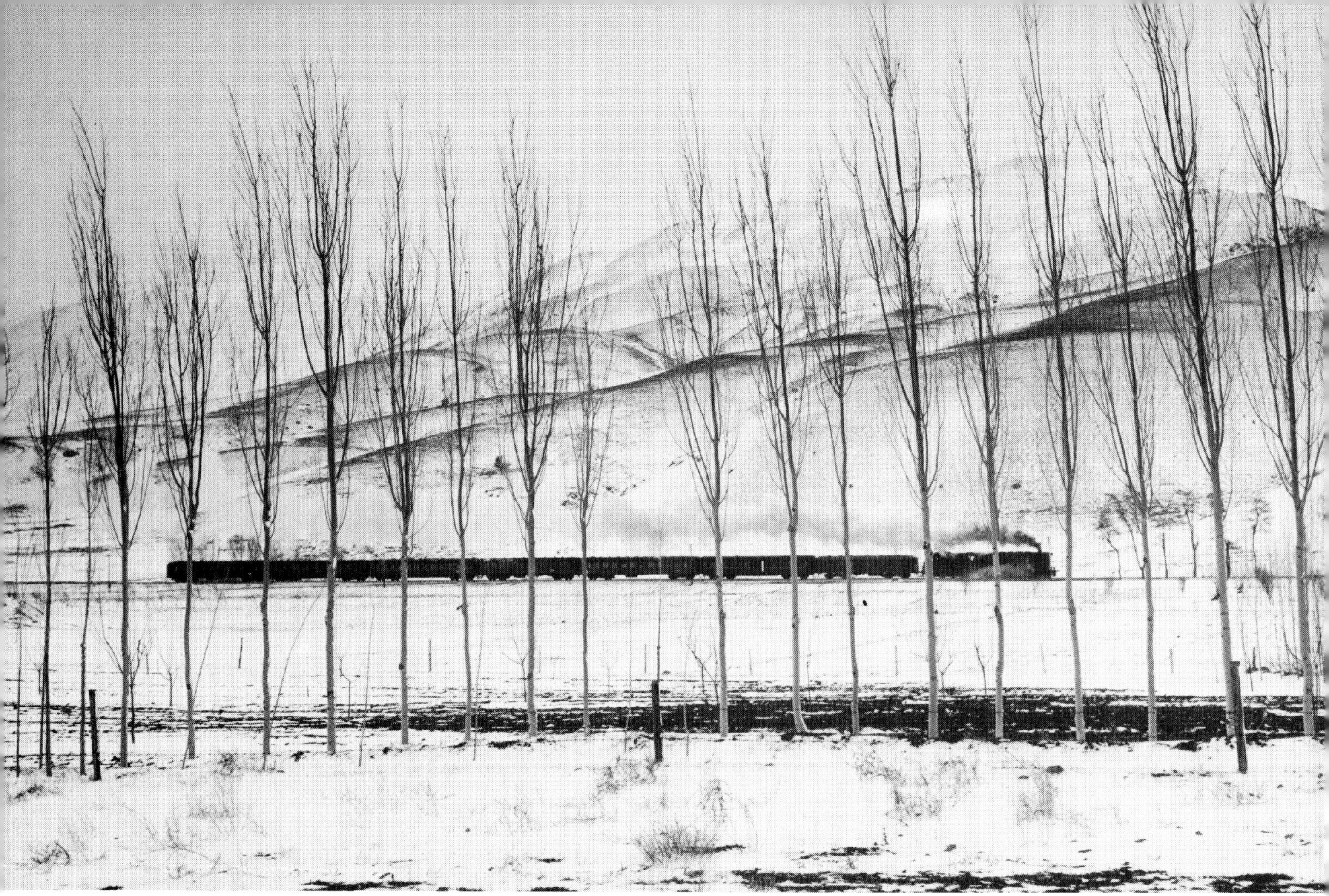

Rows of trees are used here to break the monotony of repeating horizontal lines. In this photograph a viewpoint was chosen such that the tops of the trees followed, at least approximately, the contours of the distant mountains. Note that the success of this picture depends rather extensively upon the snow-covered landscape from which the train is immediately identified as a black silhouette.

A Turkish Railways 3-cylinder 2-10-0 approaches the summit of the long climb from Adana, at Ulakisla, with a westbound express in March 1975.

Minolta Autocord 6 × 6 75mm Rokkor Tri-X D76 (1:1) 1/250th second f 8.

Two gnarled trees frame 45.010 as she crosses Smardale Viaduct on the Settle & Carlisle line with a down express on 13 May 1978. This location is quite some distance from the nearest road and an enthusiastic railway photographer will soon find that the discovery of interesting and out-of-the-way locations is so much easier if one owns, or has access to, a comprehensive selection of Ordnance Survey maps. This in turn identifies a problem of the lineside railway photographer abroad; detailed maps are not easily available and those which are may often include numerous inaccuracies. Those countries with political regimes which are not particularly sympathetic to railway photographers may regard enthusiasts laden with cameras, detailed maps and extracts from working timetables with more than a little suspicion.

Pentax 6 × 7 105mm Takumar Tri-X Perceptol (1:1) 1/125th second f 8/11.

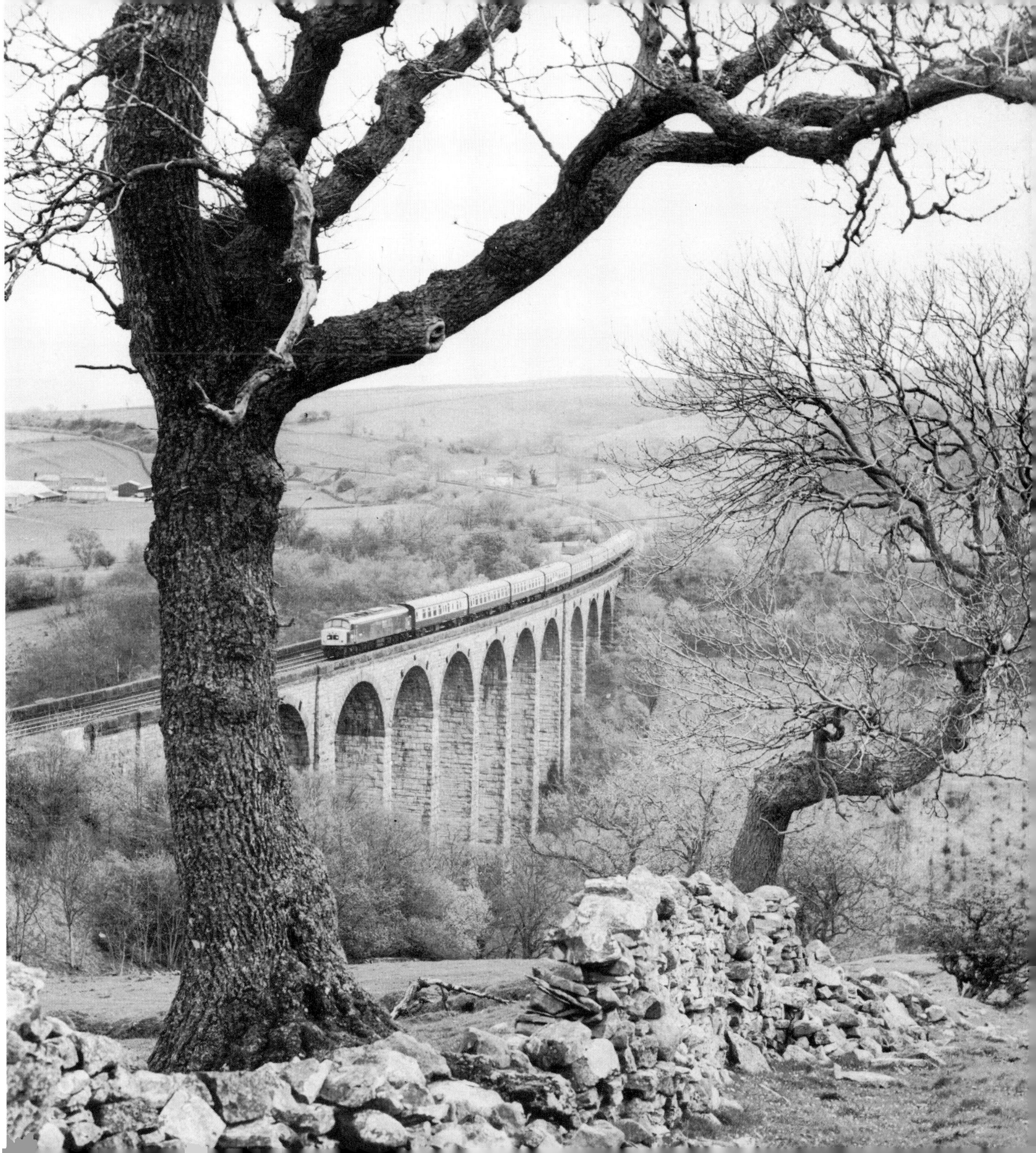

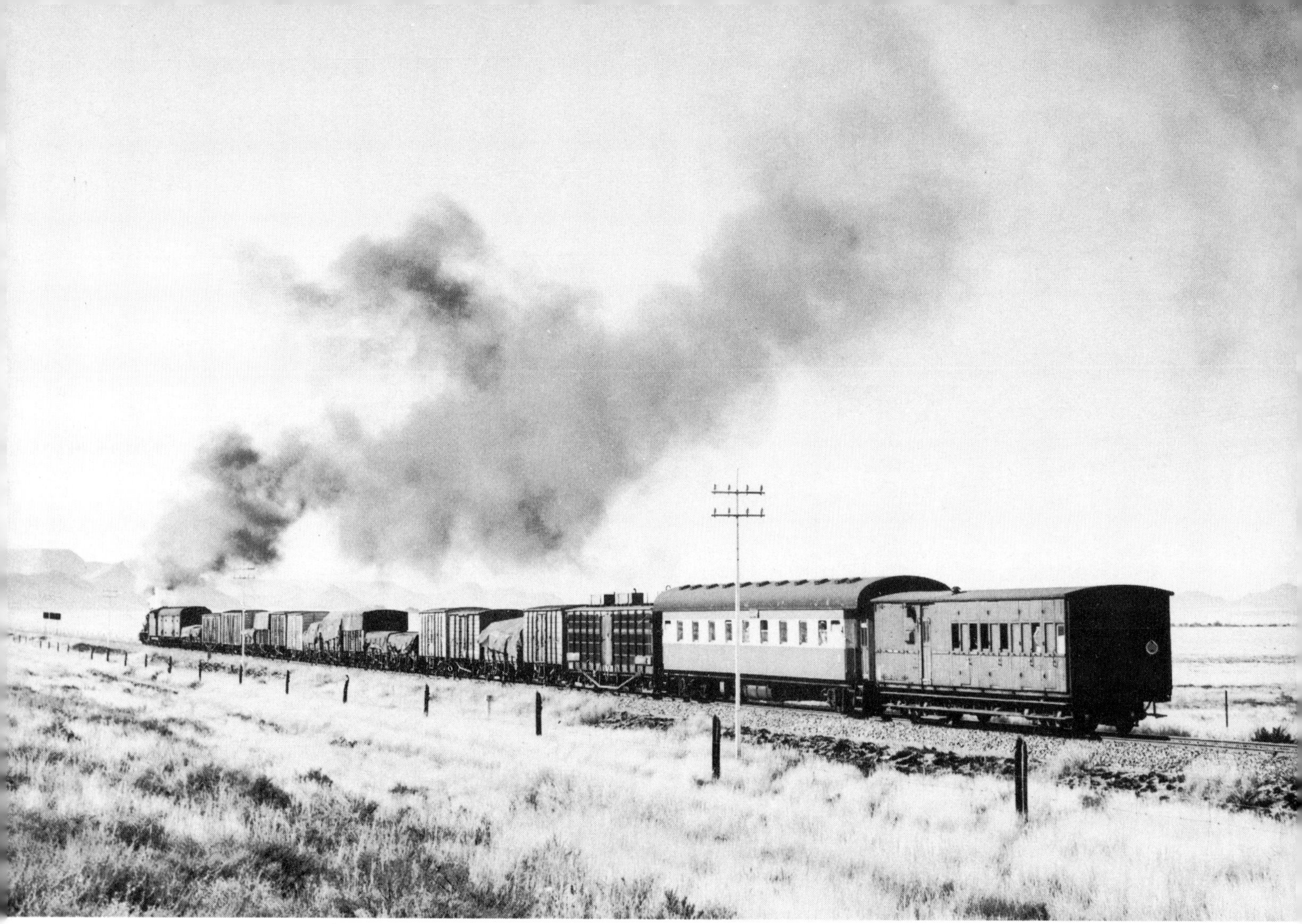

Very few outstanding photographs have been taken of trains moving away from the camera. The focal point of interest of a train is usually the locomotive, with the coaches or wagons playing an almost incidental role; indeed, most railway photographs are classic three quarter front studies. Occasionally, however, interest will be centred upon the train itself, and a viewpoint with the locomotive furthest away from the camera will provide a more pleasing perspective than one where the train crosses the field of view. Apart from ensuring that the prevailing wind direction was favourable, photographing this interesting South African Railways mixed train, as it meandered across the Karoo desert to the east of Rosmead, presented few problems. The train was travelling at a mere 30 m.p.h. in bright sunny weather; 1/250th second at an aperture of f8/11 on FP4 film developed in half strength D76 for twelve minutes produced a perfect negative.

Pentax 6 × 7 105mm Takumar FP4 D76 (1:1)
1/500th second f 6.3.

To produce an interesting photograph of a train of Mark I stock such as this one, represented by a Sheffield to St. Pancras express, is something of a challenge. A location which emphasises the elderly rolling stock rather than the locomotive is again required, and preferably one where sunlight would be reflected from the sides of the coaches towards the camera; this provides more interesting modelling than if the sun is behind the photographer. This up train approaching Chesterfield in the early afternoon in mid-winter admirably fulfils both of these criteria. Note the footbridge which frames the locomotive and takes the eye into the distance. The dramatic sky gives this photograph additional impact.

Pentax 6 × 7 200mm Takumar Tri-X Perceptol (1:1) 1/500th second f 8.

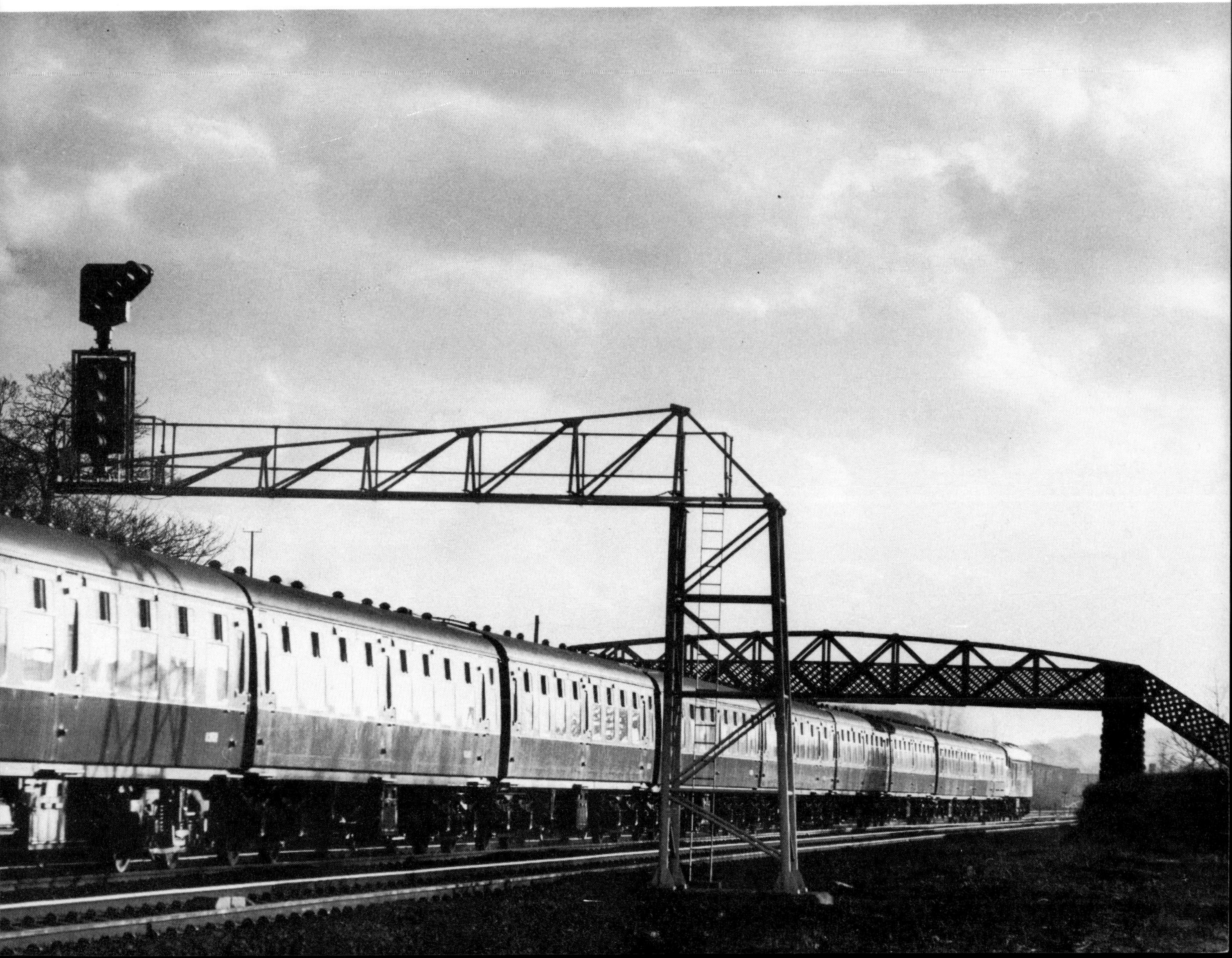

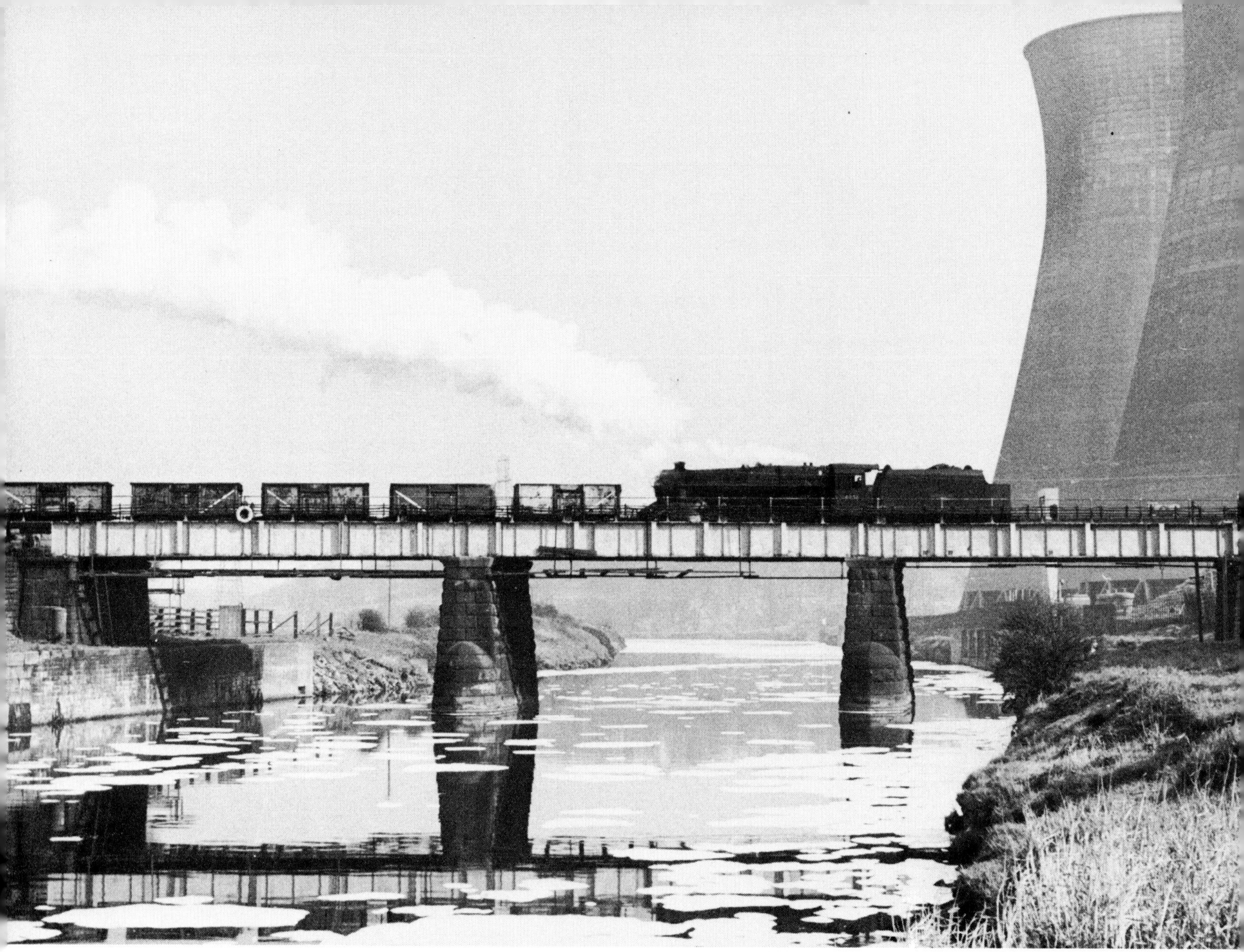

Steam locomotives travelling tender-first are among the more difficult railway subjects to photograph but even though the conventional three quarter front approach is usually unacceptable, interesting and occasionally outstanding photographs may be obtained if the photographer is prepared to use a little imagination. One obvious solution to the problem is to select a location where the train crosses the field of view of the camera as shown in the scene above depicting Stanier Class 5 No.44896 crossing the polluted Calder & Hebden Navigation canal at Wakefield in October 1965. In contrast the photograph opposite was not planned. I had watched the Class 9F 2-10-0 arrive at Hathersage in the Hope Valley, deposit its train in the up siding and then begin to move off, light engine, back to Sheffield. This scene appeared and disappeared in a matter of seconds but a camera at the ready, and complete familiarity with its controls, secured a quite unusual photograph.

Above: Exakta Varex IIa 50mm Pancolar FP4 Acutol 1/250th second f 6.3.

Opposite: Exakta Varex IIa 135mm Sonnar FP4 Acutol 1/500th second f 6.3.

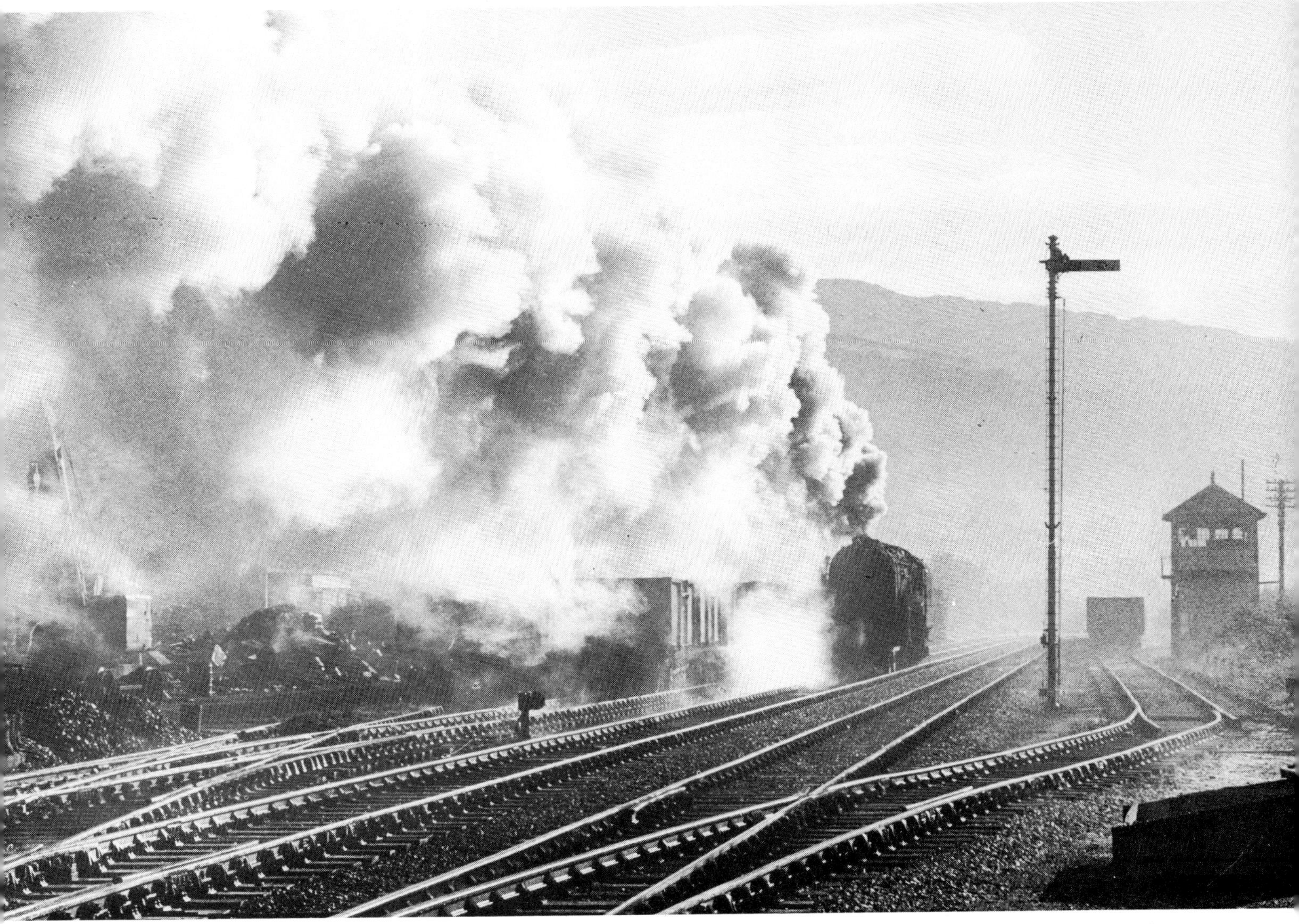

Overleaf: Some of the most impressive photographs of steam locomotives have been taken in those rather special winter conditions of frost and clear sun. The exploitation of this technique, where back lighting can be used to such tremendous effect, is a post-war development partially due to significant improvements in the performance of coated lenses in these demanding circumstances. In such weather each leak of steam condenses into a white cloud and frequently the driving wheels of a locomotive hard at work are completely hidden from view. Inevitably, contrasty negatives will result and it becomes difficult to retain adequate shadow detail. The detail of the front of this B R Class 9F has been almost totally sacrificed in optimising the exposure for the all-important exhaust. Not that this matters a great deal, for the totally black smokebox helps to create a feeling of immense power.

B R Class 9F 2-10-0 approaches Horton-in-Ribblesdale station with a freight for Carlisle on 4 November 1967.

Exakta Varex IIa 35mm 80mm Biometer FP4 Acutol 1/500th second f 8.

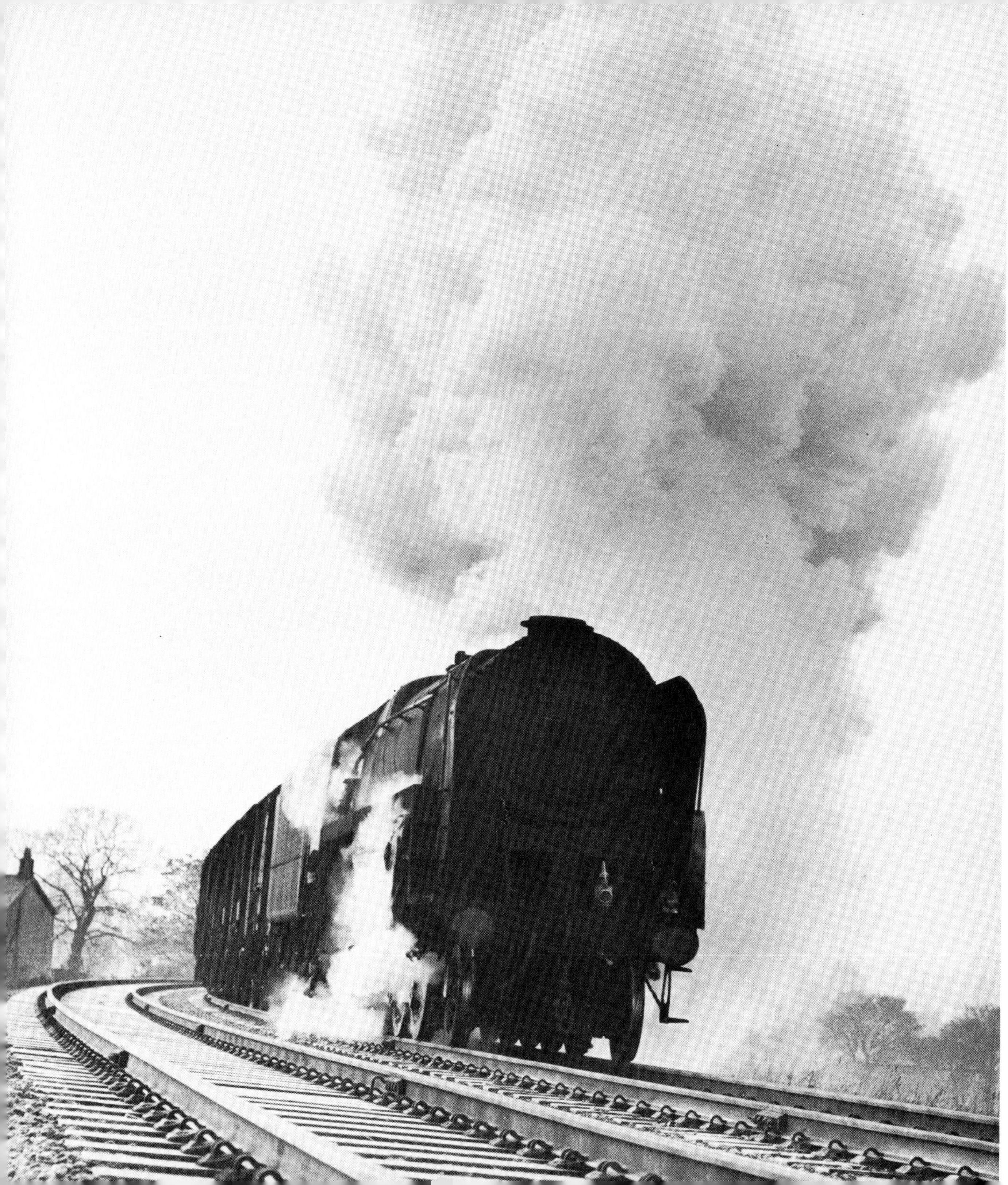

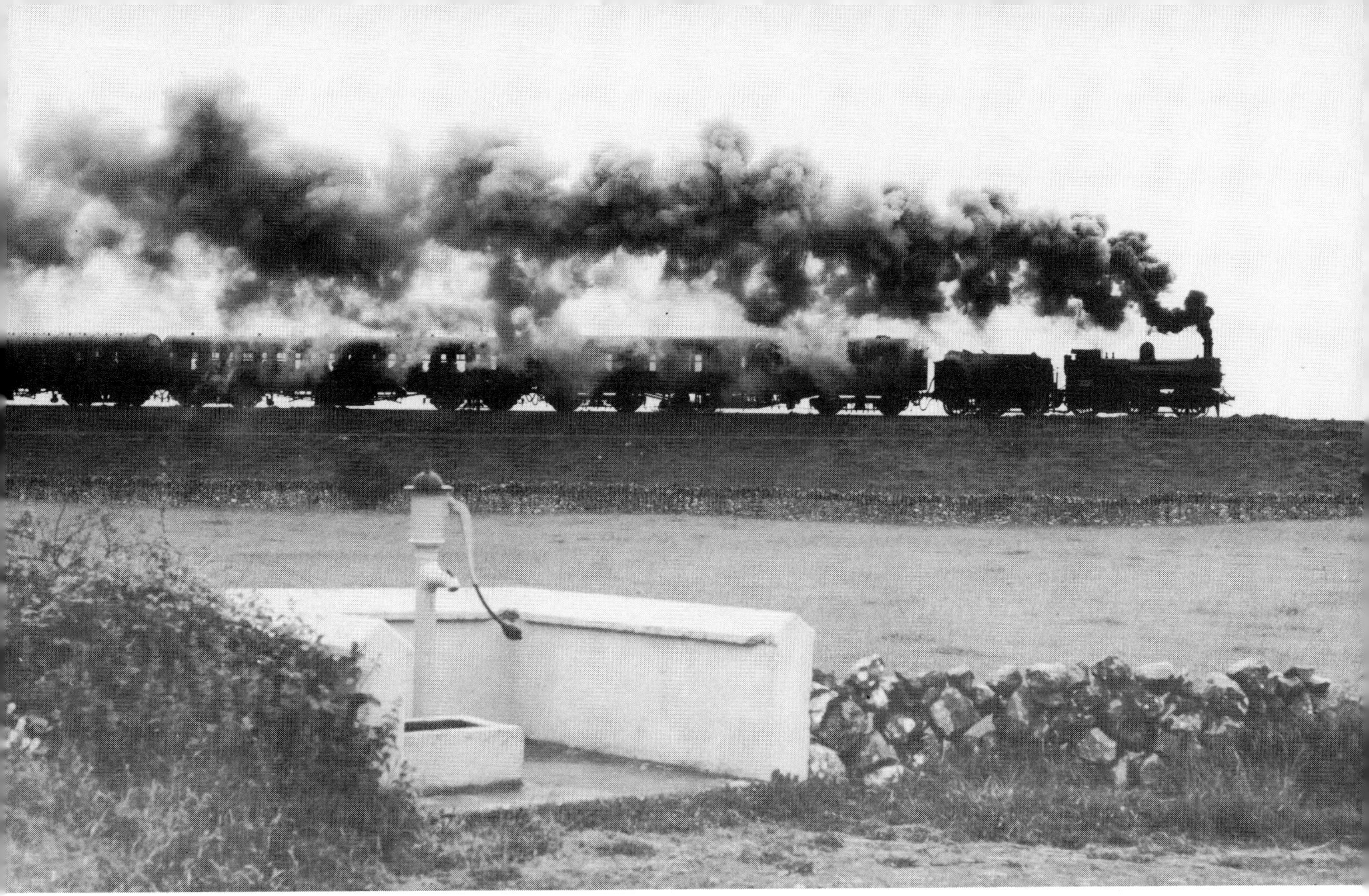

The more usual silhouette formula is one where the train is photographed against the sky as it traverses a high embankment. The best results are usually obtained when the subject is at an angle of 90° to the camera lens so that every detail of the outline of the locomotive and train is shown to maximum advantage. An open stretch of line with no lineside bushes, trees or buildings is to be preferred otherwise the attractive form of the train may well be spoiled. Trains hauled by steam engines provide the most spectacular subject material, particularly if the locomotive is smoking profusely. Modern motive power on the other hand, with no exhaust and a basically unattractive shape, does not easily lend itself to this treatment. In colour, superb photographs may often be obtained in the half hour preceding sunset or after sunrise. A location where the sun is shining into the camera lens should be selected and the shutter released at the moment when the engine obscures the sun. Exposure should be minimal, just enough to yield perfect sky tones. The composition of this photograph became the subject of some debate when it was recently circulated in a Rail Camera Club photographic portfolio. Some members suggested that the water pump in the foreground should be excluded, others that the pump should be in sharper focus, while some thought that it should be to the right of the picture rather than to the left. Suffice to note that such matters are subjective rather than definitive. The open debate of differing points of view is one of the many advantages which accrue from membership of a photographic portfolio.

Railway Preservation Society of Ireland preserved ex-G S W R 0-6-0 No.186 between Galway and Athenry Junction with an enthusiasts' excursion in 1976.

Pentax 6 × 7 105mm Takumar FP4 D76 (1:1)
1/250th second f 4.5.

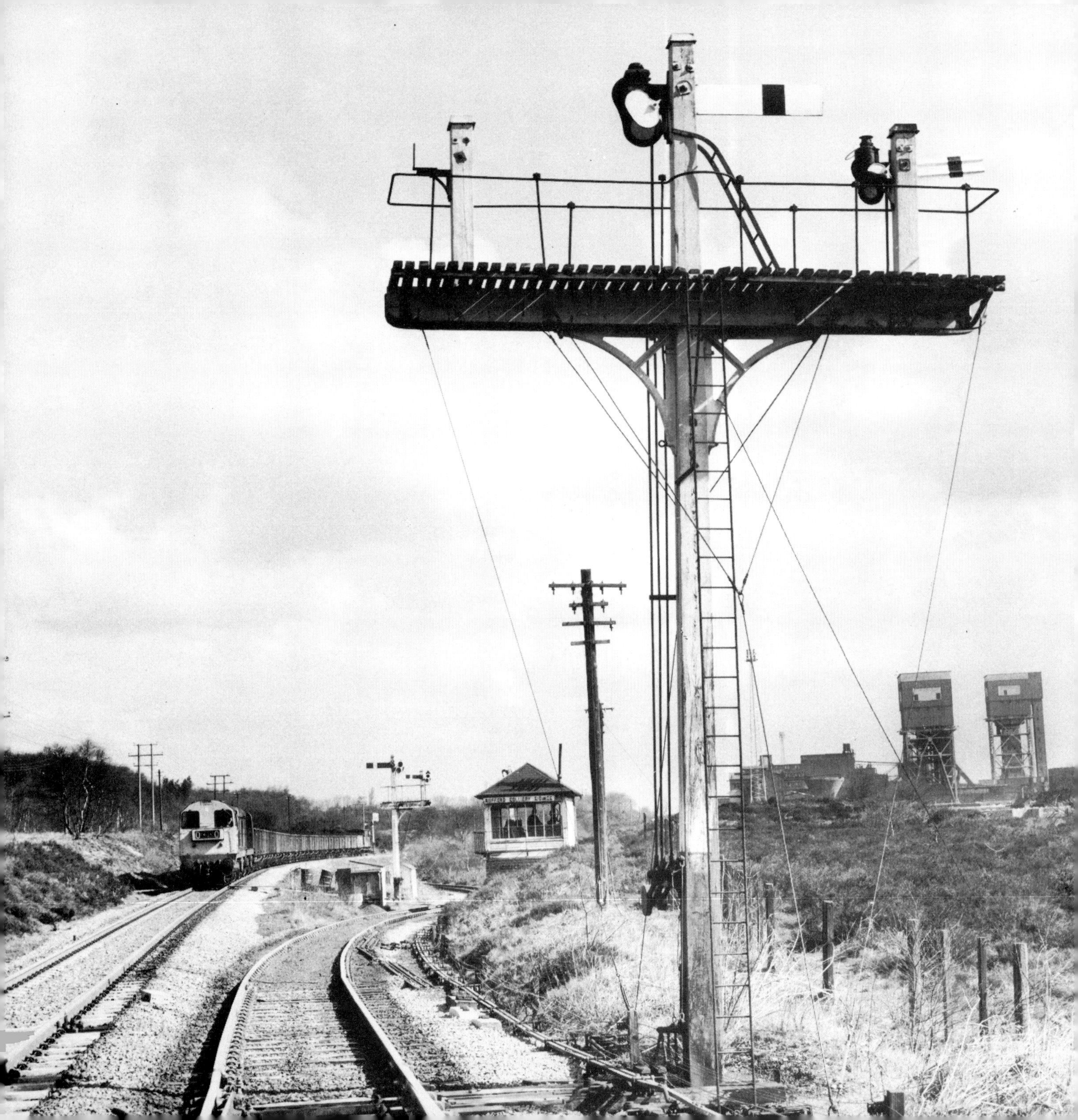

◀

A quite mundane location is often transformed by the intelligent inclusion of signals. A selection of photographs in which signals play a dominant role in the picture composition are presented in the next four pages. On the left the photograph is primarily a record of a fine pair of former Midland Railway lower quadrant signals at Rufford Colliery near Mansfield. A standard lens was used to obtain a perspective in which the signals dominate the rest of the scene. The use of a telephoto objective, from a more distant viewpoint, would have placed much more emphasis for example on the signal box and the train. The pictorial quality of this scene is considerably enhanced by the interesting sky tones. Cloud effects on sunny days are easily emphasised by the use of a pale yellow filter placed in front of the camera lens. An additional exposure of one and a half to two stops will normally be required.

Class 20 diesel-electrics Nos.20134/136 pass Rufford Colliery Sidings signal box on 14 April 1977.

Pentax 6 × 7 105mm Takumar Tri-X Perceptol (1:1) 1/250th second f 11.

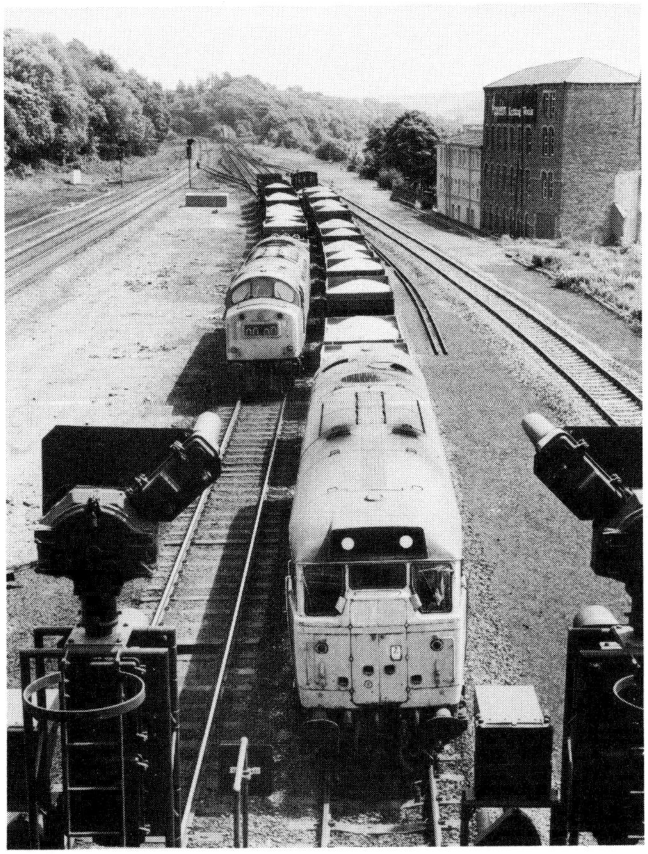

Colour light signals are visually much less attractive than their semaphore counterparts, but nonetheless appropriate to the modern railway scene. Part of a gantry of modern colour light signals on the site of Horbury and Ossett station forms an impressive foreground in this study of a Class 31 and a Class 40 diesel electrics simultaneously approaching Healey Mills marshalling yard from the east. A small aperture of f11 was necessary to provide sufficient depth of field; a shutter speed of 1/60th second was sufficient to arrest the 5 m.p.h. movement of the trains.

Pentax 6 × 7 105mm Takumar Tri-X Perceptol (1:1).

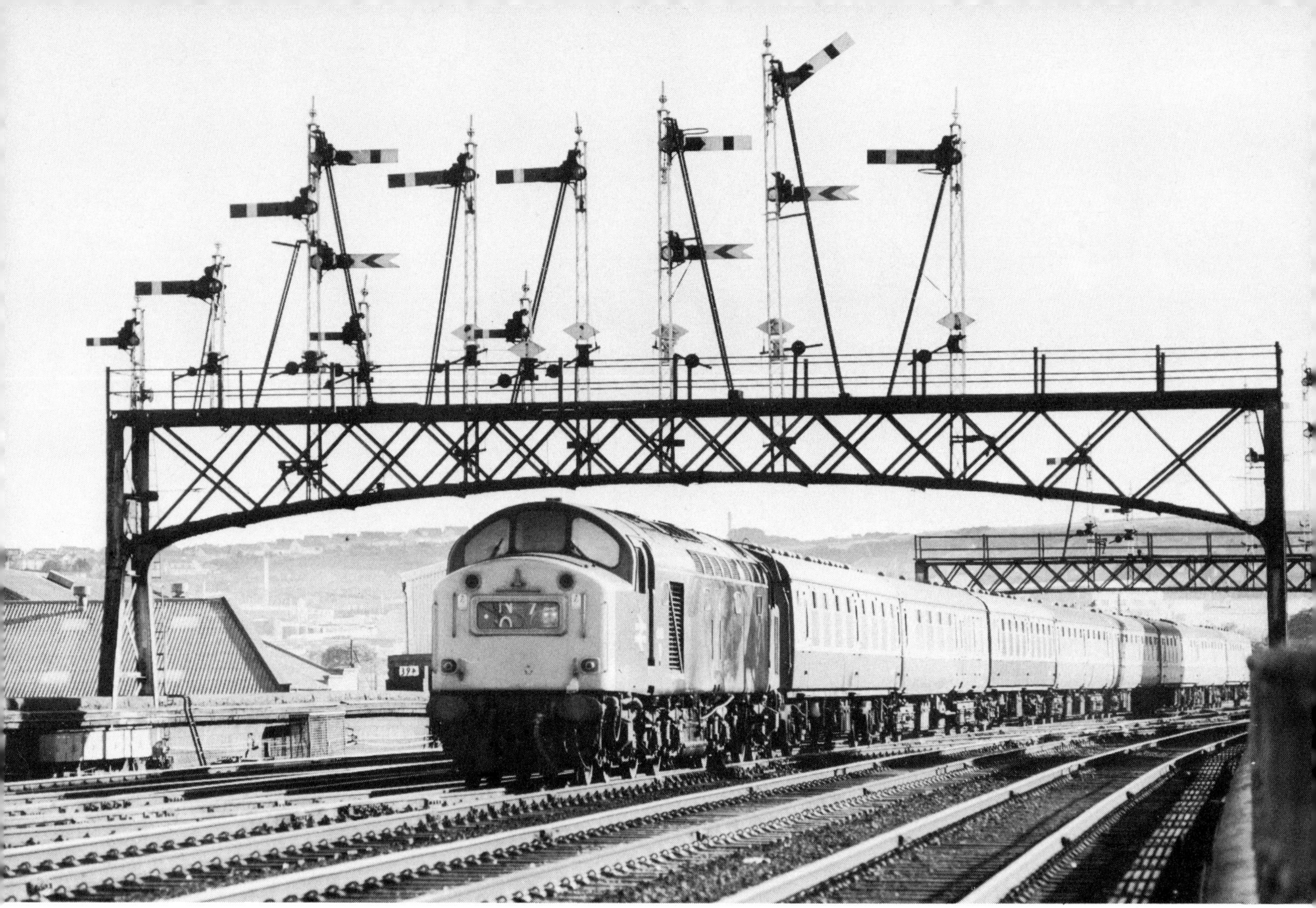

Gantries of semaphore signals were commonplace at most large stations in this country but few now remain. At the time of writing Aberdeen is a pleasant reminder of the pre-electronic railway signalling age. The attractive arch of this gantry, alongside Ferryhill signal box, superbly frames Class 40 No. 40 184 with an Edinburgh–Aberdeen express on 3 September 1977. Assessing the optimum point for making an exposure is not as easy as it may appear. In this case the careful observation of the preceding down train was necessary to ensure that the locomotive would be clear of the gantry and that the whole of the train would be included in the field of view.

Pentax 6 × 7 200mm Takumar FP4 D76 (1:1)
1/500th second f 6.3.

Semaphore signals serve to precisely identify a location; an important point to bear in mind when photographing locomotives or trains in unusual territory. It would be quite pointless to photograph, for example, a Deltic on the Western Region in a rural location which could perhaps be anywhere on the East Coast main line. Here Class 52 diesel-hydraulic No. 1023 *Western Fusilier* is clearly in unusual surroundings as she negotiates the intricacies of Black Carr Junction, Doncaster, with an enthusiasts' excursion for York on 20 November 1976. Note how the top of the right hand foreground signal has been placed between the signal box and the signals in the middle distance but it does, unfortunately, tend to bisect the train. Were it possible, a slightly higher viewpoint would have avoided this problem.

Pentax 6 × 7 200mm Takumar Tri-X D76 (1:1)
1/500th second f 8.

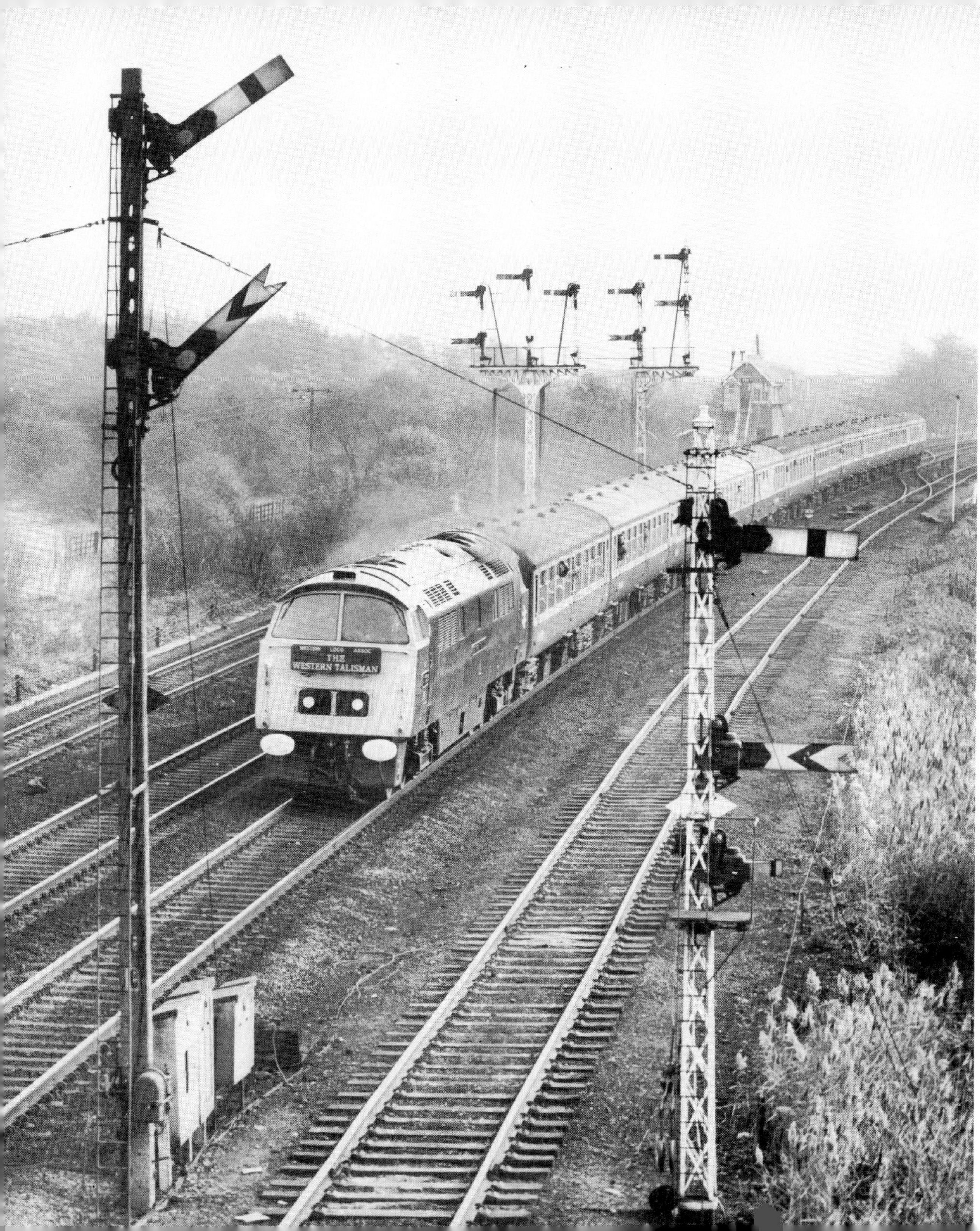
THE
WESTERN TALISMAN

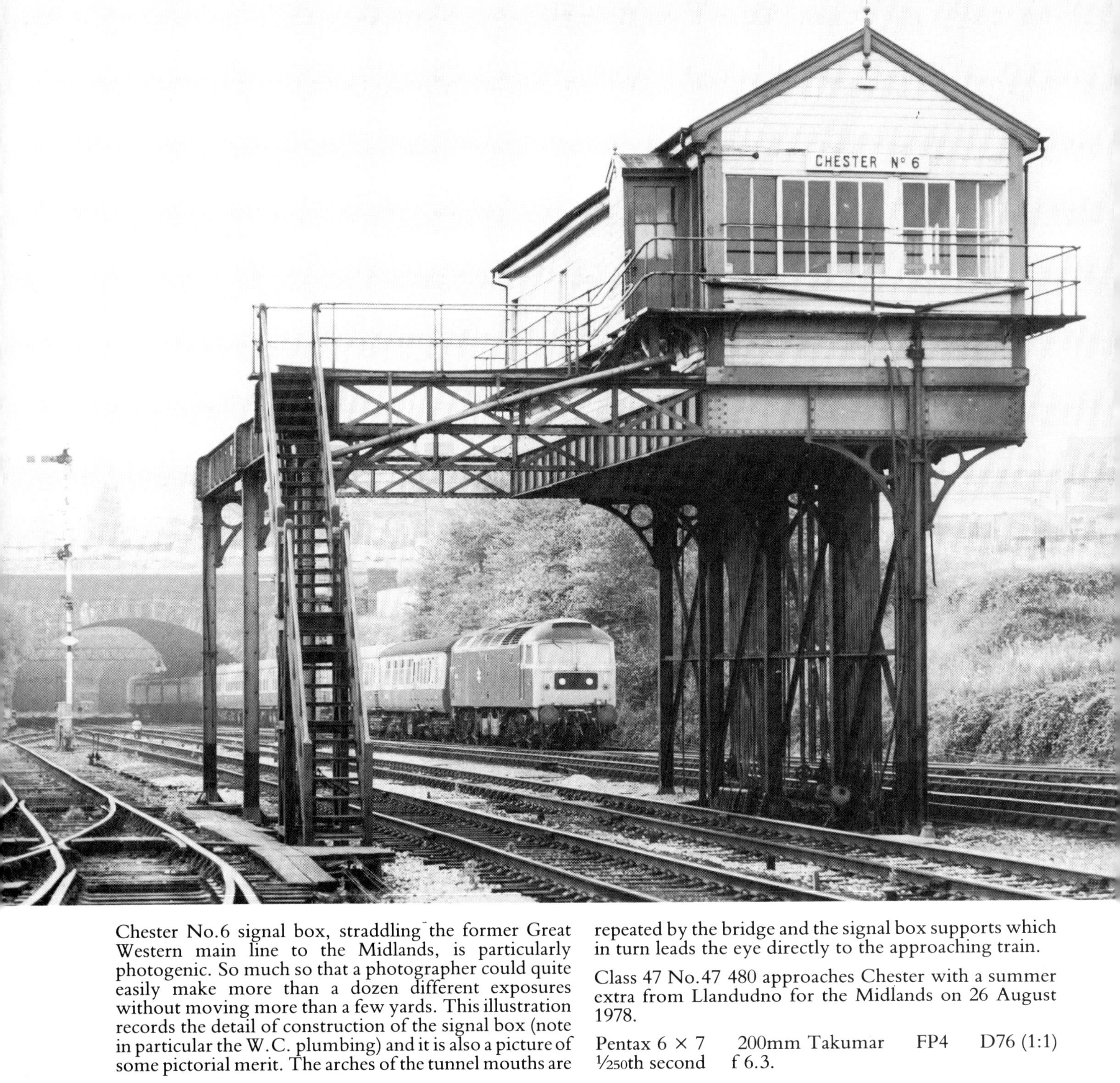

Chester No.6 signal box, straddling the former Great Western main line to the Midlands, is particularly photogenic. So much so that a photographer could quite easily make more than a dozen different exposures without moving more than a few yards. This illustration records the detail of construction of the signal box (note in particular the W.C. plumbing) and it is also a picture of some pictorial merit. The arches of the tunnel mouths are repeated by the bridge and the signal box supports which in turn leads the eye directly to the approaching train.

Class 47 No.47 480 approaches Chester with a summer extra from Llandudno for the Midlands on 26 August 1978.

Pentax 6 × 7 200mm Takumar FP4 D76 (1:1) 1/250th second f 6.3.

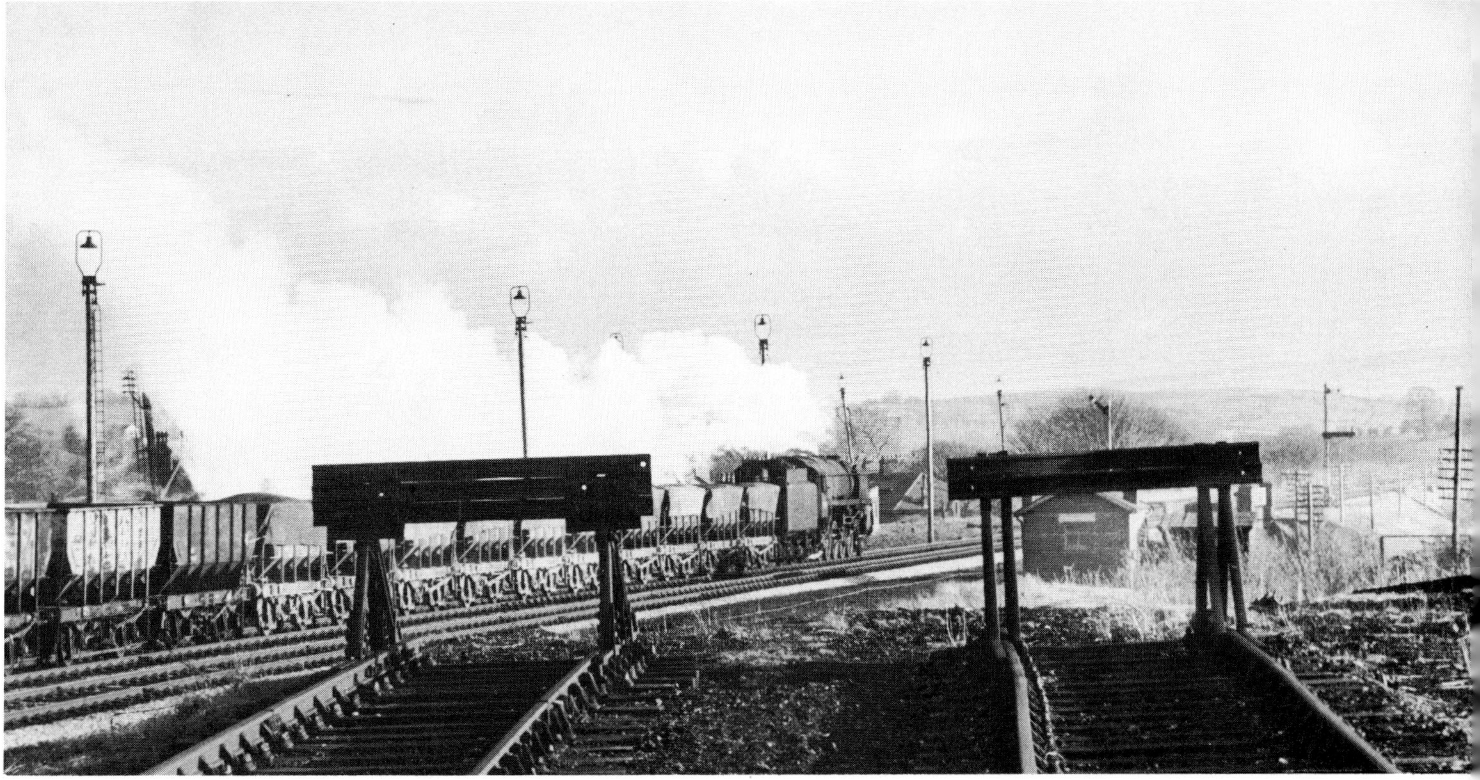

Buffer stops are rarely the main feature of a railway photograph. Two, at the end of the down sidings at Hellifield, are used to good effect in this study of a B R Class 9F 2-10-0 leaving with an up Long Meg anhydrite train in 1966. Note the apparent grain in this photograph which was caused by reticulation. This phenomenon frequently occurs when a film suddenly experiences a sudden downward temperature change; the emulsion, relative to the support, rapidly contracts and thus gives an overall grainy appearance to the negative. The problem is usually encountered in the winter and spring months when the water used for washing a film, if taken directly from the tap, may have a temperature as low as 2 or 3°C. Since the temperature of the developer and fixer are usually maintained at about 20°C the thermal shock experienced by a film will be considerable. The problem is quite simply solved by strict temperature control of all solutions throughout the processing and washing procedures.

Exakta Varex IIa 135mm Sonnar FP4 Acutol
1/250th second f 6.3.

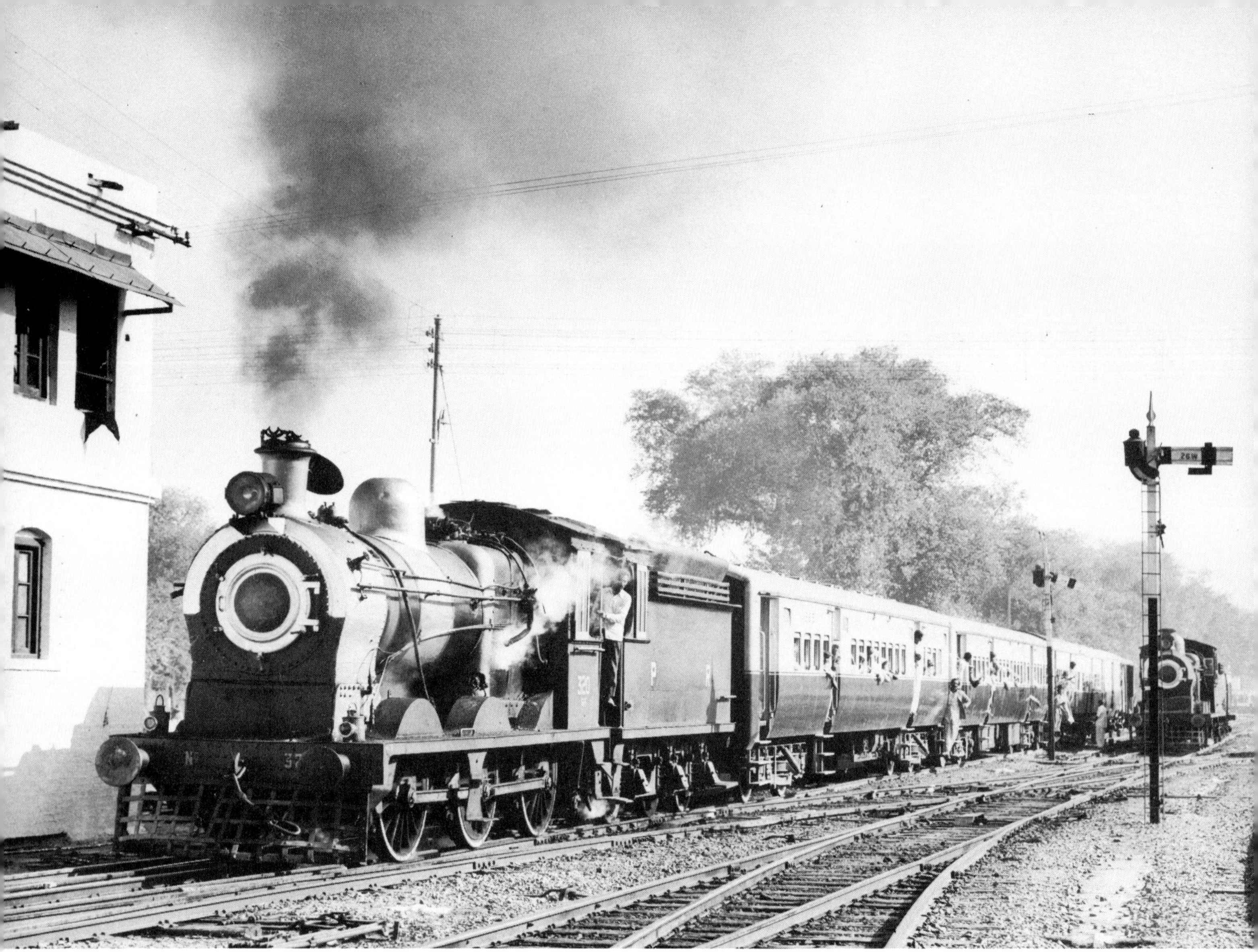

Telegraph poles, lamp posts and wires are the bane of the railway photographer. On many occasions it is possible to avoid these difficulties, or at least to minimise the problem, by the careful choice of a viewpoint but the exclusion of all wires and poles from the picture above was virtually impossible: a recurrent problem incidentally in many urban Asian locations. In this case a strong composition, where the locomotive is placed on a third and is framed by part of the signal box and the trees, successfully counters the pole which appears to emerge from the top of the boiler. In a completely open location a pole in this position would tend to be unacceptable although better here than apparently sprouting from the chimney of the engine. Removal of offending poles by techniques such as those outlined on page 14 will rarely succeed. A white ghost image is very difficult to spot so that it convincingly merges with the other sky tones, even if a viewer is prepared to accept obviously unsupported wires.

Pakistan Railways Class SGS 0-6-0 No.320 leaves Malakwal Junction with a local passenger train for Bhera.

Pentax 6 × 7 105mm Takumar FP4 D76 (1:1) 1/500th second f 5.6.

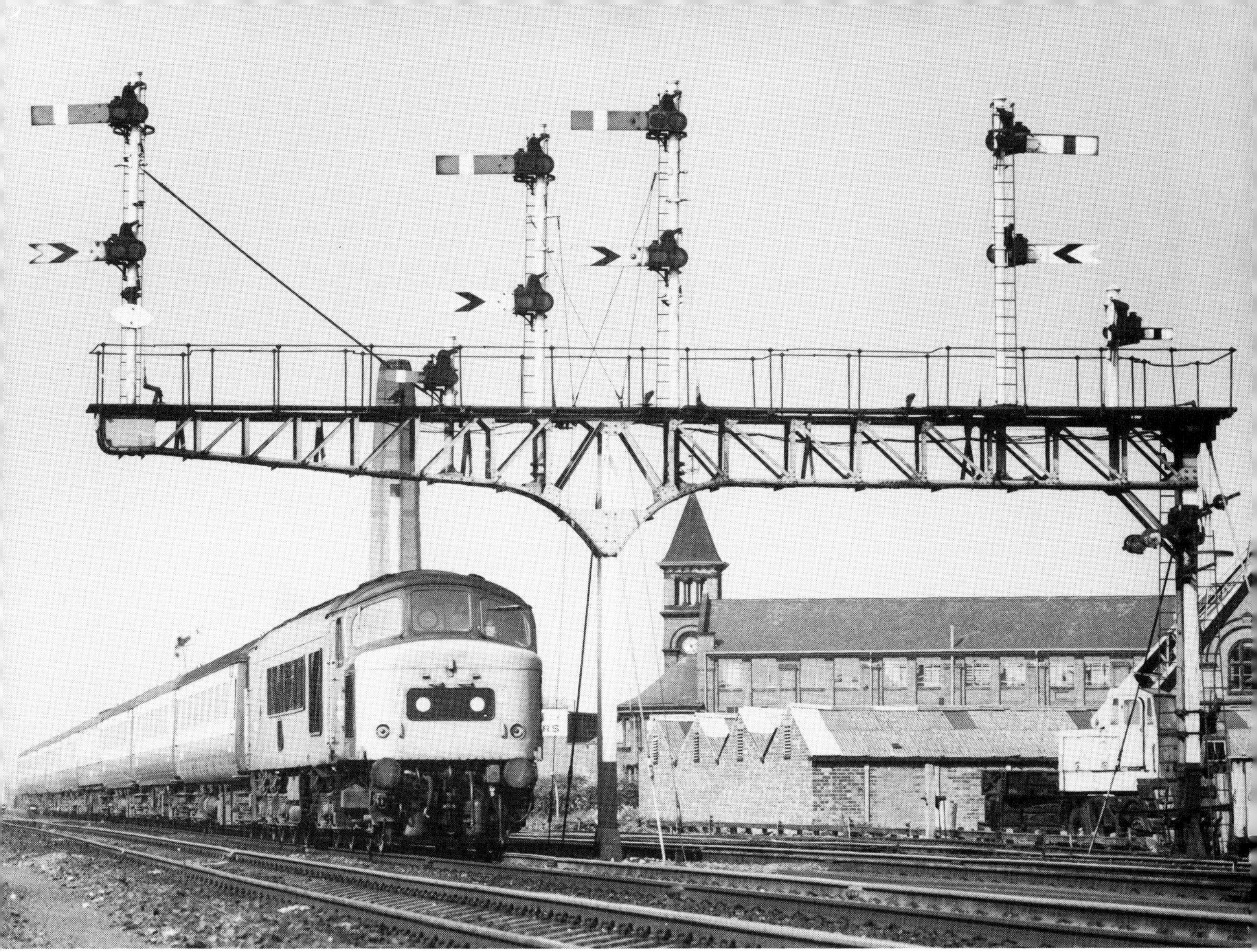

This photograph is, compositionally, a failure. At least three problems are apparent. A fundamental error is the way in which the central support of the gantry, and the two signals immediately above it, divide the picture into almost two equal halves, indeed the right hand half of the photograph is almost superfluous. Further the huge chimney which appears to sprout from the top of the diesel locomotive is immediately obvious whilst in addition the exact coincidence of the apex of the triangular roof of the clock tower with the gantry is less than ideal. This location was studied at length and a satisfactory picture of a train approaching this gantry from the north could not be obtained in the afternoon. A photograph taken in the morning, from the other side of the line and through the arch of the gantry, is entirely satisfactory.

A Sheffield to St. Pancras express approaches Bell Lane signal box to the north of Leicester with Class 45 No. 45 101 in charge; photographed 29 May 1978.

Pentax 6 × 7   200mm Takumar   Tri-X   Perceptol (1:1)   1/500th second   f 8.

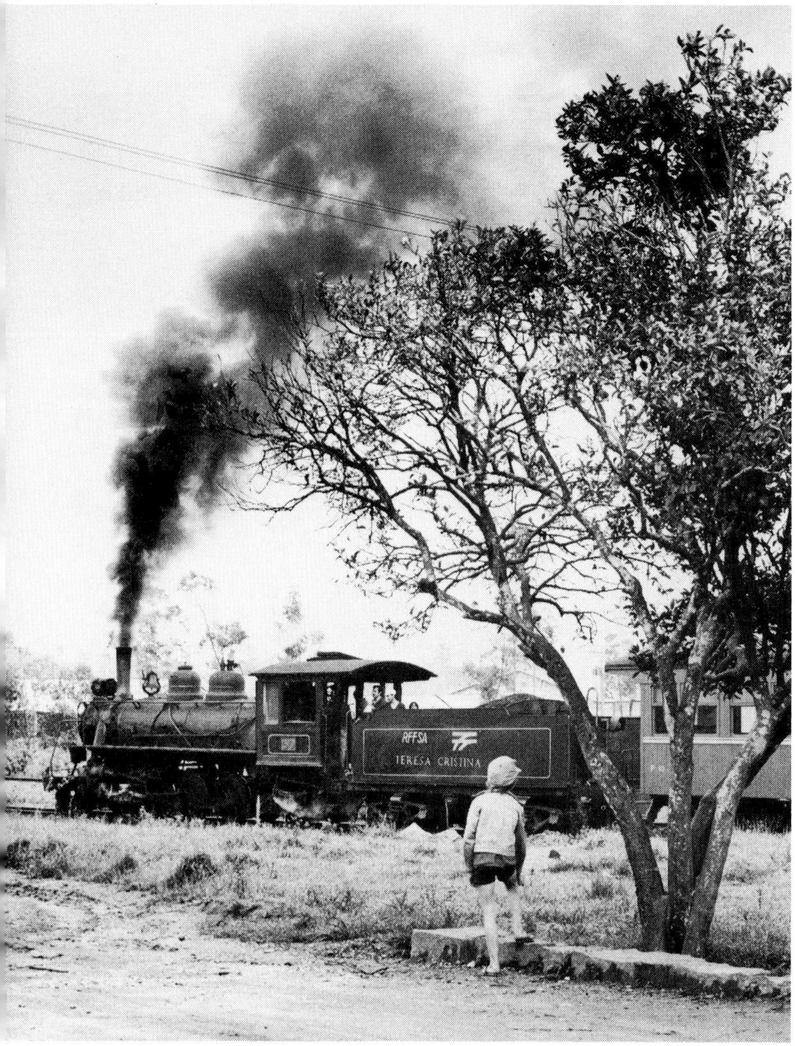

HUMAN INVOLVEMENT

The international fascination of the steam engine; a small boy admires the handsome lines of Brazilian Federal Railways (Estrada de Ferro Dona Teresa Cristina) metre gauge Baldwin 4-6-2 No.50 as she pauses for water at Esplanada with a weed-killing train in August 1976. The definition of this photograph is rather suspect — the results of making a hasty exposure before the boy had a chance to move.

Pentax 6 × 7 105mm Takumar Tri-X D76 (1:1) 1/250th second f 4.5.

People are an integral part of most railway scenes, yet so many photographers will go to extraordinary lengths to exclude fellow beings from the field of view — an attitude which is perhaps understandable if the human involvement is a group of brightly dressed, camera bedecked fellow enthusiasts . . . Obviously there is a place for views of trains on the move in lonely, out-of-the-way locations. However, the spontaneous involvement of passengers, railway personnel or even spectators will often transform an adequate record of an event into a scene which also tells a story. This is illustrated by the photograph opposite of Indonesian Railways (P N J A) wood-burning Class 26 0-6-0T on the daily Kediri to Paré local service in August 1977. The amorous attentions of the fireman of the engine towards the girl are superbly countered by her interested but passive behaviour. Note that the locomotive, and the fireman in particular, are the focal point of interest. A weakness is the rather blank highlight area at the bottom lefthand corner, which could have been darkened by 'burning in' slightly at the printing stage.

Pentax 6 × 7 105mm Takumar Tri-X Perceptol (1:1) 1/500th second f 6.3.

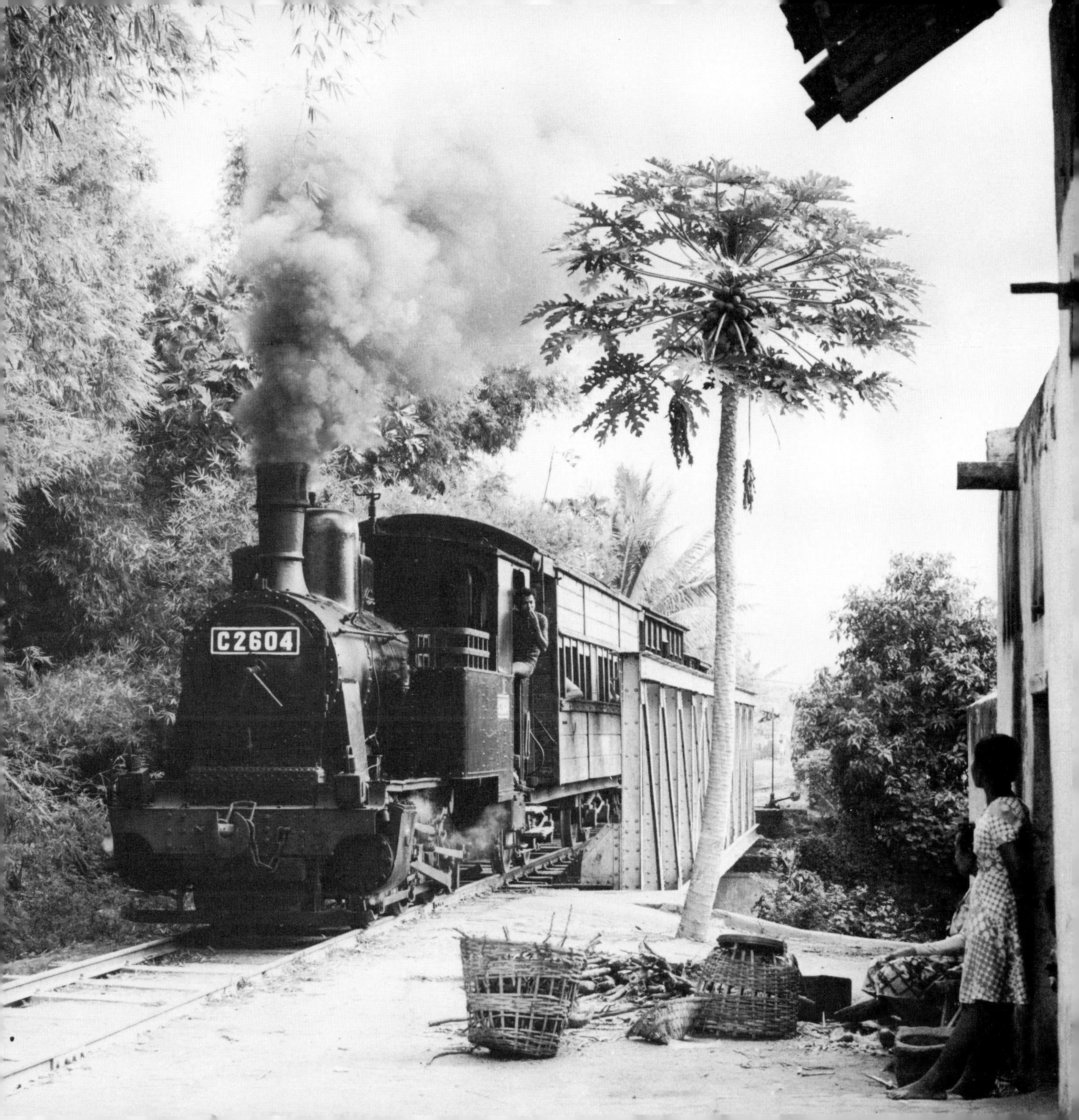
C2604

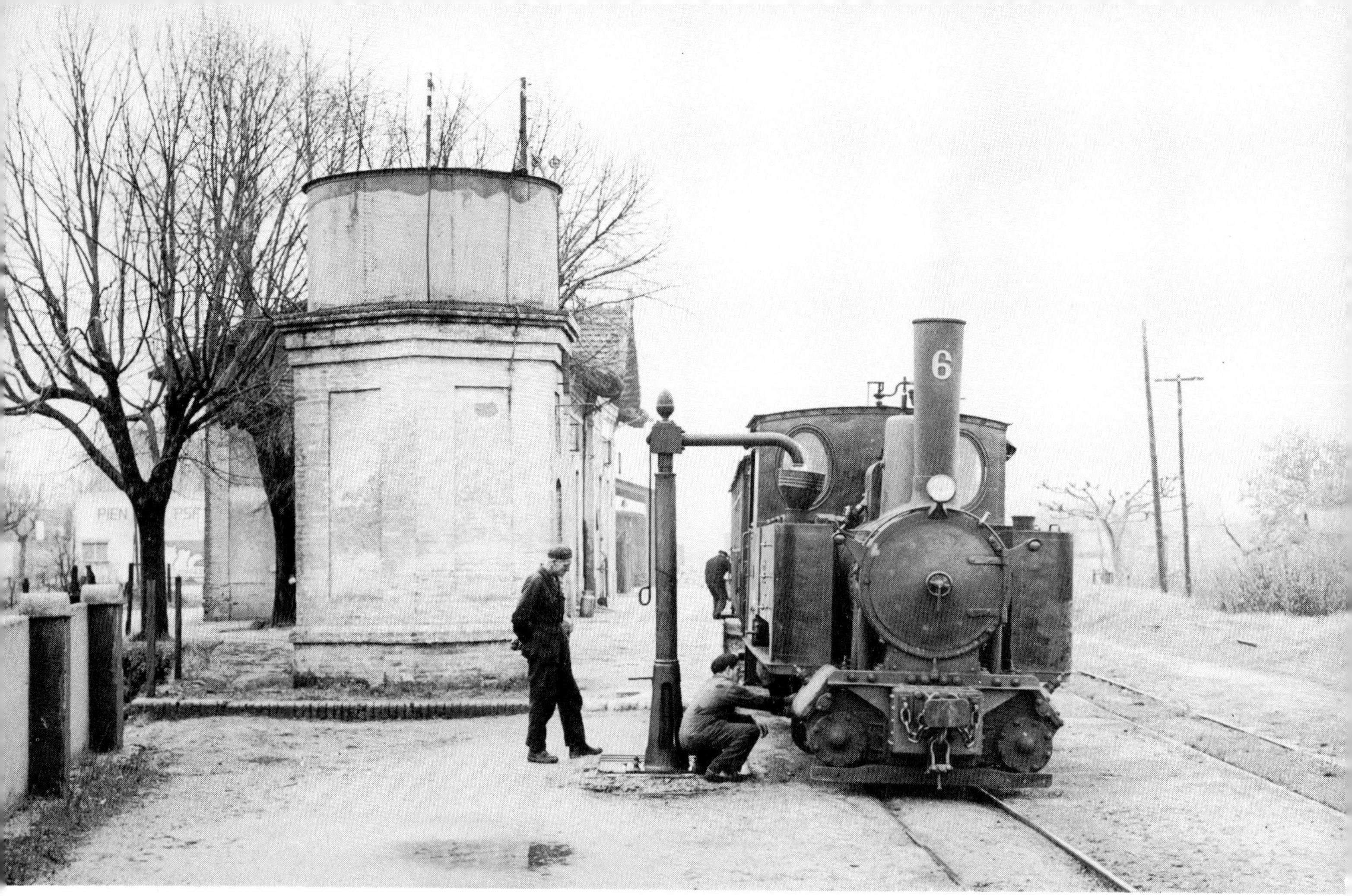

Railwaymen at work. No.6, a narrow gauge 0–6–2T of the San Felui to Gerona (S F G) railway in Spain, is apparently giving the crew some cause for concern as she pauses for a lengthy stop at the deserted station of Llagostera in 1969. The presence of the driver, to the left of the water column, is of vital importance; note how, through him, attention is focused upon the fireman and the locomotive.

Minolta Autocord 6 × 6 75mm Rokkor Tri-X D76 (1:1) 1/125th second f 4.5.

A much lower viewpoint was deliberately selected for the scene opposite, which features a Class 40 diesel electric at Earl's Sidings, Hope, on a misty morning in December 1978. The camera was a mere eighteen inches or so above the ground, and this has emphasised the interesting trackwork, which takes the eye into the picture and to the locomotive. On frosty rails, No. 40 016 was faced with the arduous task of moving a heavy cement train out of the siding and on to the main line, hence the secondman's manual sanding activity. This procedure took quite some time, and the photographer had ample opportunity to make several exposures. This was the best of three; in the other two the driver and guard, just visible to the left of the locomotive were in a dominant position detracting from a simplicity of presentation. ▶

Pentax 6 × 7 200mm Takumar Tri-X Perceptol (1:1) 1/500th second f 8/11.

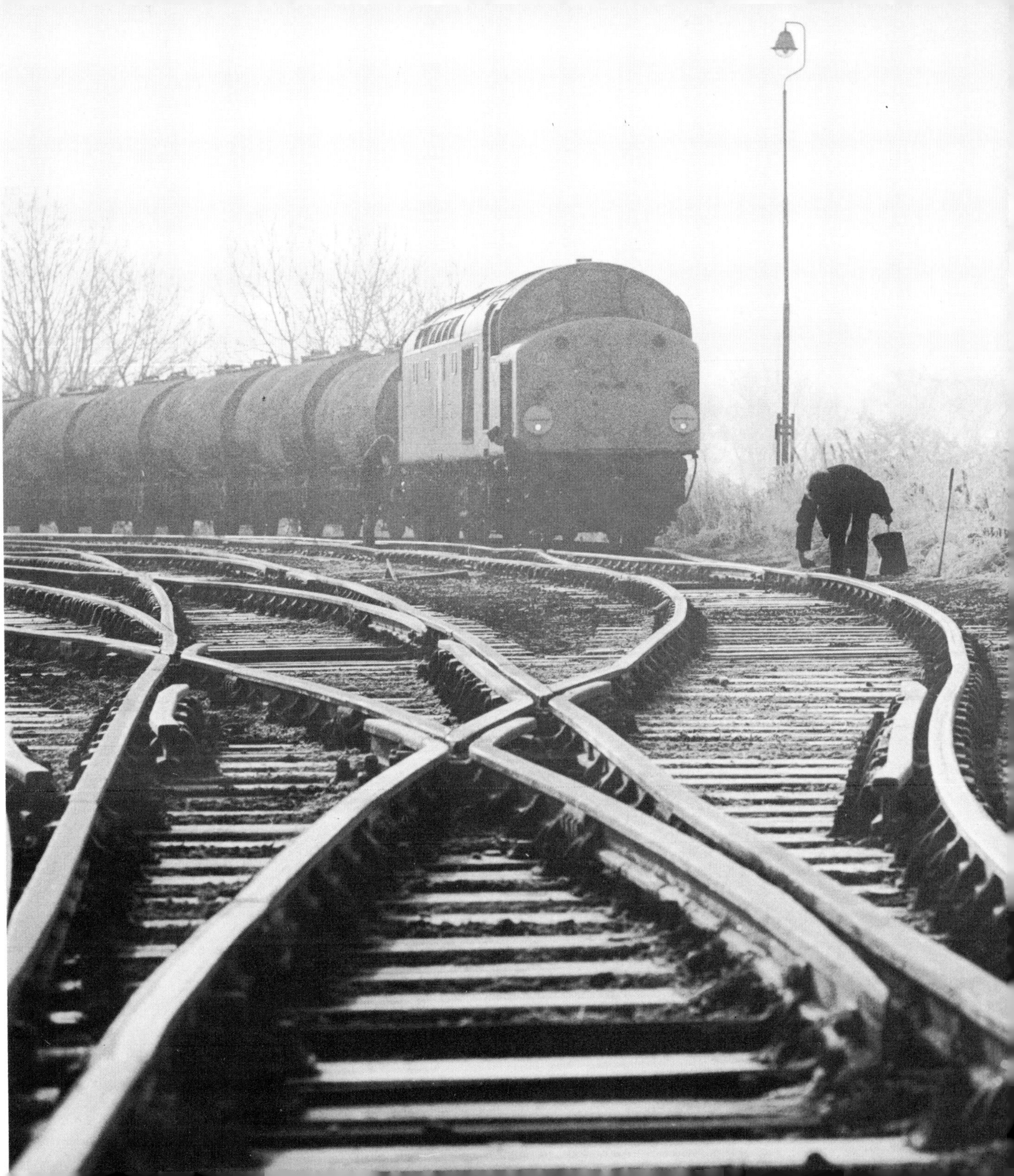

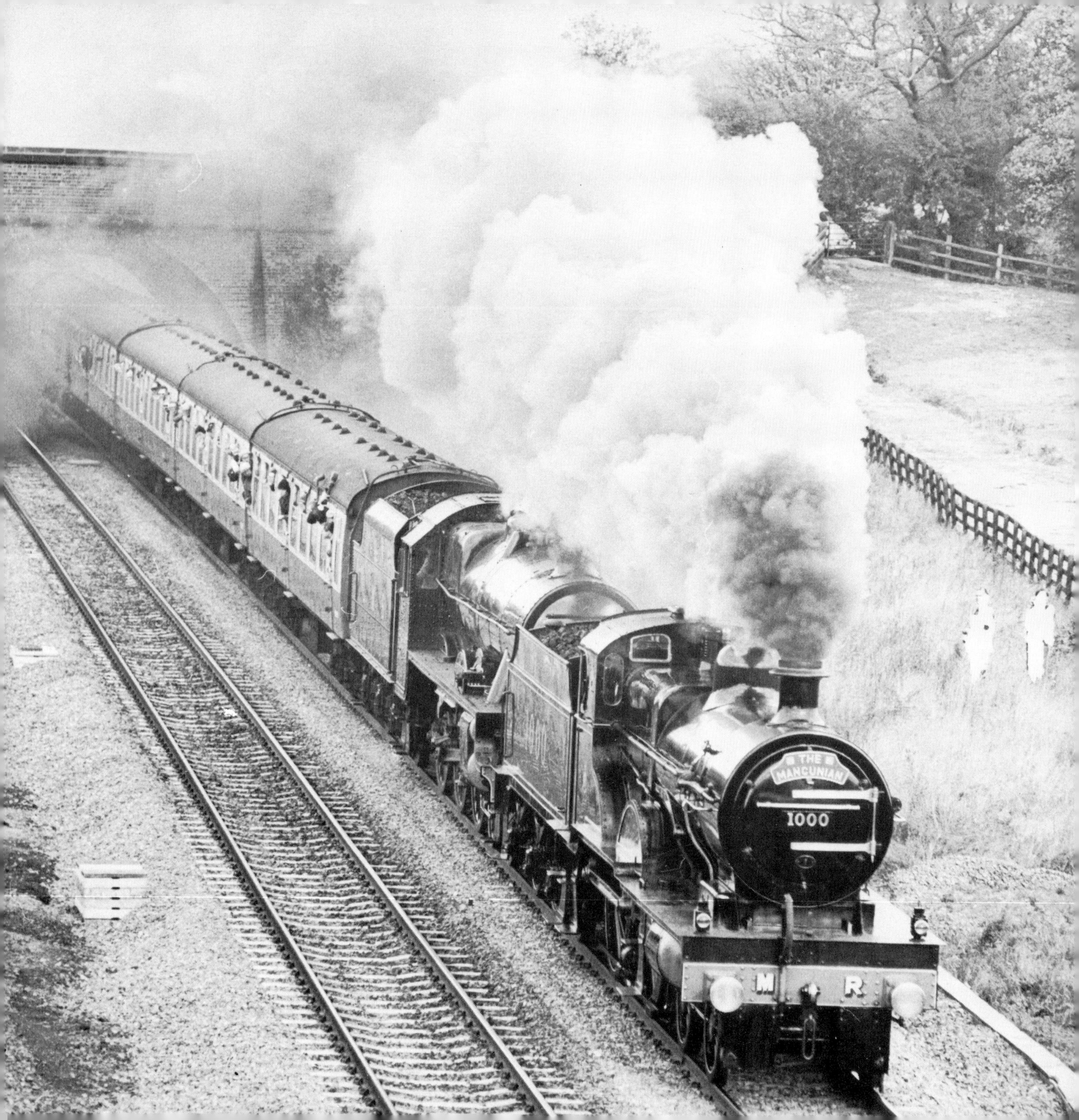
THE MANCUNIAN
1000
M R

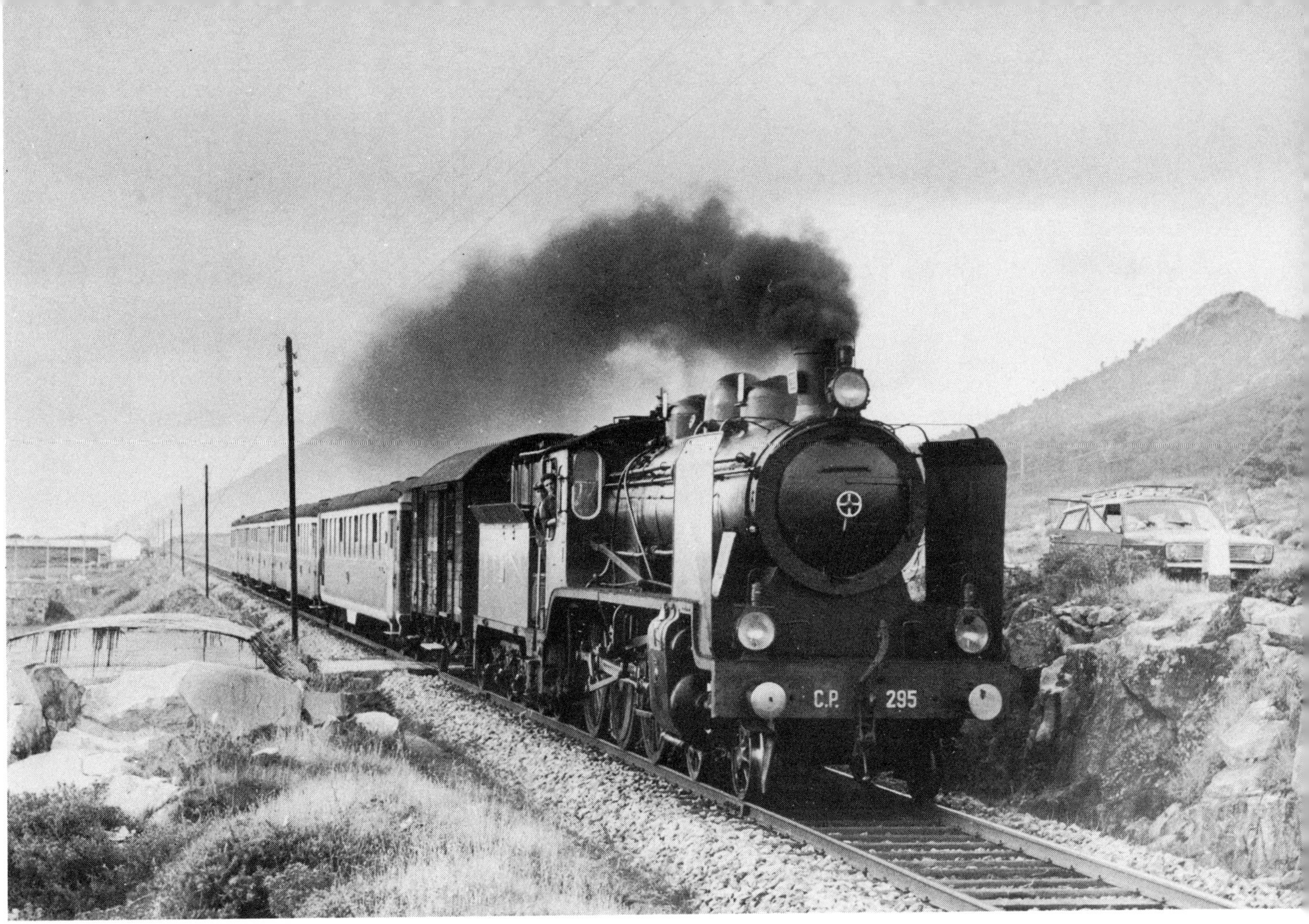

◀ Since so many enthusiasts now turn out to photograph the mainline excursions of preserved steam it often becomes difficult to exclude them from your own field of view; particularly at the more popular locations. Fortunately, at least in black-and-white photography, it is often possible to remove them after the exposure has been made. The best technique, with larger format negatives, is to carefully paint out the appropriate images using photographic opaque as detailed on page 14. Two enthusiasts have been so treated in this photograph of 'Jubilee' No.5690 *Leander* and former Midland Compound 4-4-0 No.1000 as they approach Copmanthorpe with an excursion bound for Dinting on 30 September 1978. Normally the resultant white images would be carefully spotted; a fairly easy task when the immediate background is an intimate blend of a variety of tones.

Pentax 6 × 7 200mm Takumar Tri-X D76 (1:1) 1/500th second f 6.3.

To have one's own car spoil your own photograph is unforgivable! Inevitably situations such as this arise when a photographer is attempting to repeatedly photograph a train by following it along nearby roads. Chasing is not conducive to photographic excellence since very little time is allowed for the critical assessment of a potential location and unforeseen difficulties and problems have to be reluctantly accepted. The photographer's car, complete with open doors, is certainly in on the act in this view of Portuguese Railways 4-6-0 No.295 working a Porto-bound local train on the coast line near Viana do Castelo. In colour, the result is even more disastrous since the red car totally dominates the scene.

Minolta Autocord 6 × 6 75mm Rokkor Tri-X D76 (1:1) 1/500th second f 4.5.

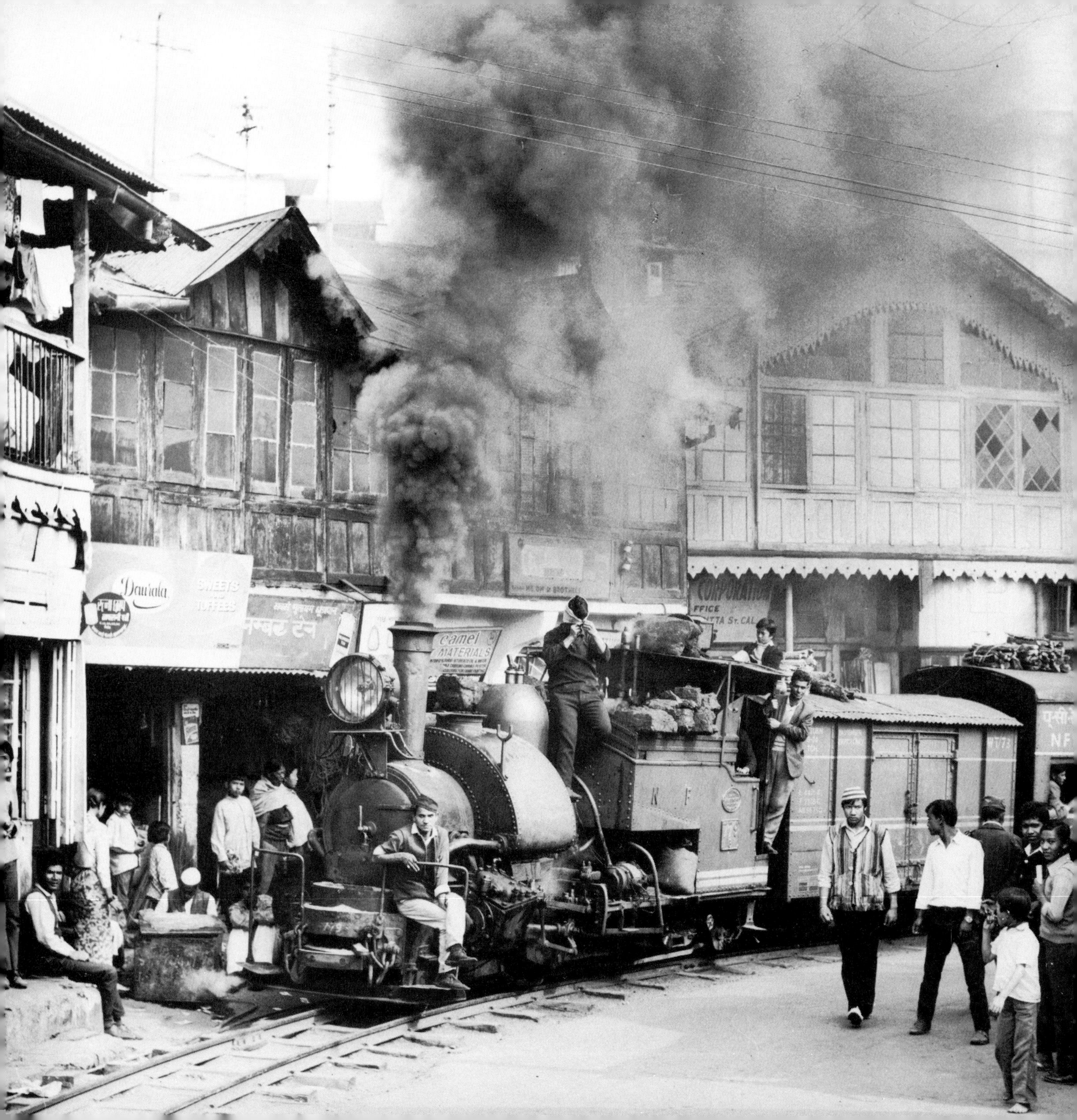
Daurala
SWEETS
TOFFEES
camel
MATERIALS
CORPORATION
FFICE
N F

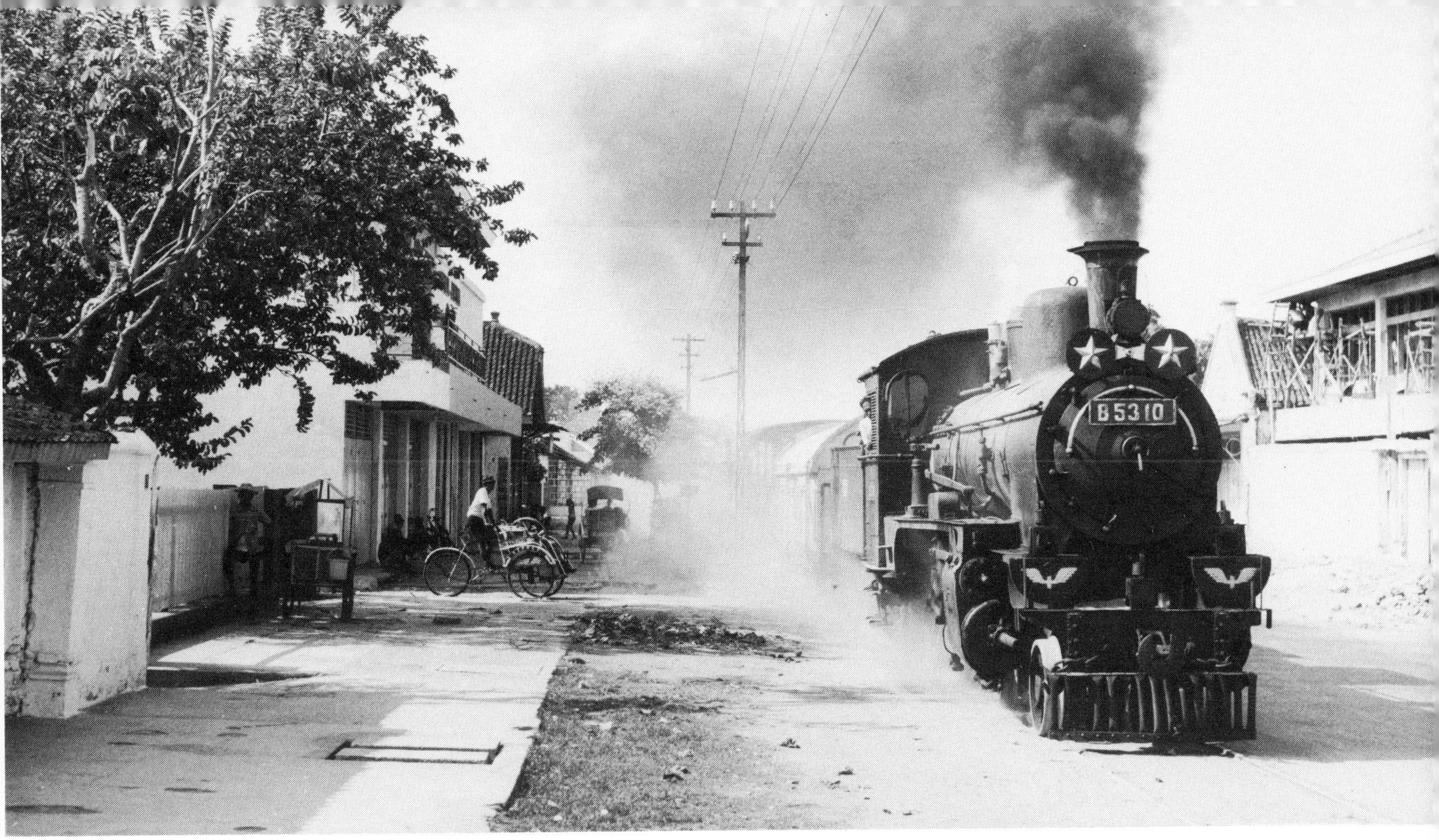

Here the major concern of the photographer was personal safety and the exclusion of dust and airborne rubbish from the cameras.

Indonesian Railways Class 53 4-4-0 No. B53 10 races down the main street of Maduin with the daily 14.15 mixed to Ponorogo and Slahung on 15 October 1973.

Minolta Autocord 6 × 6 75mm Rokkor FP4 D76 (1:1) 1/500th second f 6.3.

◀ A train negotiating the main street of a provincial town is a rare occurrence and one which immediately attracts the attention of the enthusiast. It is however one of the most exasperating subjects imaginable since little of the subject is under the control of the photographer. This is particularly true of Asian towns where streets are invariably crowded with pedestrians, animals and every conceivable form of transport. Add to this the endeavours of small boys to stand in front of a camera at all costs and it is surprising that anything worthwhile could possibly be obtained. This is a situation where it is best to make a number of exposures; indeed there may even be an arguable case for the use of a camera fitted with a motor-driven film advance. The majority of the negatives will, inevitably, be rejected but one or two will hopefully be of a reasonable standard. The scene opposite is the best of a series of seven exposures. The attitudes of most of the passers-by, along with the composition, are near ideal. It seems quite remarkable, in retrospect, that at the moment of exposure, not a single person impeded the view of the track on the left or of the locomotive. Note the wealth of detail in this scene; a viewer may look at this photograph time and time again and still discover some new minor item of interest.

Darjeeling-Himalayan railway Class B 2′0″ gauge 0-4-0ST No. 779 negotiates the main street of Kurseong with a mixed train bound for Darjeeling.

Pentax 6 × 7 105mm Takumar FP4 D76 (1:1) 1/250th second f 6.3.

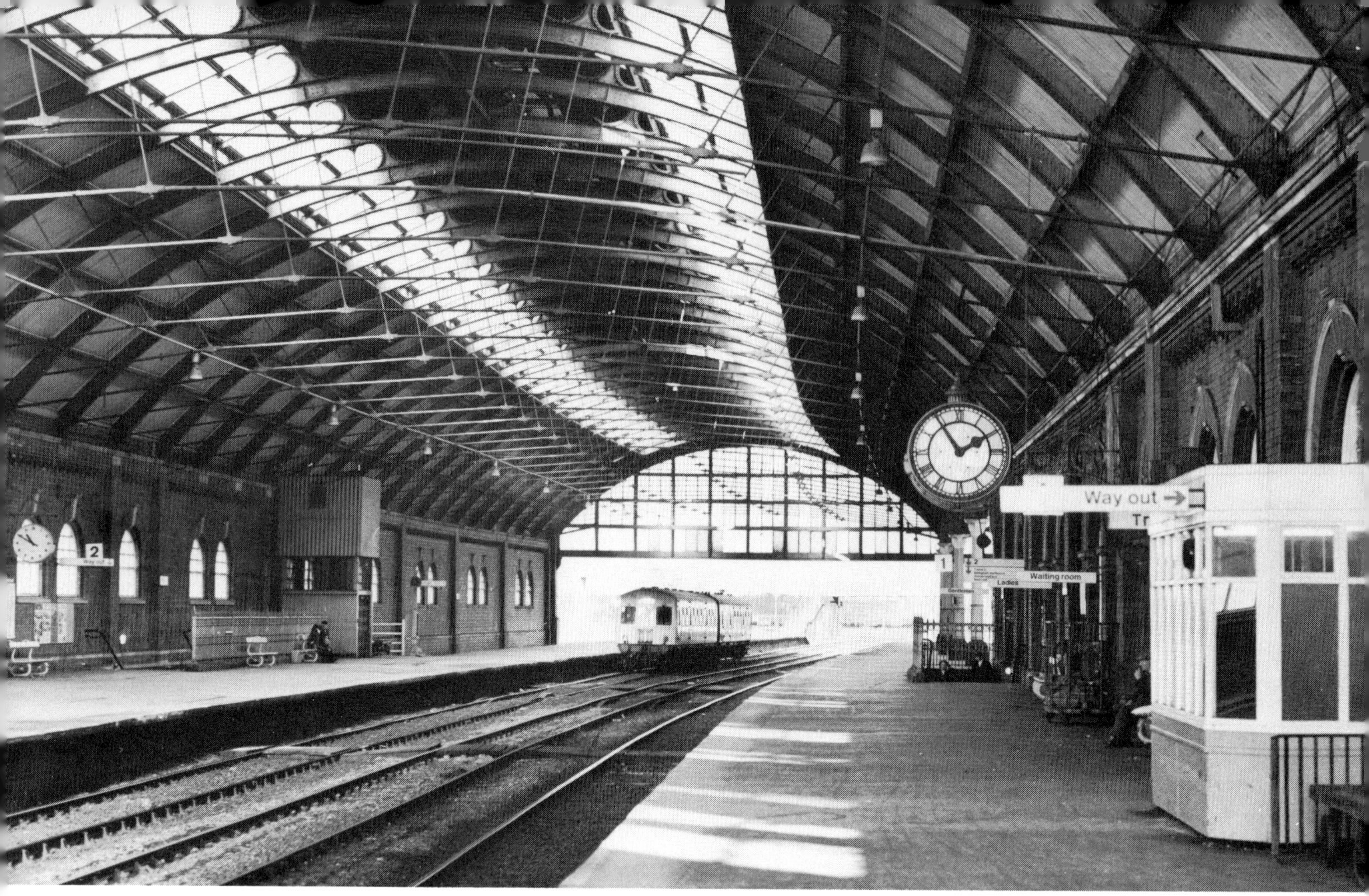

STATIONS

Stations are some of the more important architectural features of a railway. Variations in style and size are immense, ranging from the pseudo-Gothic masterpiece of St. Pancras to a simple wayside halt in Pakistan. Stations, and the people who use them, present the photographer with a kaleidoscope of opportunity. In the scene above the prime objective was to record, pictorially, the train shed of Stockton-on-Tees station which is threatened, at the time of writing, with demolition. The two car dmu (located at the focal point of the curved roof) is a minute, but pictorially essential part of the scene. Note too how the curve of the track leads the eye into the picture.

Pentax 6 × 7 105mm Takumar FP4 D76 (1:1) 1/125th second f 5.6.

To produce an evocative railway photograph at Kings Cross station early on a Sunday morning is not the easiest of tasks. Certainly one could record, yet again, a down express leaving and approaching Gas Works tunnel, but originality would be sadly lacking. The suburban side of the station, on the other hand, is rather neglected by photographers. A two car dmu, forming the 10.40 to Potters Bar, standing alongside a deserted platform seemed a very uninspiring subject, but the subtle use of two large puddles provides necessary additional interest, while patience was rewarded by the appearance of two railwaymen adding a little life to the scene. A slow shutter speed, and hence a relatively small aperture, was used, to ensure that the reflections in the water were critically sharp. The lack of shadow detail will be noticed; a result of slight underexposure.

Pentax 6 × 7 105mm Takumar Tri-X D76 (1:1) 1/125th second f 6.3.

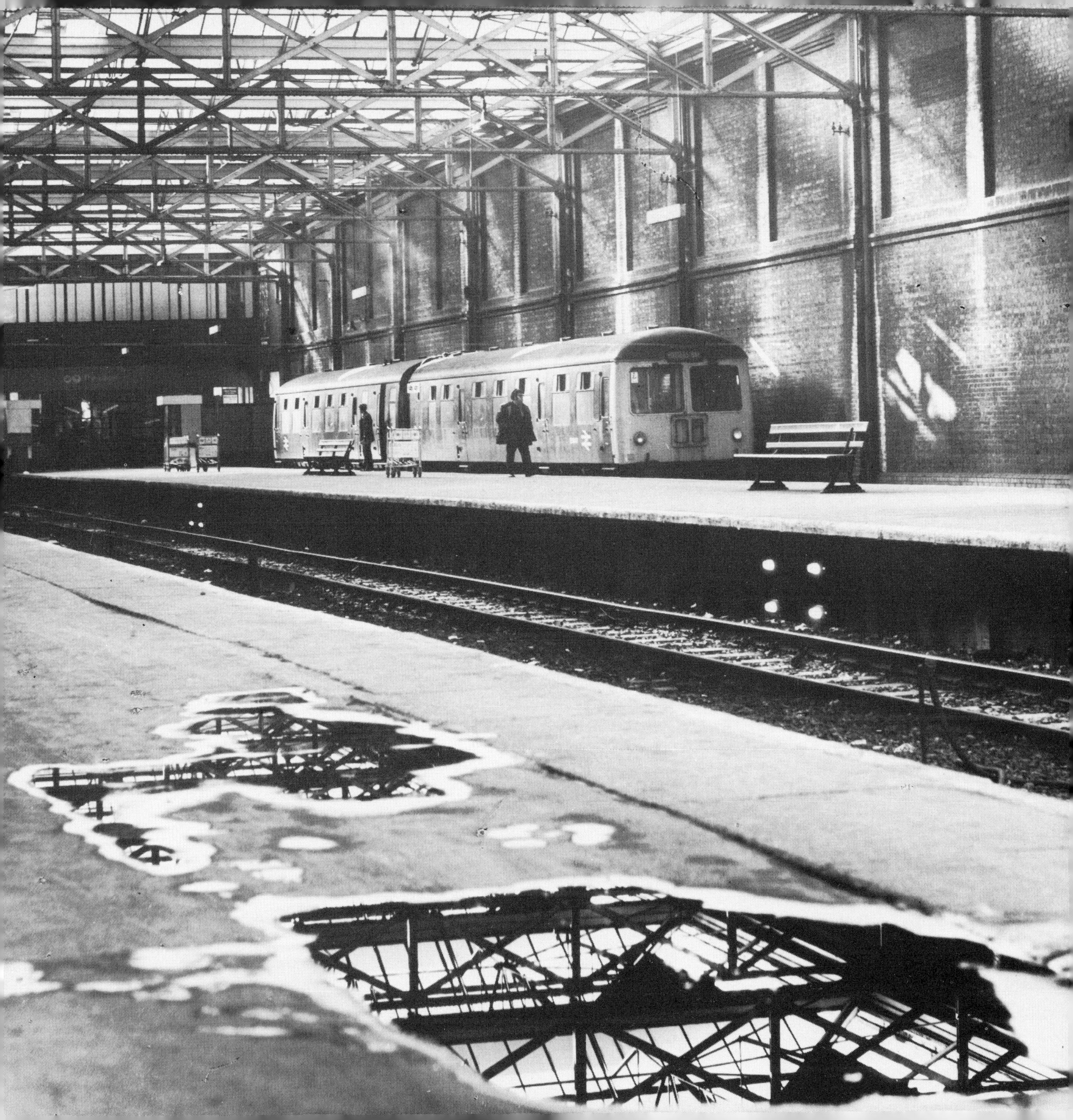

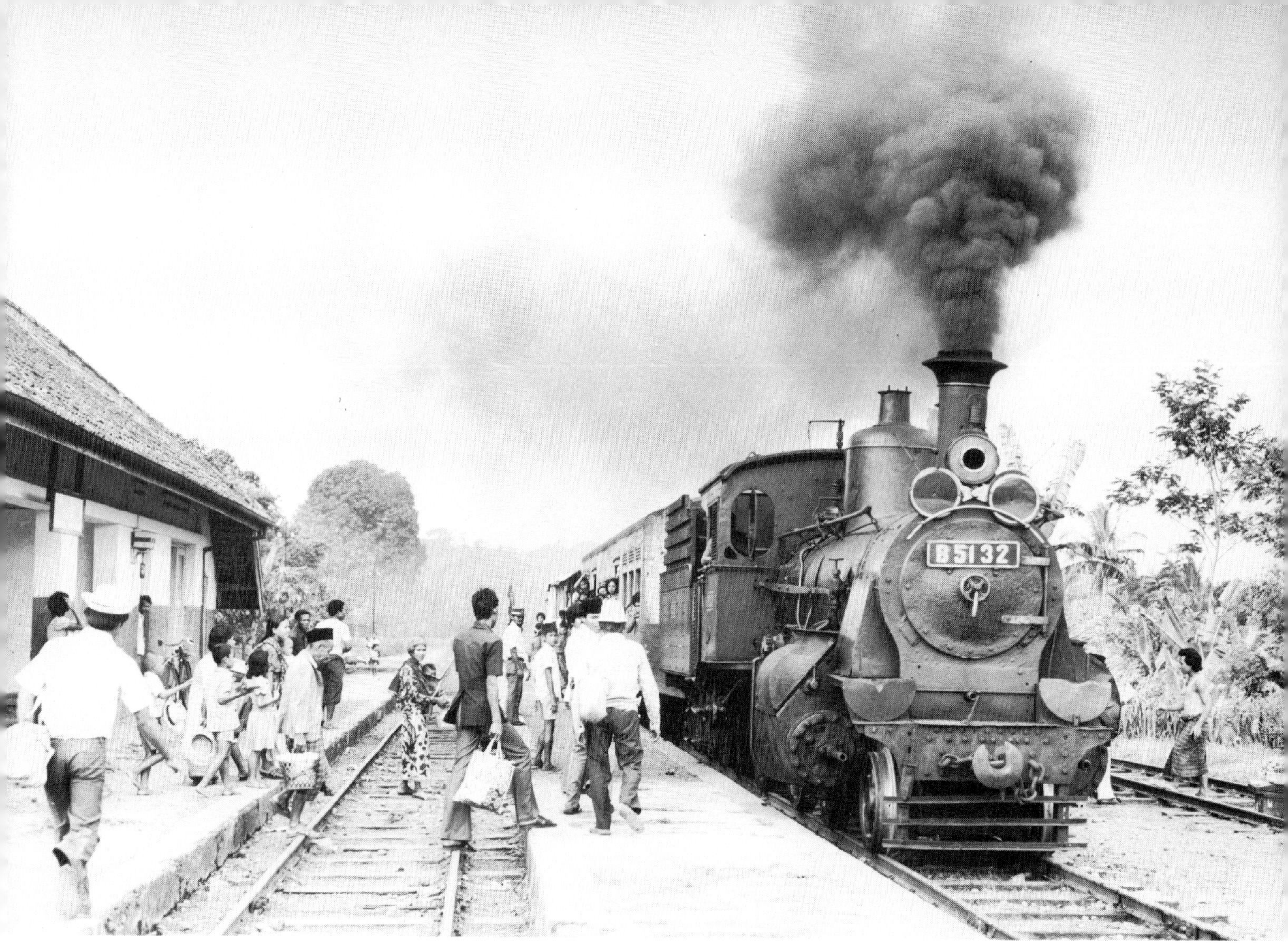

The daily mixed from Rankasbitung to Labuin rolls to a halt at the wayside station of Pandeglang in West Java. None is more inquisitive and demanding of the foreign enthusiast than the people of India and Indonesia. In spite of this note the delightful spontaneity of this picture with not a single person watching the photographer; all are completely preoccupied with attempting to find a place on the train. The appearance of the young man on the extreme left hurrying along the platform was particularly fortunate. The technique used here often succeeds. Feign casual interest in something completely different to the railway, perhaps a nearby ox and cart, and at the last moment swing round for the exposure. But for each success anticipate at least one failure.

Indonesian Railways (P N J A) Class B51 oil-burning compound 4-4-0 at Pandeglang, August 1977.

Pentax 6 × 7 105mm Takumar FP4 D76 (1:1)
1/500th second f 5.6.

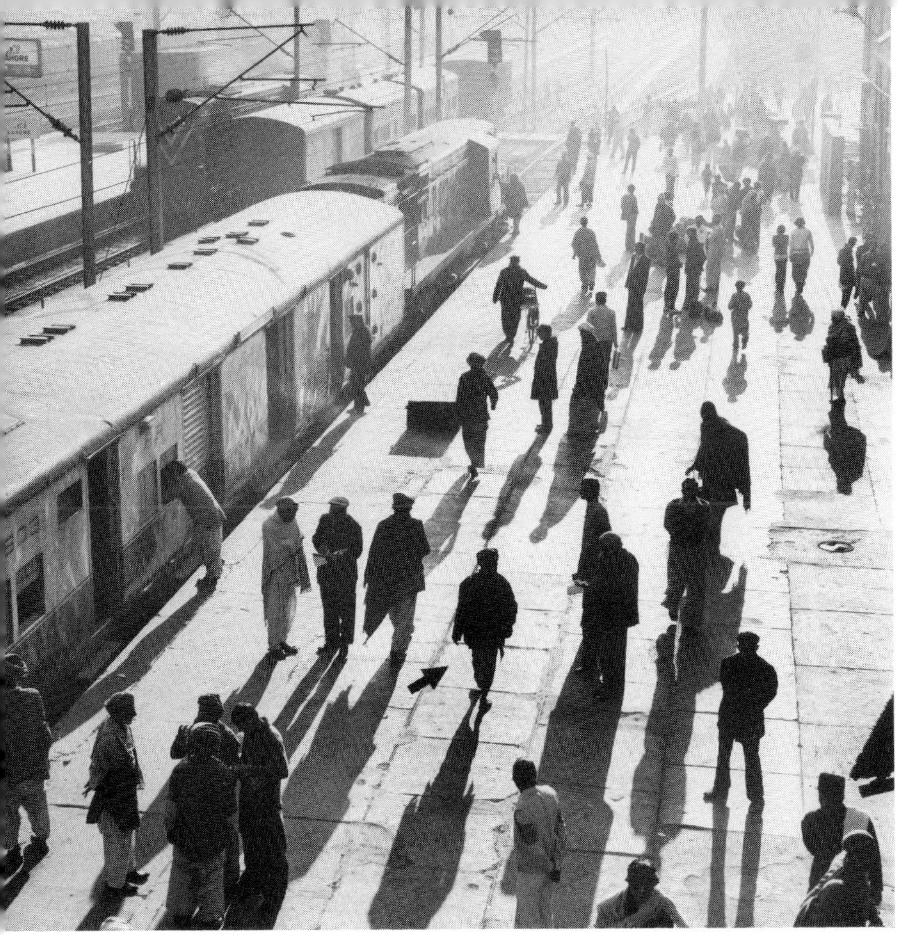

This early morning scene of Lahore station in Pakistan was taken from a foot overbridge with a camera pointing almost directly into the sun. At the moment of exposure the camera was deliberately tilted downwards so that the image of the sun could not be seen through the viewfinder. A certain amount of flare, or light scatter at the various air glass interfaces, is inevitable in these conditions but modern coated lenses, such as the Pentax Takumar SMC series, reduce the effect to a minimum. If significant flare is present the overall contrast of the negative will be reduced and, in consequence, a hard grade of printing paper required for enlargement. The value of an efficient lenshood, one which is designed specifically for the lens being used, cannot be overemphasised in contre jour work. The hood should restrict the light falling upon the lens to that which is required for image formation.

Note here how the camera has captured a moment of a period of intense activity. The numerous human figures are randomly distributed but of sufficiently low density for each, and the attendant shadows, to be seen separately. Note also the particular compositional importance of the arrowed figure; without him, the photograph would be much less attractive. Photographs involving large numbers of human beings are very difficult to plan; optimum conditions will occur for a fraction of a second and the camera must capture that precise fleeting moment. Patience, and a camera at the ready, are the ingredients of success.

The down Khyber Mail (Peshawar to Karachi) pauses at Lahore with an Alco 2000 hp diesel-electric in charge; January 1979.

Pentax 6 × 7 105mm Takumar FP4 D76 (1:1)
1/500th second f 8.

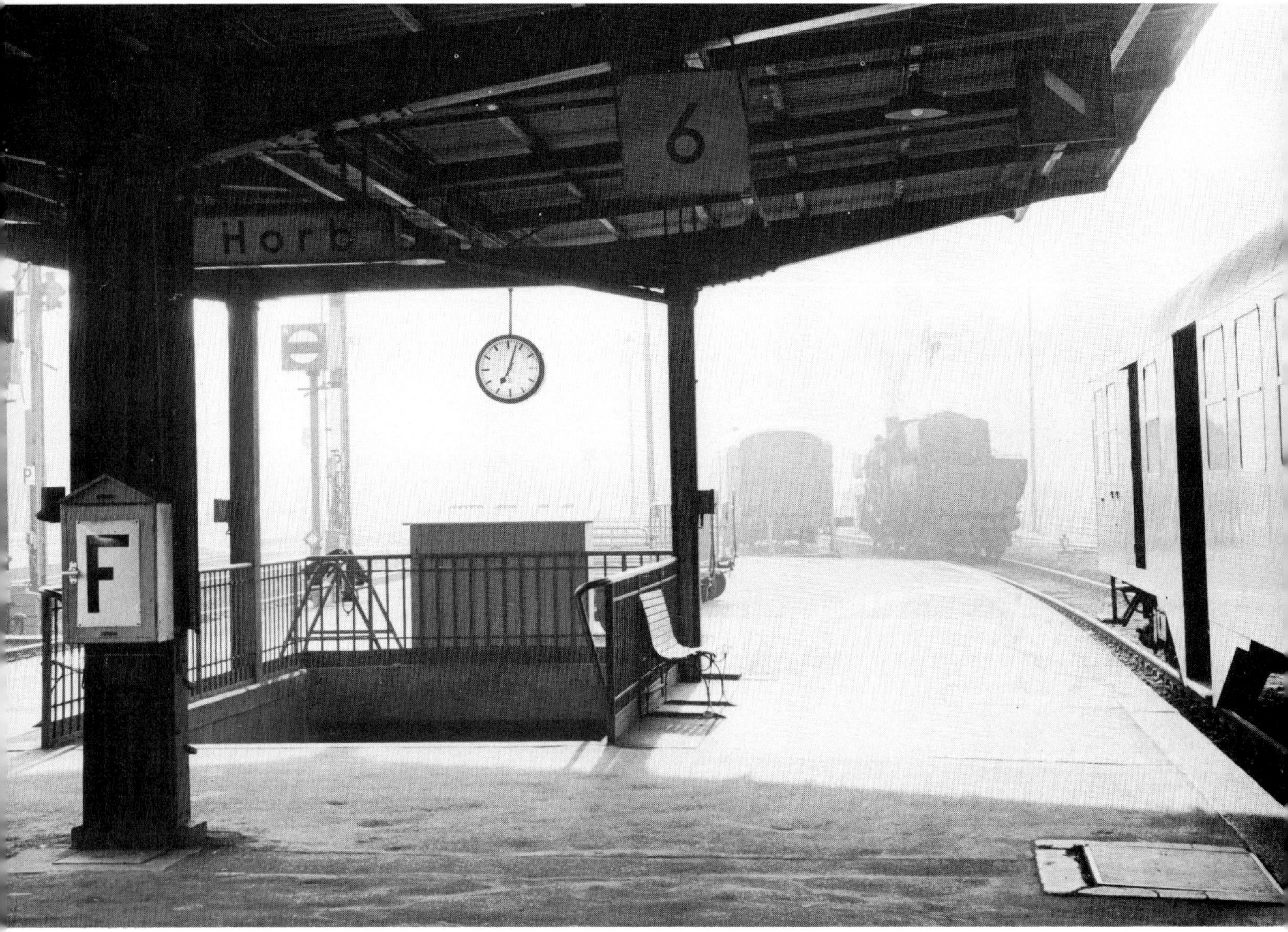

This view of West German Railways (D B) Class P8 4-6-0 No.3156 at Horb is another morning scene but the mood contrasts the earlier view of Lahore station. Large numbers of passengers would not be in keeping with the sleepy rural atmosphere of a small Bavarian town in early summer. The complete absence of people, passengers or railway staff, is however a weakness; after all, stations are associated with people just as much as they are with trains. Early morning mist is the secret of success here. A feeling of depth is created by the recession of the planes of interest; the dark prominent station building and clock in the foreground, the locomotive in the middle distance, and the misty, barely visible trees and hills as a backdrop. Recession in a photograph can be emphasised at the printing stage by holding back or underexposing the highlight areas; but it is a process which requires considerable manipulative skill if halos or areas of uneven density in the final print are to be avoided.

Minolta Autocord 6 × 6 75mm Rokkor FP4 D76 (1:1) 1/250th second f 6.3.

Nowadays many enthusiasts attempt to photograph preserved steam locomotives either as static exhibits or during their occasional visits to mainline stations. Both are fraught with difficulties, not least of which is the presence of other enthusiasts. It becomes an almost impossible task to obtain a photograph which excludes all camera-laden admirers. A patient wait of five minutes was necessary to obtain this relatively clear view of 'Jubilee' No.5690 at Sheffield Midland on 24 September 1977. It could be argued that the enthusiasts at the extreme right and left are part of the scene and therefore, as such, should be accepted. Again note the inclusion of the colour light signal to create a recession of planes and a feeling of depth to the picture.

Pentax 6 × 7 105mm Takumar Tri-X Perceptol (1:1) 1/250th second f 8.

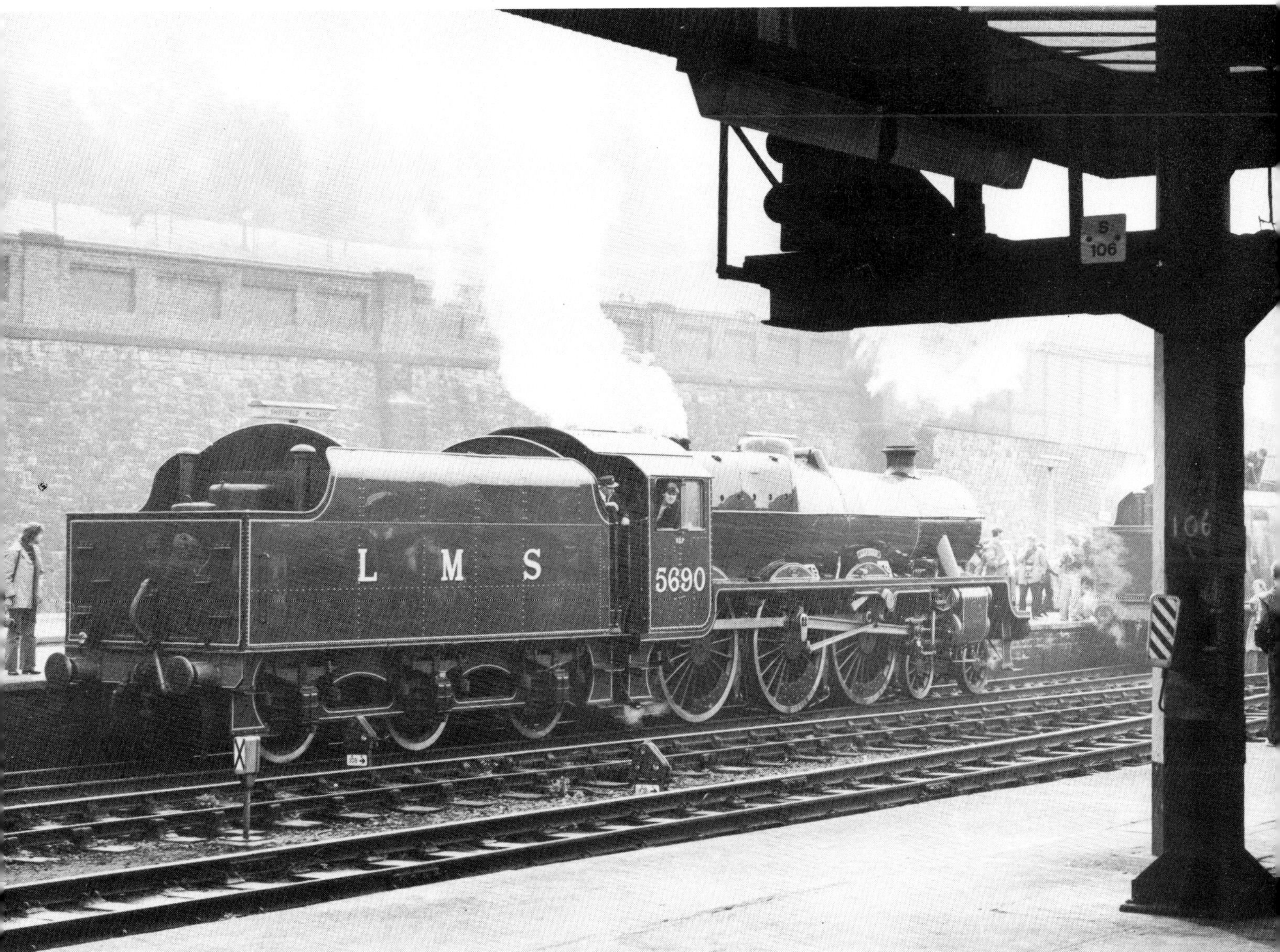

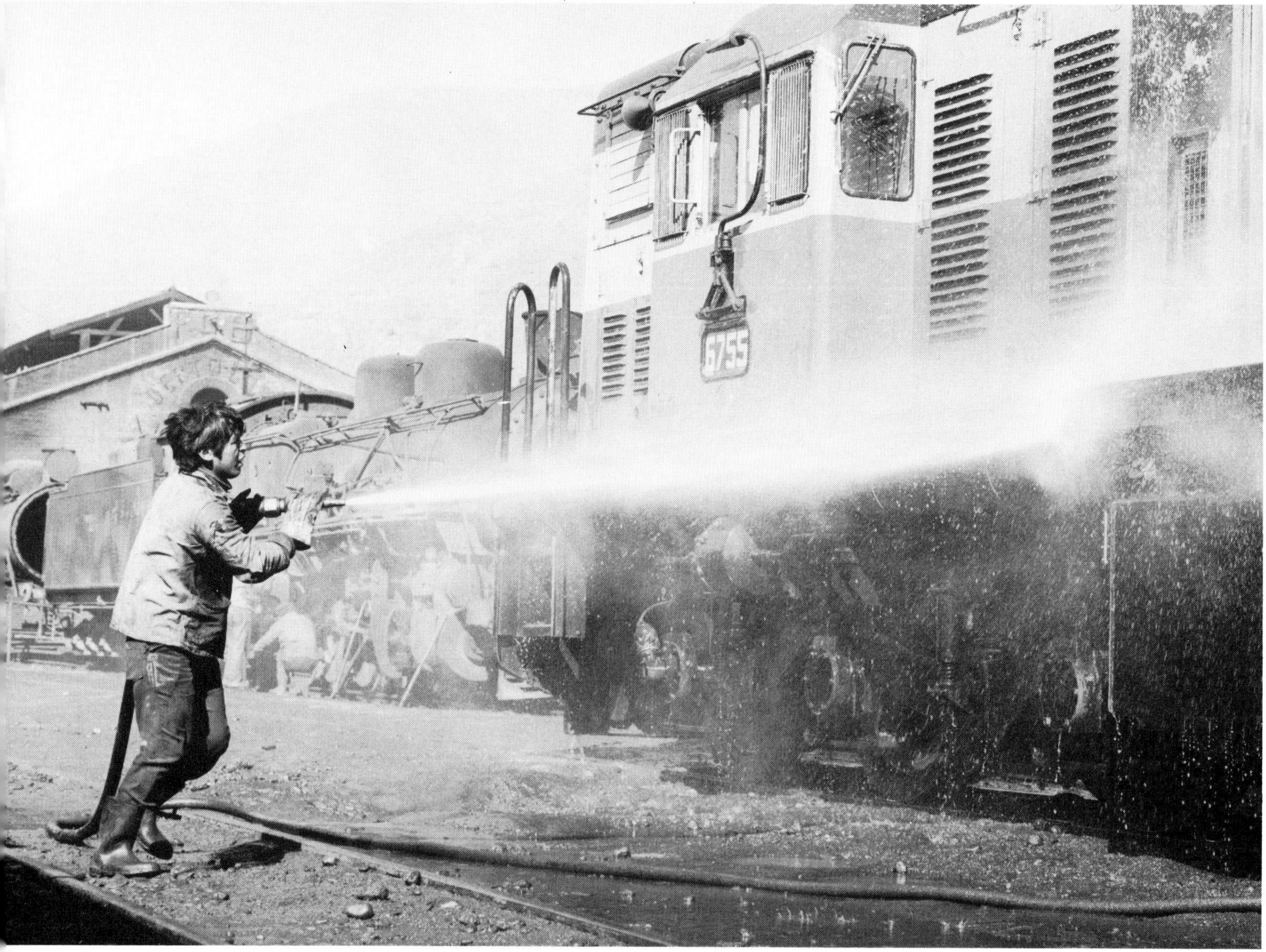

This is an interesting and rather unusual scene at the motive power depot at Volcan in North West Argentina but one which would have been considerably improved by the more obvious use of differential focusing. The steam locomotives in the background compete for attention; the use of a large lens aperture would have recorded all save the principal subject as an indistinctive blur. In good lighting conditions this is not too easy to achieve in black-and-white photography. Here the exposure on FP4 film was 1/500th second at f 6.3; to use an aperture of f 2.2 would require a shutter speed of 1/4000th second unless a neutral density or colour filter is used. A further solution of course would be to use a telephoto lens which has for a given aperture, a much more limited depth of field.

Pentax 6 × 7   105mm Takumar   FP4   D76 (1:1)
1/500th second   f 6.3.

During an early morning visit to York shed in May 1966 Class V2 2-6-2 No. 60886 was noted, out of steam, at the back of the depot. Photography was out of the question since the most optimistic exposure meter reading for FP4 film was 1/30th second at f 2.8. Two hours later the scene was transformed with shafts of sunlight superbly highlighting the smokebox of the locomotive. Deciding upon the correct exposure was a problem since pointing the exposure meter towards the tender gave a totally different reflected light intensity to that reflected from the driving wheels. No fewer than four exposures were therefore made, each differing from the previous one by half a stop, i.e. exposures of 1/60th second at f 4, f 4.5, f 5.6 and f 6.3 (a procedure technically known as bracketing the exposure). An aperture of f 5.6 afforded the best negative with adequately recorded shadow detail and manageable highlights.

Exakta Varex IIa 50mm Pancolar FP4 Acutol
1/60th second f 5.6.

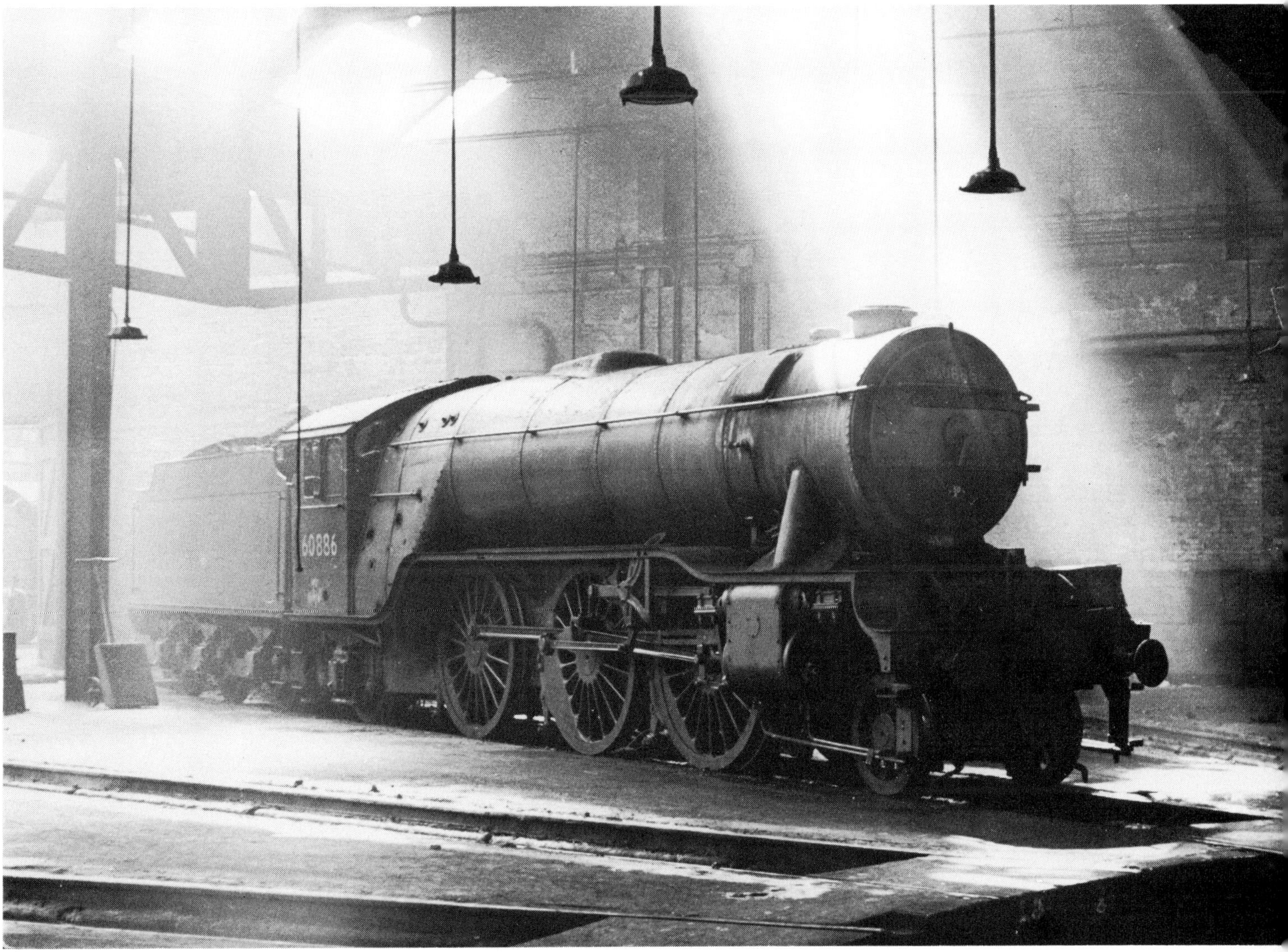

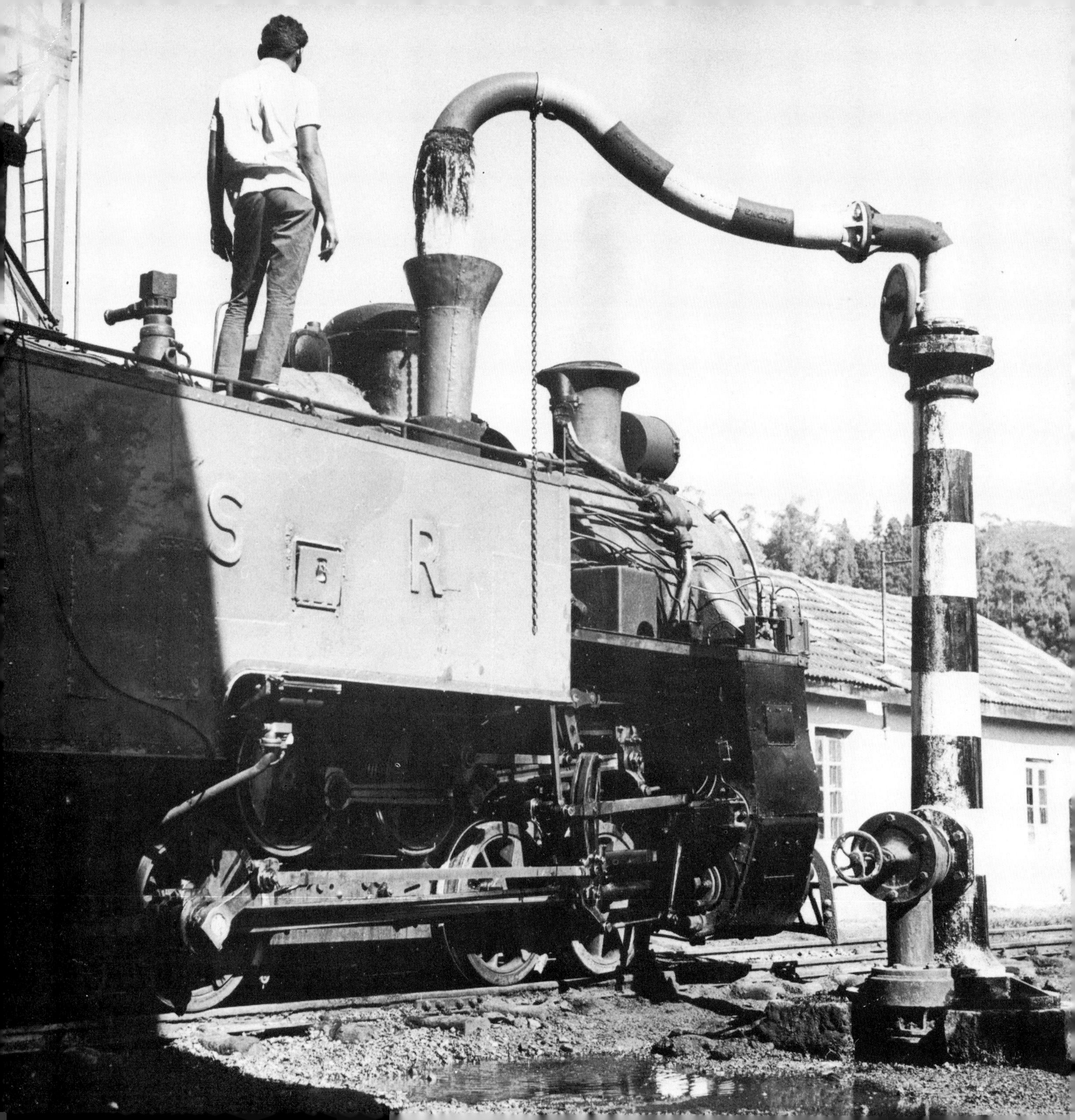
S R

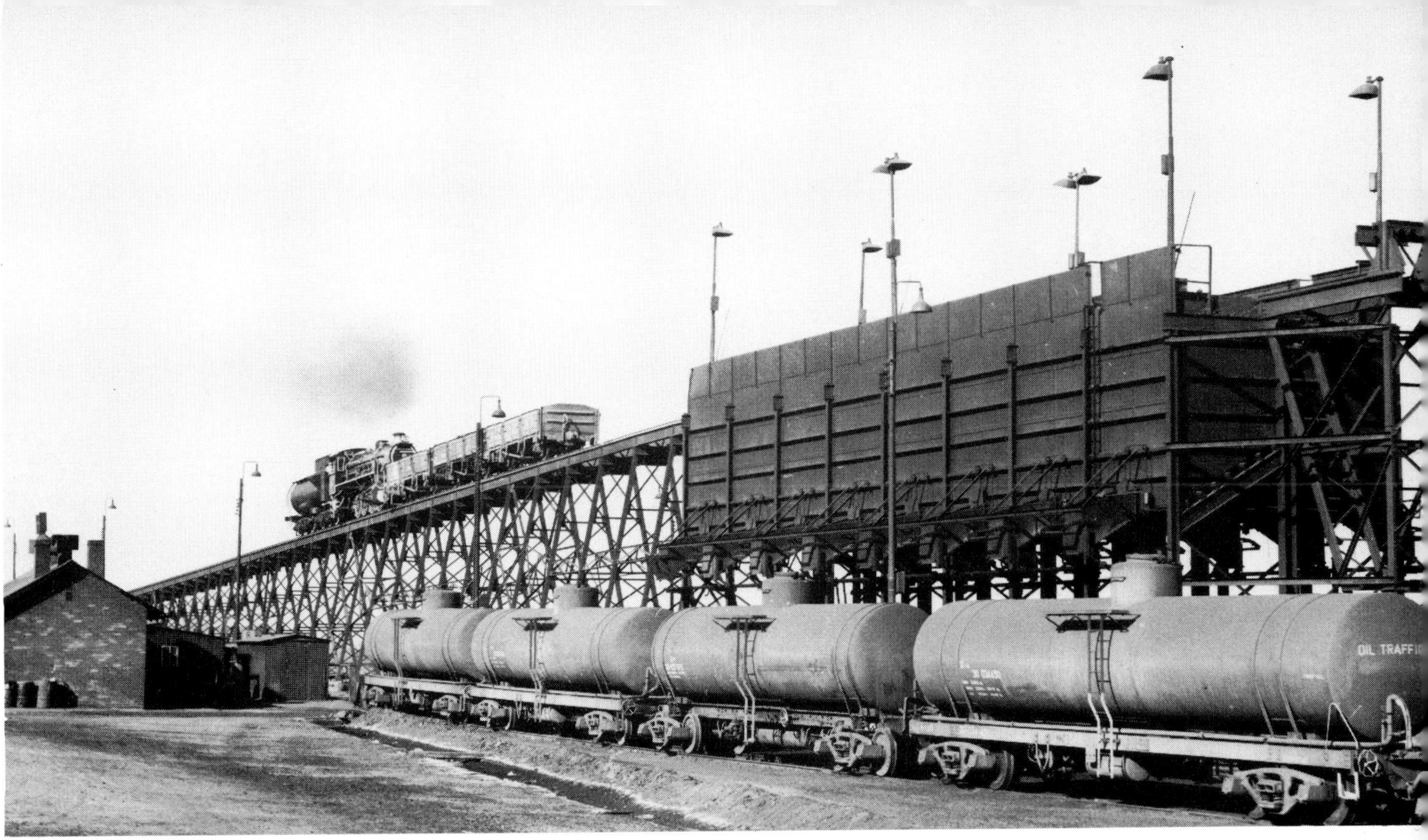

SHEDS

More photographs have been taken of locomotives on shed than at any other type of location and most are locomotive portraits. These require little compositional skill other than an ability to position the camera to exclude or to minimise the effects of unwanted poles or sundry objects which may otherwise appear to 'grow out of' the engine. An engine shed of course is a place where people work as well as a place where off duty engines are housed and it is inevitable, and indeed desirable, that some photographs should graphically record this human/machine interface. This has been brilliantly done in the past by a few select photographers; the work, for example, of Colin Gifford is highly regarded. For success in this sphere the camera must become an unseen eye, momentarily recording a fleeting glimpse of activity. Most people, upon noticing that a camera is pointing in their direction will immediately adopt a quite unnatural pose, usually a situation to be avoided. The man opposite, busy supervising the watering of Indian Railways Class X 0-8-2 rack tank locomotive at Ootacamund shed in South India was completely unaware of the presence of the photographer.

Minolta Autocord 6 × 6 75mm Rokkor FP4 D76 (1:1) 1/250th second f 8.

There is tremendous variety in the facilities for refuelling and watering locomotives, indeed this specialised subject almost warrants a separate publication. A good photograph of the unique and interesting arrangement used at most locomotive depots of South African Railways should be self explanatory, making a caption, other than one which identifies location and date, superfluous. The photograph above is compositionally quite attractive, clearly showing a steam engine hard at work pushing loaded coal wagons up the incline to the top of the coaling stage. However, the story is incomplete. It would have been so much better if the oil tankers in the foreground, which after all are in no way related to the subject, had been replaced by a locomotive in the process of taking coal from the storage hoppers. In summary a pleasant record of the event but one which falls short of the apparent objectives of the photographer.

A South African Railways Class S2 0-8-0 pushes loaded coal wagons on to the coaling stage at Pietersberg in August 1975.

Pentax 6 × 7 105mm Takumar FP4 D76 (1:1) 1/250th second f 8/11.

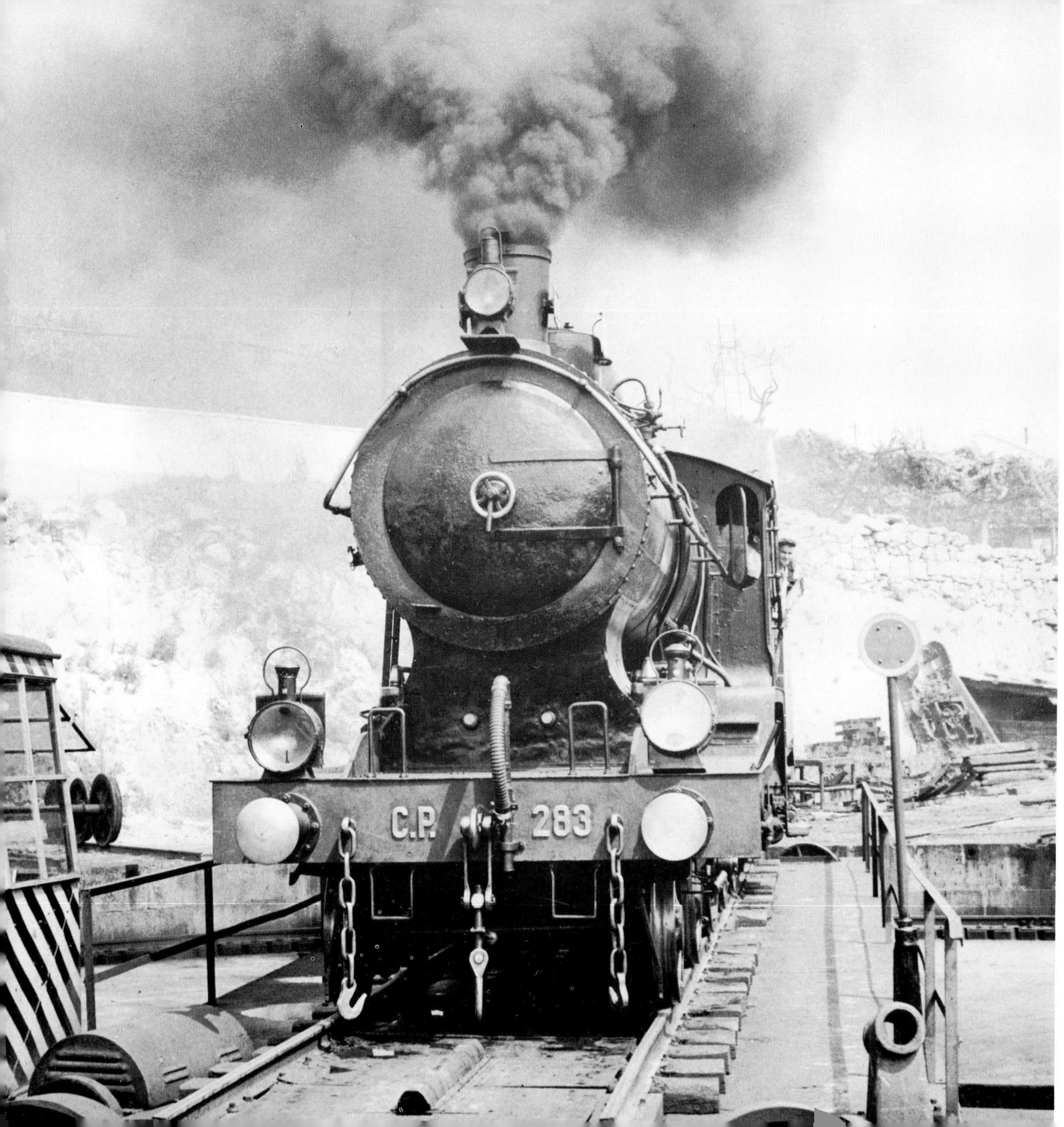
C.P. 283

◀ A Portuguese Railways 4-6-0 poses on the turntable at Contumil shed, Porto. A friendly word with the driver and a few English cigarettes soon persuaded him to place his engine in the most favourable spot for the sun while the fireman obliged with black smoke to hide some of the distracting bric à brac of the background. A contrived picture perhaps but no less satisfying for that.

Minolta Autocord 6 × 6 75mm Rokkor FP4 D76 (1:1) 1/250th second f 8.

Lines of locomotives on shed have a fascination of their own; yards of film have been expended on scenes such as the one depicted below. Technical excellence is of paramount importance with particular attention to depth of field. A small aperture must be used if both near and distant locomotives are to be seen in sharp focus. A row of stationary engines parked in a line will inevitably tend to take the eye out of the picture and it is usually good practice to include some object, though not too dominant, to counter this effect. A building, human figure or even a telegraph pole may be used but here the exposure was made at the precise moment when a fourth locomotive had been moved onto the roundhouse turntable. This helps to hold the picture together but the photograph would have been improved by the inclusion of more of the shed building.

Class 57 2-6-0s and a Class 58 4-6-0 at Temuco shed, Chile, August 1976.

Pentax 6 × 7 105mm Takumar FP4 D76 (1:1) 1/125th second f 11/16.

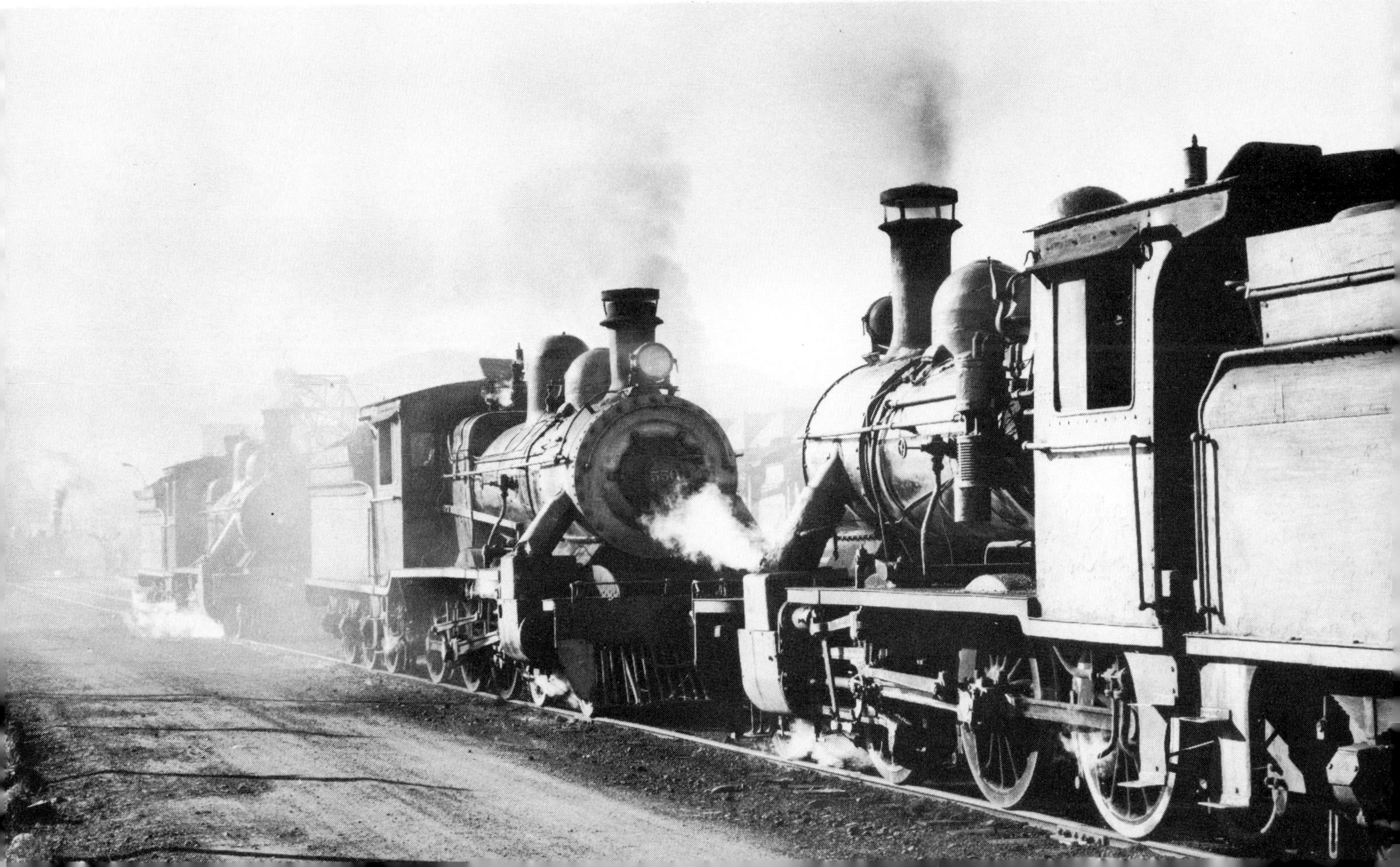

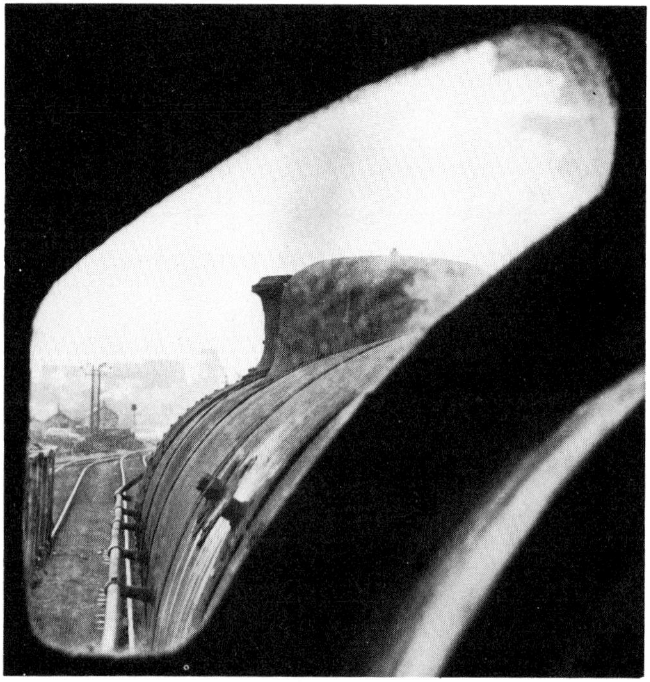

FROM THE TRAIN

What the fireman saw! A view through the cab spectacle — previously cleaned by the photographer — of a former L N E R Class 04/8 2-8-0. Again the need for a reasonable depth of field is apparent. In these circumstances it is almost impossible to fill the viewfinder with the subject and to record near and distant features in sharp focus; indeed to do so would be pictorially less satisfying. It is far better for the boiler, chimney and the road ahead to be clearly seen through a slightly out of focus frame.

The optimum focusing point is probably about half way along the boiler which is not too easy to assess unless a camera fitted with a reliable rangefinder is used.

Exakta Varex IIa 50mm Pancolar FP4 Acutol
1/125th second f 8.

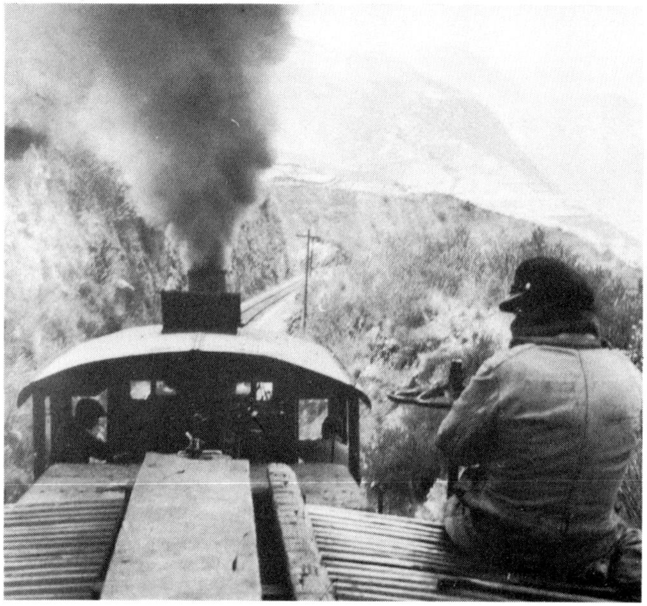

Travelling on the roof of a passenger train is possible in a few relatively remote corners of the world, and photographers are well advised to enquire in advance of the precise locations of tunnels and low bridges! Sudden lurching or swaying movements even if unsuccessful in unseating the enthusiast can be guaranteed to reduce the best camera to the level of the Box Brownie particularly if slow shutter speeds are used. This view of 2′6″ gauge Baldwin 2-6-0 No.103 of the F C H H at work near Ingahuasi in Peru with a Huancayo to Huancavelica train in August 1976 was the best of four exposures. The overall definition is very poor and with hindsight it is clear that a 400 ASA film should have been used along with a shutter speed of 1/500th second.

Pentax 6 × 7 105mm Takumar FP4 D76 (1:1)
1/125th second f 8/11.

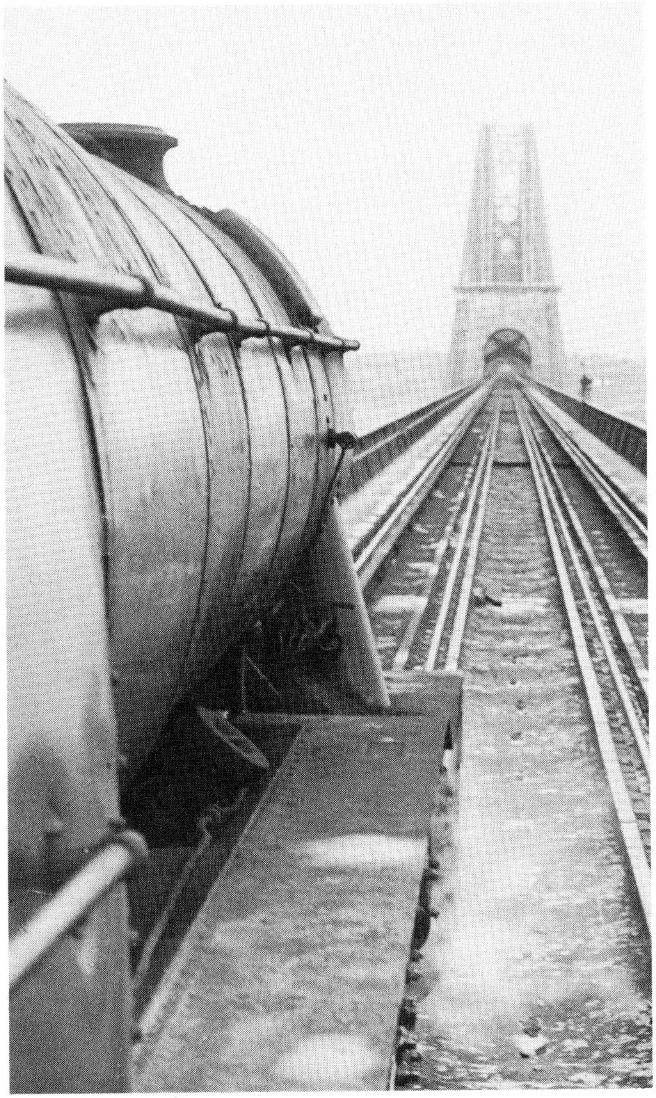

One would rarely advocate making an exposure while holding the camera with one hand but this was the only way to obtain such a dramatic view of the approach to the Forth Bridge from the footplate. Several exposures were rejected because of blur due to camera shake.

Exakta Varex IIa 50mm Pancolar FP4 Acutol 1/250th second f 6.3.

Overleaf:
The monotonous box-like appearance of electric and diesel multiple units inherently makes them, at least photographically, one of the least attractive forms of rail transport. Traditional three quarter front studies of multiple units, even if technically beyond criticism, are unlikely to captivate the attention of a viewer for more than a moment or two unless the environment plays a more dominating role in the scene. The sinuous exits from Victoria station for example are ideal for this sort of railway photography. Interesting viewpoints may be found from vantage points on nearby high rise buildings but another possibility is to indulge in photography from a moving train. As a passenger on an up train, which had been reduced to walking pace due to a signal check, the photographer here had ample time to assess the pictorial implications of an approaching train. The inclusion of both trains in the photograph gives a feeling of depth but it is unfortunate that the buildings in the middle distance are slightly out of focus. A slow shutter speed and hence a smaller aperture should have been selected.

Pentax 6 × 7 105mm Takumar FP4 D76 (1:1) 1/250th second f 4.5.

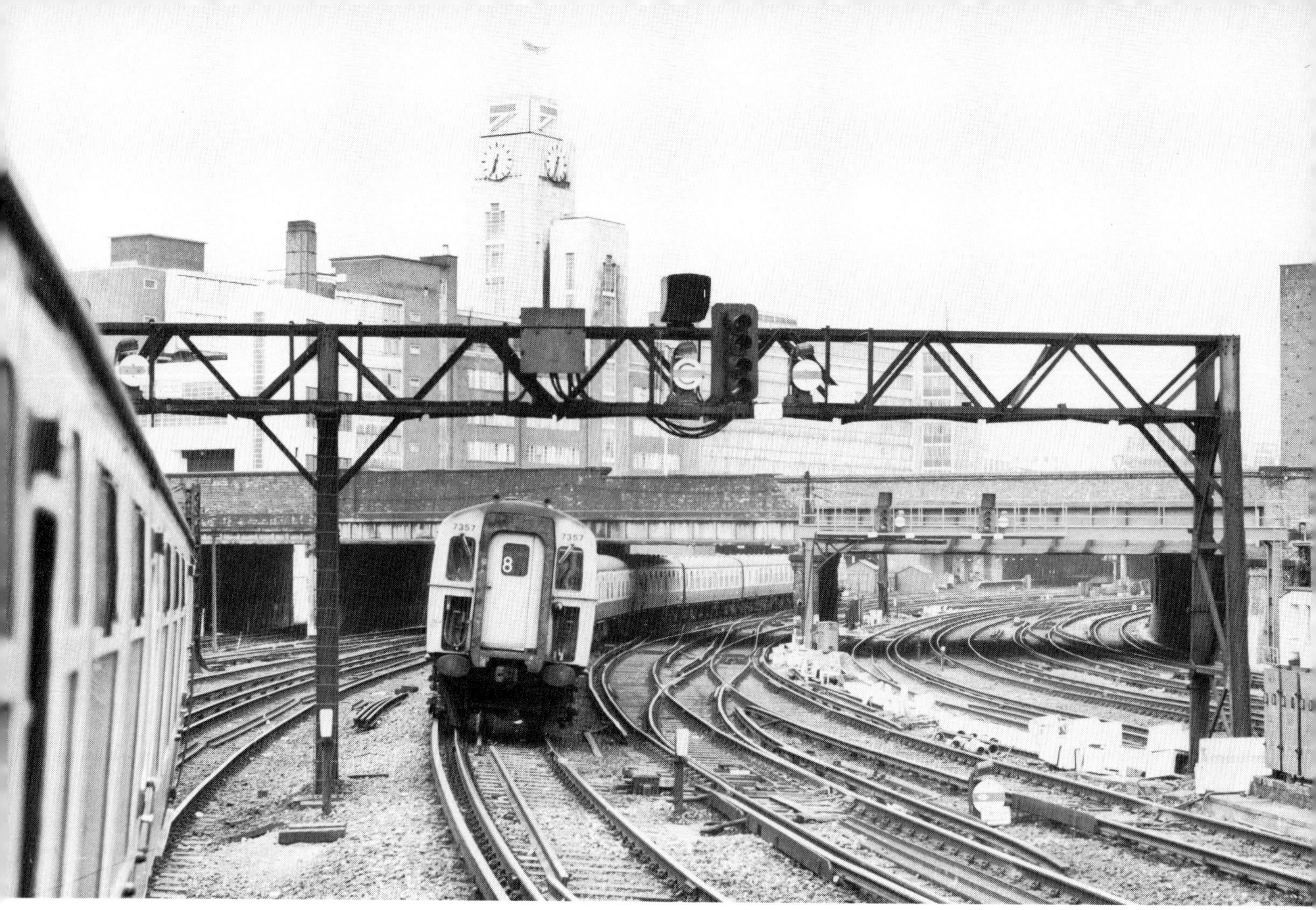

Successful photography from moving trains is one of the most difficult and possibly one of the most dangerous aspects of the hobby. Often an exposure will be made while the train is traversing an acute curve so that the locomotive and the way ahead are shown to good advantage. This leads to a degree of unwanted camera movement particularly in situations where the permanent way is in poor condition. A minimum shutter speed of 1/250th second is advisable even though this may result in depth of field problems. This train was travelling at a mere 10 m.p.h. on the very poorly maintained track of one of the logging branches of the Ali Shan Forestry Railway in Taiwan. It will be noted that the limited shutter speed of 1/250th second has not produced a critically sharp image and the human figures, a railway official and several Japanese climbers, are clearly out of focus. The picture is, however, rescued by strong compositional features; in particular the curve of the train leading the eye to the locomotive, the rather fortunate fall of the exhaust, and the near-ideal position but not dominance of the human interest.

Ali Shan 2 cylinder 2 truck Shay No.12 pushes a track lifting train up the Tzu Chung branch on 30 March 1978.

Pentax 6 × 7 105mm Takumar Tri-X D76 (1:1)
1/250th second f 5.6.

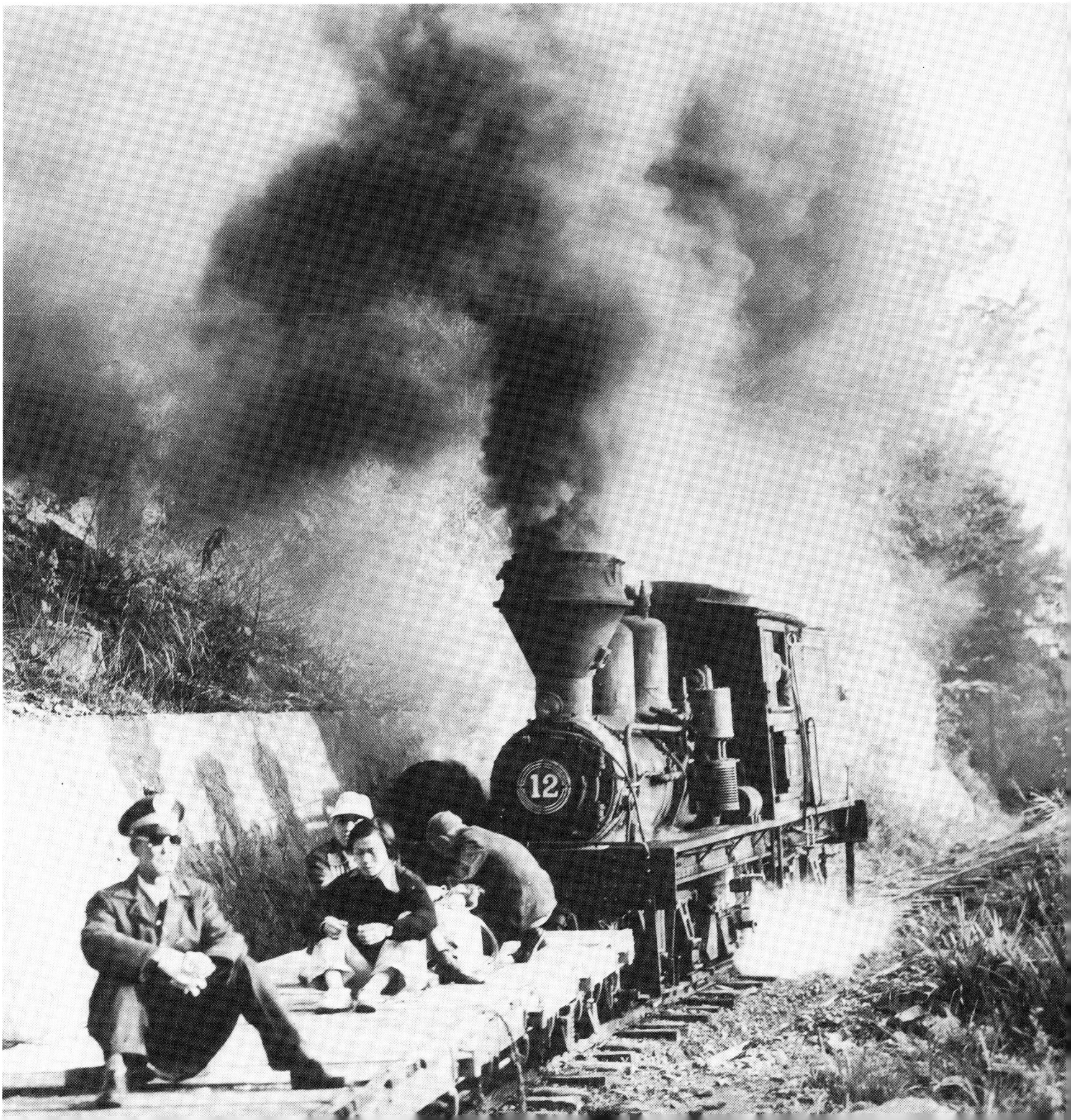
12

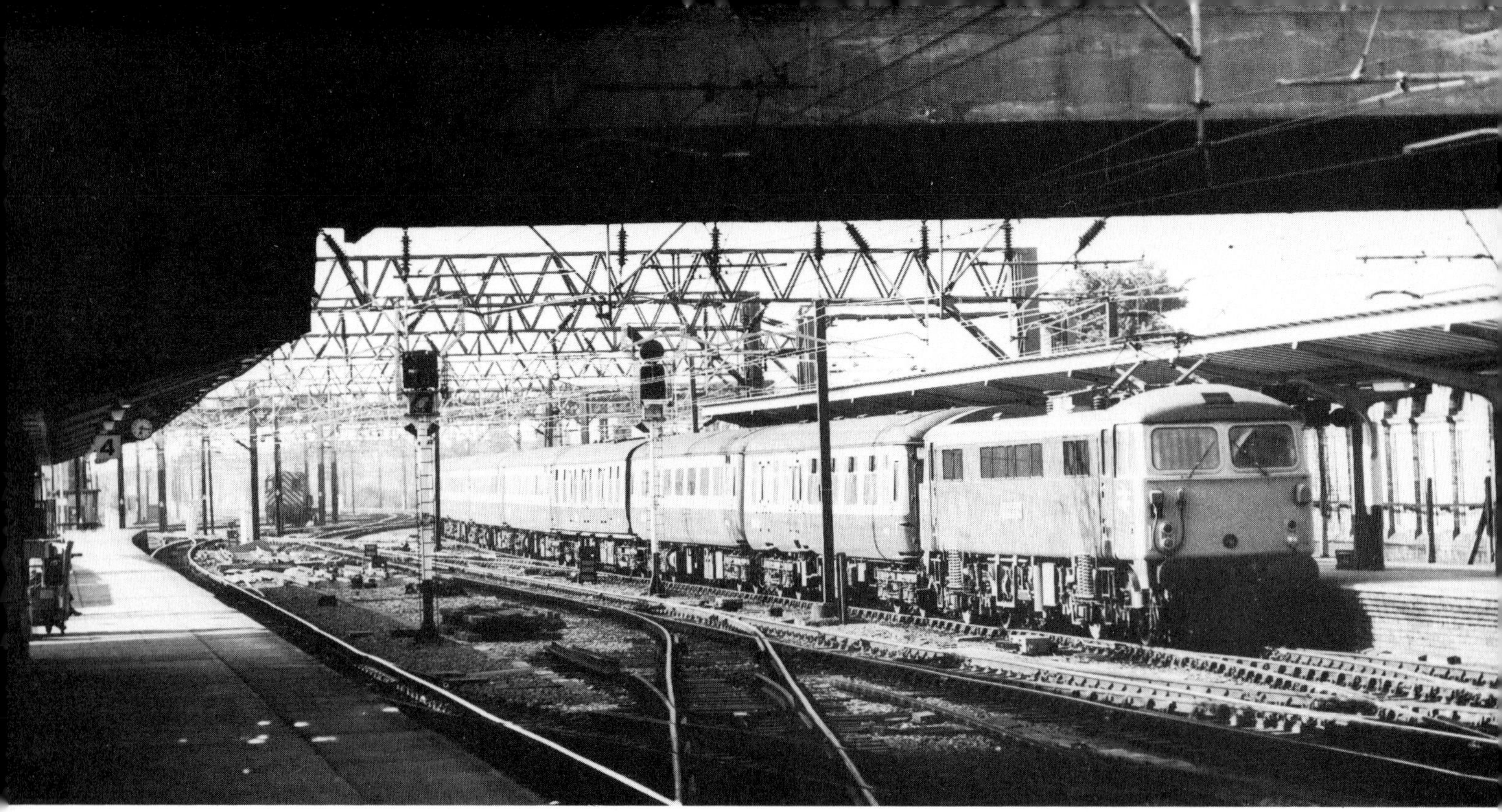

Class 87 electric locomotive No.87021 *Robert the Bruce* arrives at Crewe with the up 'Clansman' on 11 July 1978.

Pentax 6 × 7 200mm Takumar FP4 D76 (1:1) 1/250th second f 8.

ELECTRIFIED LINES

Electrified lines with overhead catenaries are, potentially, a photographic nightmare. Poles and wires will be present in every field of view and it becomes difficult to obtain unimpeded photographs of a locomotive and train; indeed it is almost impossible if a location overlooking the train is selected. A telephoto lens when used in an almost head on track level position can produce quite spectacular results since the catenary supports will appear to be closely spaced, producing a tunnel effect. This is partially evident in the scene above although only a medium focal length lens was used. Note how the impact of the subject has been conveniently enhanced by framing the subject, this time with an overbridge. The preparation of a railway line for electrification presents an interesting challenge; a location is likely to be untidy with equipment and partially erected catenaries very much in evidence. It is, of course, a transient scene and one which is well worth photographing if only from a record point of view; but how much better if the photographer can also make the scene visually appealing. In this example the vertical exhaust pattern emerging from the Austrian Railways Class 93 2-8-2T is emphasised, and repeated, by the vertical catenary supports. The locomotive has been photographed at a position between the poles; those on the extreme right and left help to frame the subject.

OBB Class 93 2-8-2T No.93 1362 at Hieflau in August 1969. ▶

Minolta Autocord 6 × 6 75mm Rokkor Tri-X D76 (1:1) 1/500th second f 5.6.

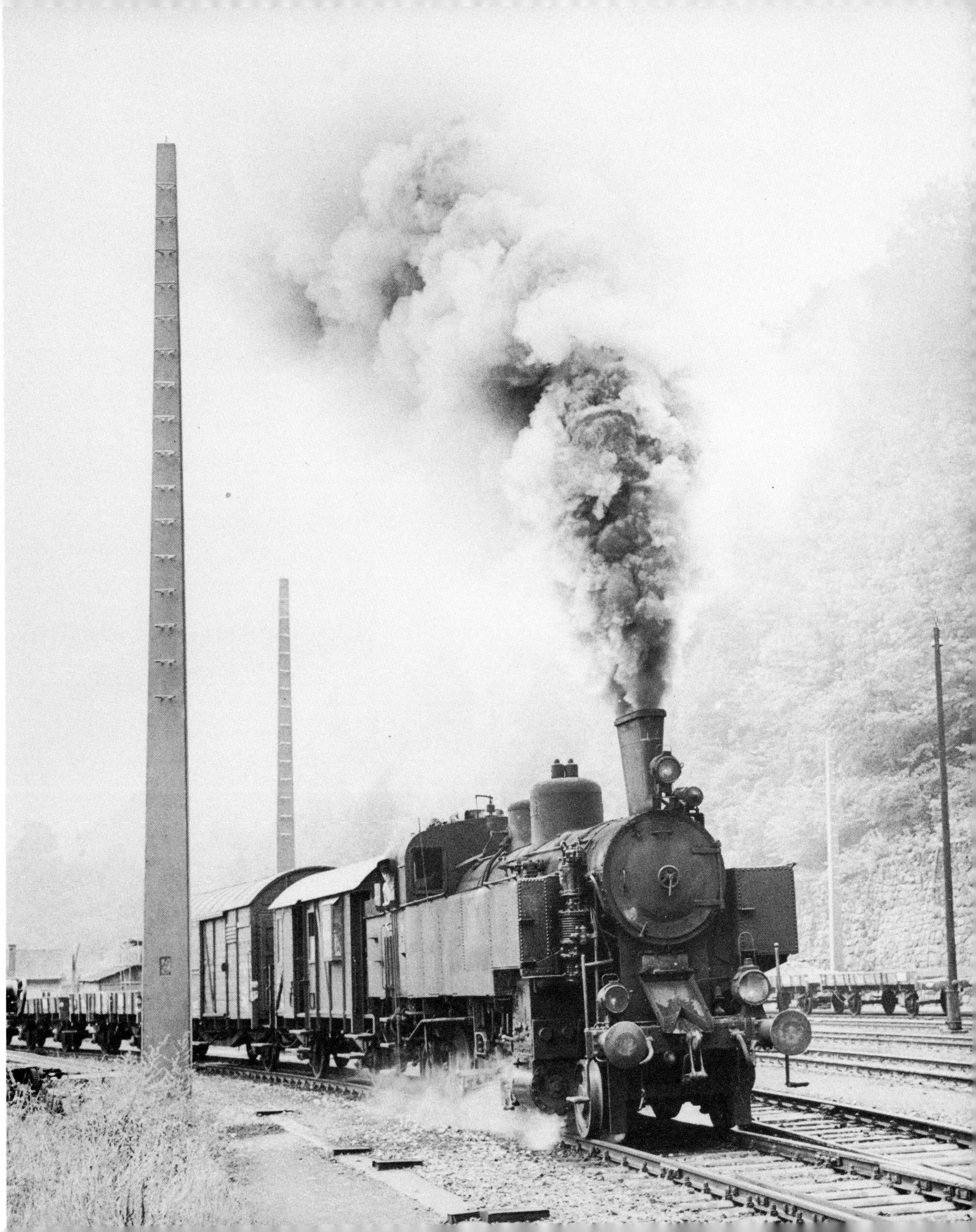

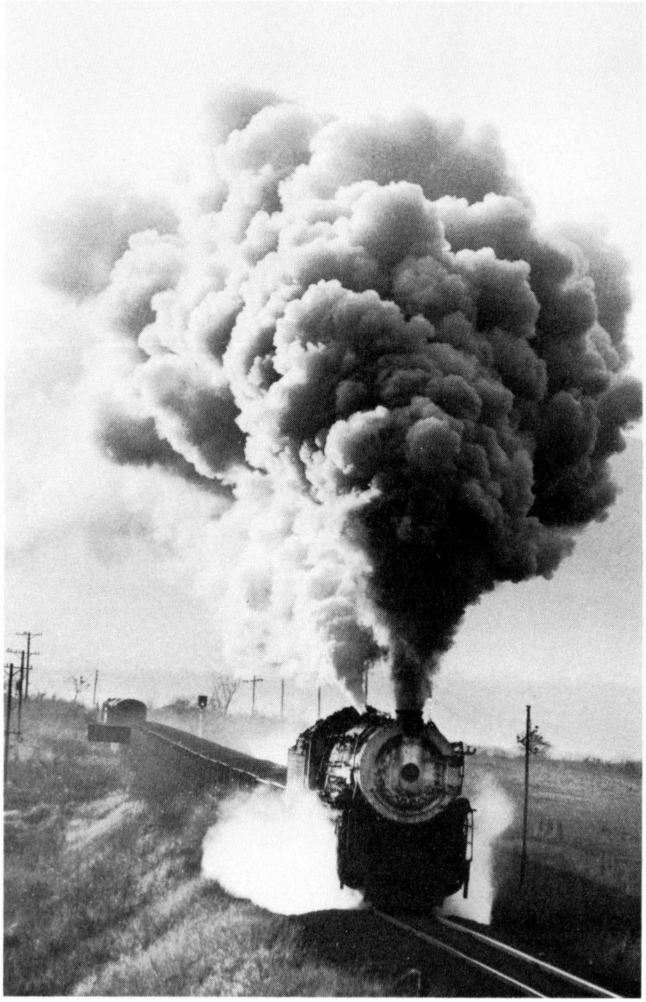

POWER OF STEAM

In tropical and semi-tropical countries only occasionally do temperatures fall sufficiently to produce superb 'cotton wool' exhausts. Moreover these conditions will last for only thirty minutes or so after sunrise. A photograph such as this, depicting C F M (Mozambique Railways) 4-8-2 No.703 leaving Sidvokodvo in Swaziland for the mines at Kadake in August 1975, is therefore the reward of very careful planning. The working timetable must be consulted and maps studied to locate east-west stretches of railway line with reasonable access. All this is to no avail, of course, if the train runs behind schedule!

Pentax 6 × 7 200mm Takumar FP4 D76 (1:1)
1/250th second f 6.3.

A classic three-quarter front study of two Hunslet saddle tanks hard at work at Bickershaw Colliery in Lancashire in April 1977. More or less every factor was favourable on this occasion; the superb exhaust was enhanced by cold damp atmospheric conditions and the interesting background, balanced by the spoil heap and the fence on the left, combined to portray steam in action at its best. Although this is a well-worn recipe of numerous railway photographers over the years, careful thought is still required before the shutter is pressed.
At Bickershaw, for example, trains on the system's main line head in a westerly direction for most of their 1½ mile journey; a wise photographer would therefore arrive with his camera in the morning and be certain before he left home that the wind was not in the north. ▶

Pentax 6 × 7 200mm Takumar FP4 D76 (1:1)
1/500th second f 6.3.

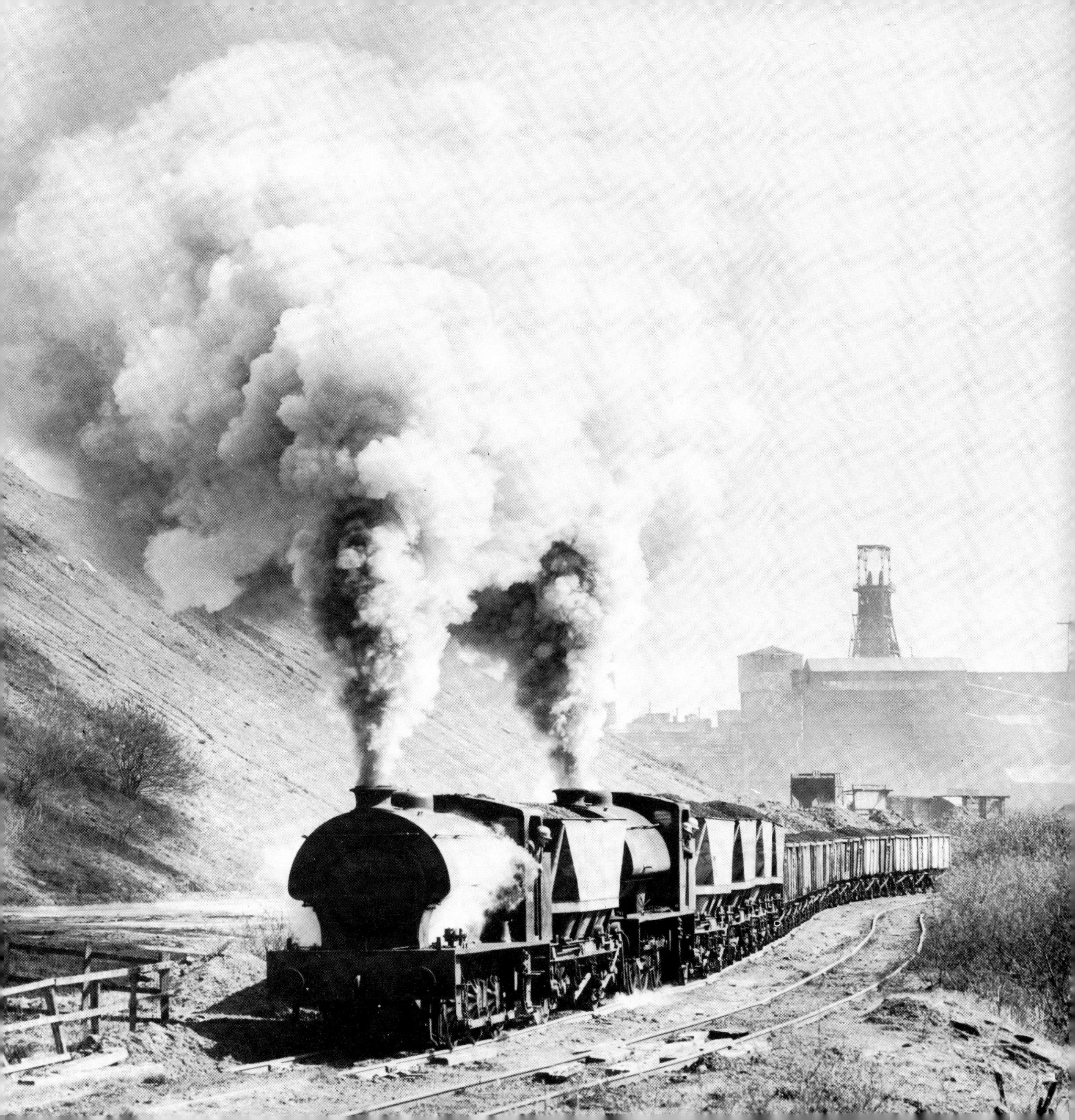

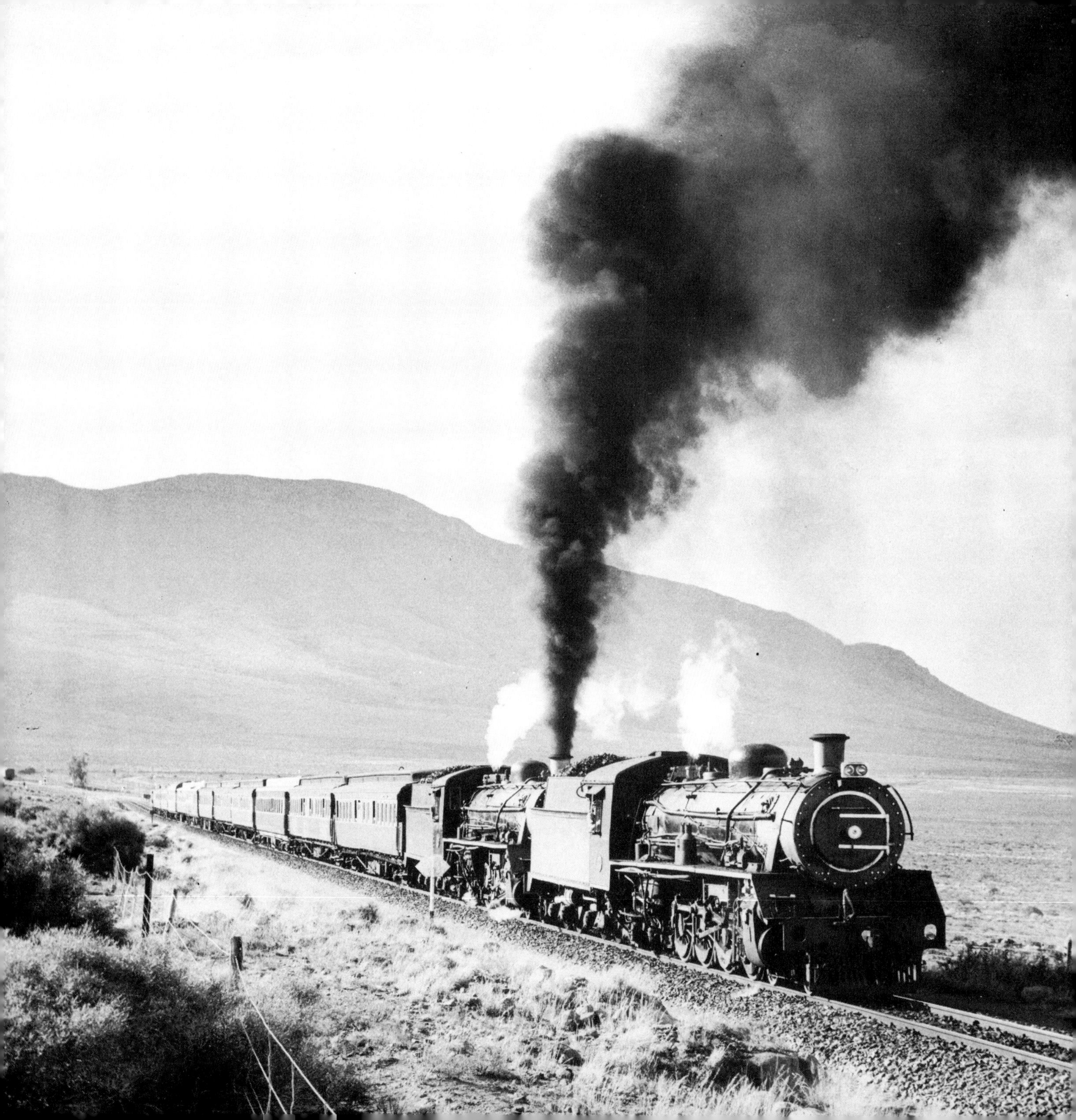

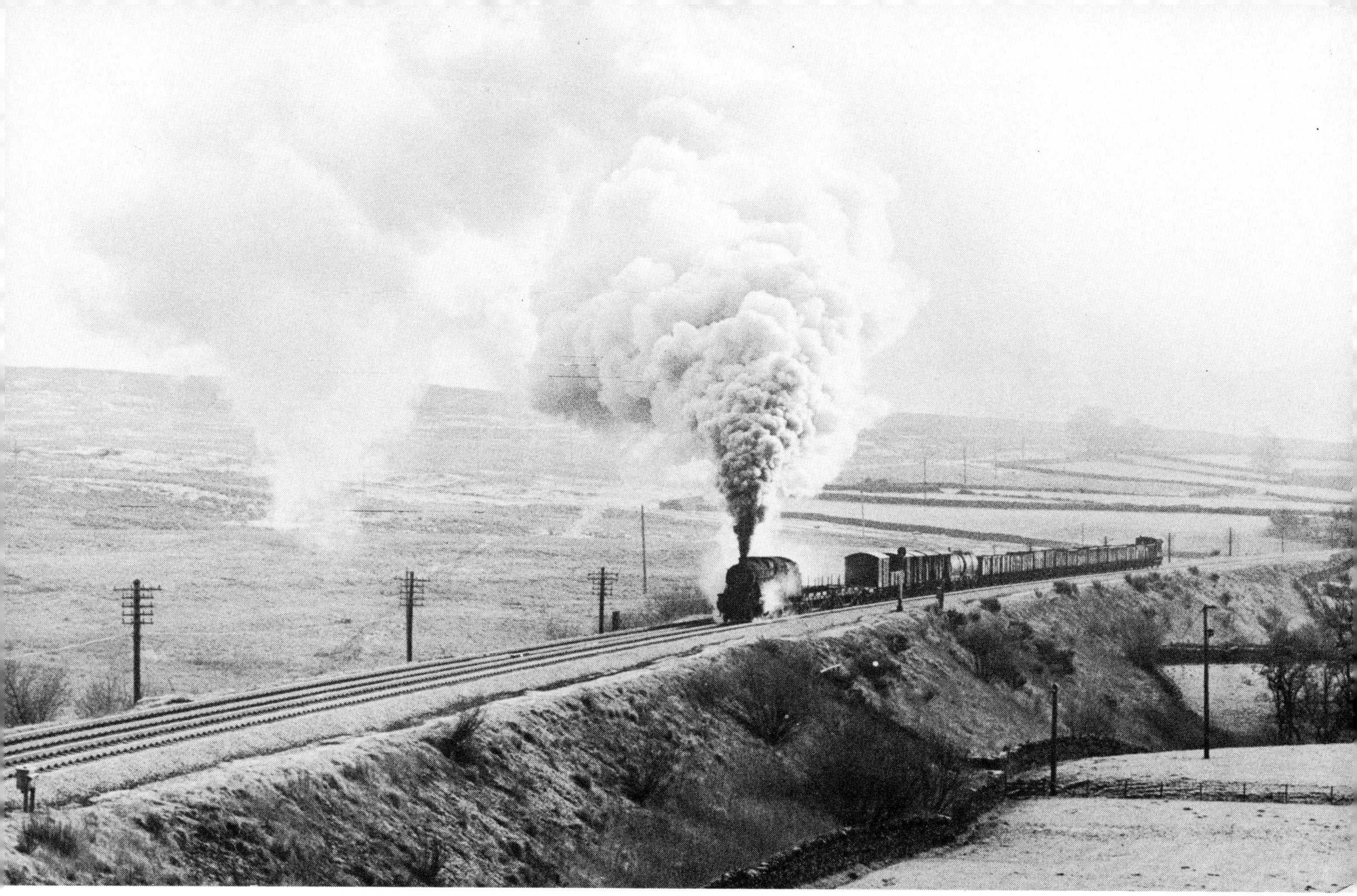

◀ South Africa offers the lineside photographer some of the best locations and, in winter, some of the best weather for photography. Away from the industrial area centred on Johannesburg exceptionally clear atmospheric conditions exist, especially on the high plateau of the Karoo desert. In these conditions even the most modest 35mm camera, handled competently, will produce an excellent photograph. On this particular day, the photograph would have been much improved if only the pilot locomotive had been producing as much smoke as the one behind. The strong exhaust pattern from the latter tends to divide the picture into two equal halves, contravening the 'rule of thirds' mentioned on page 29.

A pair of Class 19B 4-8-2s of South African Railways climb away from Rooihoogte with Train 1305, the Johannesburg-Mossel Bay express, in August 1970.

Minolta Autocord 6 × 6 FP4 D76 (1:1) 1/500th second f 5.6.

Shap was certainly the Mecca of generations of British railway photographers and it is perhaps appropriate that at least one photograph of this famous bank should be included herein. The last few days of steam operation, in December 1967, coincided with cold clear frosty weather, possibly the best conditions of all for action photography of the steam engine. Condensing steam and smoke backlit by a low sun are the magic ingredients of this scene which contrasts markedly with the present day offering of overhead catenaries and the M6.

Class 8F 2-8-0 No. 48491 climbs unassisted towards Shap summit with a 26 wagon freight on 20 December 1967.

Exakta Varex IIa 80mm Biometer FP4 Acutol 1/500th second f 8.

TRAINS IN THE LANDSCAPE

The Cromford & High Peak Railway traversed bleak, upland limestone country for much of its length. The line was noted for a number of interesting engineering features which included rope-worked inclines, an adhesion-worked gradient of 1 in 14 and the stone embankment at Minninglow. This photograph of a Class J94 0-6-0ST crossing the latter with a water tender and guard's van on an April day in 1966 was taken with an Exakta Varex IIa single lens reflex camera, fitted with a 135mm f 4 Zeiss Sonnar. This modestly priced lens, long since deleted from the Zeiss catalogue, was capable of quite exceptional performance. A recent quality f 2.8 replacement cost almost ten times as much for only a marginal improvement in resolution. One should note that expensive equipment is not an essential prerequisite of good photography; the thoughts and actions of the man behind the camera are much more important.

Exakta Varex IIa 135mm Sonnar FP4 Acutol 1/250th second f 8.

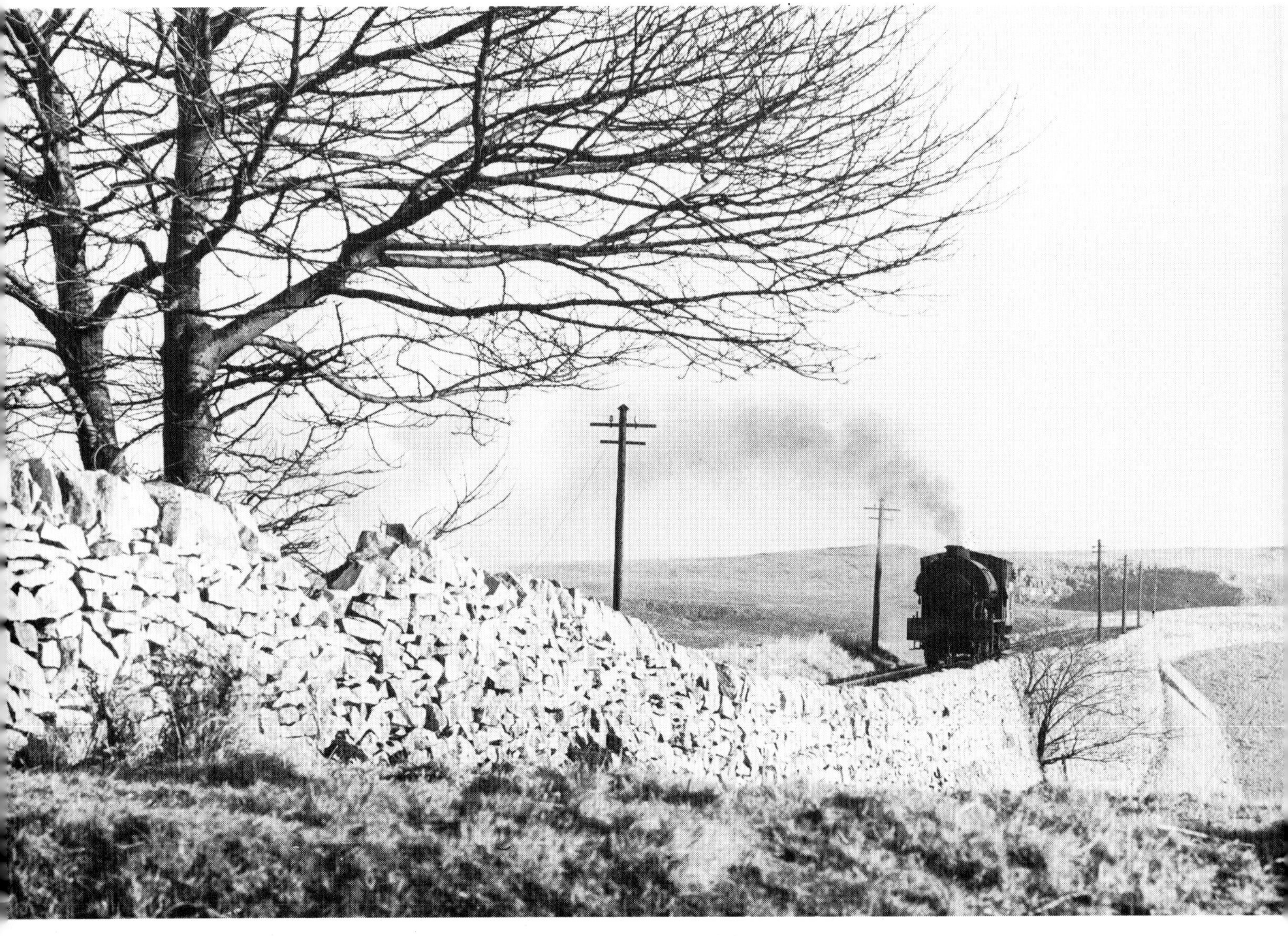

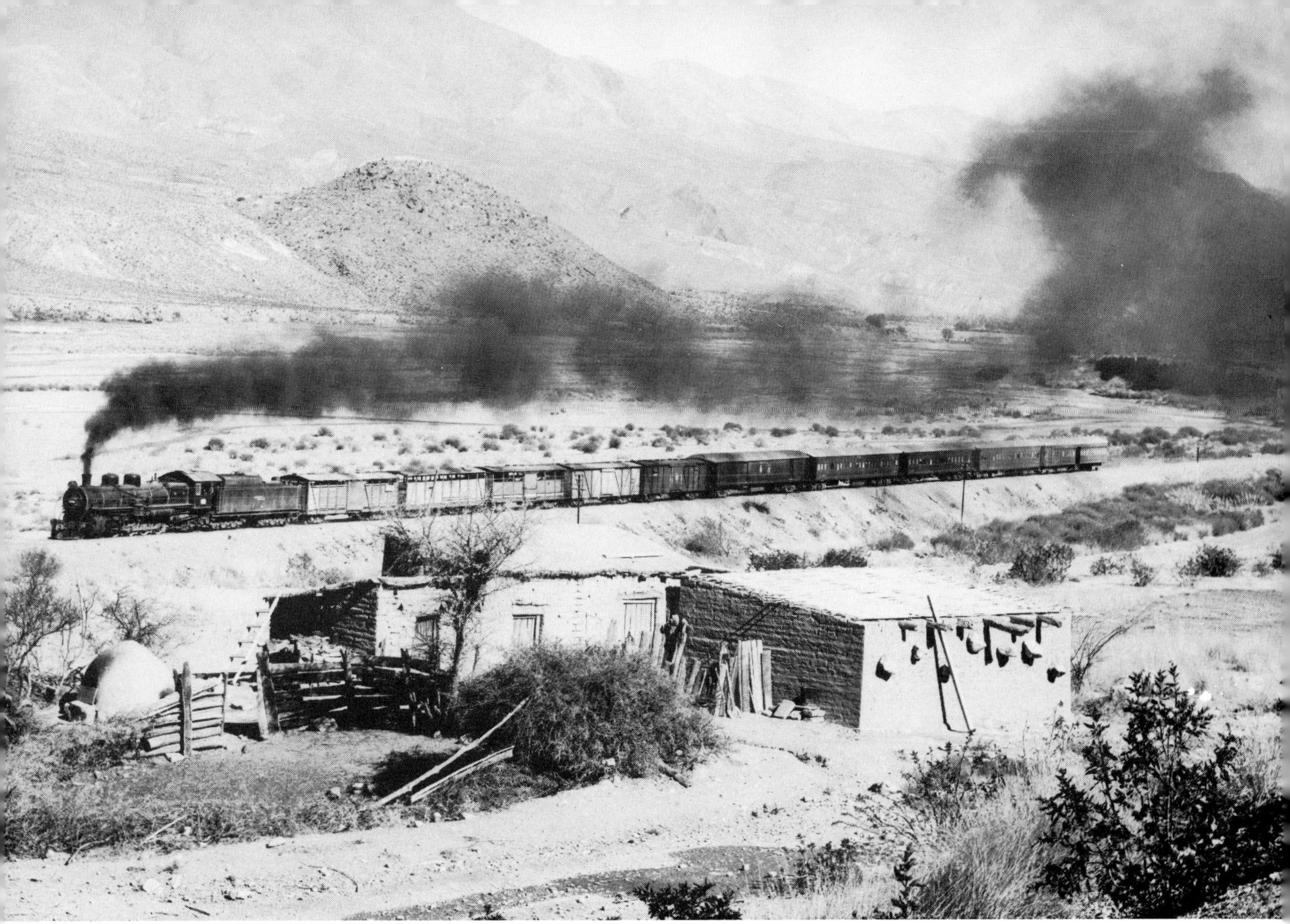

Railway photographers who work in both colour and black-and-white soon encounter the problem of achieving simultaneous exposures in two cameras. Several interesting techniques have been developed by enthusiasts in attempts to solve this difficulty; all require that the cameras be accurately located on a stout metal or wooden frame and that the focal length of the lenses be matched so that both cameras have about the same field of view. Exposures may be effected, with a little practice, by the simultaneous use of both fore-fingers; a procedure which is particularly successful in cases where a camera with a right-hand shutter release is matched with a camera whose shutter release is on the left. Alternatively a double cable release, operated by a single plunger, may be used provided provision is available for the independent adjustment of the throw of each release. Finally an electromagnetic release may be coupled to simple circuitry so that the completion of the flash circuit in one camera triggers the release which is attached to a second camera. The latter procedure was adopted to obtain this photograph; a Pentax 6 × 7 operating as a slave to a Leica M3.

General Belgrano Railway (Argentina) 4-8-2 No.881 hard at work between Volcan and Humahuaca with a mixed train bound for the border with Bolivia at Villazon in August 1976.

Pentax 6 × 7 105mm Takumar FP4 D76 (1:1)
1/500th second f 6.3.

On this page and the frontispiece are two of the finest railway photographic locations I have been fortunate enough to visit; both feature the ultimate in a snow-covered mountain backdrop. The treatment is entirely traditional in that a classic three-quarter front study of both subjects was selected. The photograph forming the frontispiece, of a diesel hauled Lima to Huancayo express on the Central Railway of Peru, was taken at an altitude of 14,000 feet. Oxygen was being administered to many of the passengers while the photographer was busy selecting the best vantage point. The air is so thin at this height that walking any distance, let alone in deep snow, requires considerable physical effort. No doubt a better viewpoint was to be had from a spot on the mountainside overlooking the train, but for once matter triumphed over mind! Photography in extremely bright snow-scapes such as these requires careful attention to technique; accurate assessment of exposure is particularly hazardous. An exposure meter will tend to give bizarre readings designed to afford perfectly exposed highlights which, of course, will invariably be open expanses of sunlit snow. In black-and-white photography it is best to be rather generous with exposure, for example overexposure by about one stop, *but* to make 15-20 per cent reduction in development time. The result should be a perfect negative with average contrast and plenty of shadow detail which will print well on soft (Grade 1 or 2) printing paper. In colour, slight overexposure vis-à-vis the exposure meter reading is also recommended, as a rough guide compromise between the exposure required for the sky and that required for the snow highlights.

Turkish Railways 4-8-2 No.46229 heads the 07.40 Erlazig to Tatvan mixed train near Murat on 1 April 1975.

Minolta Autocord 6 × 6 75mm Rokkor FP4 D76 (1:1) 1/500th second f 5.6.

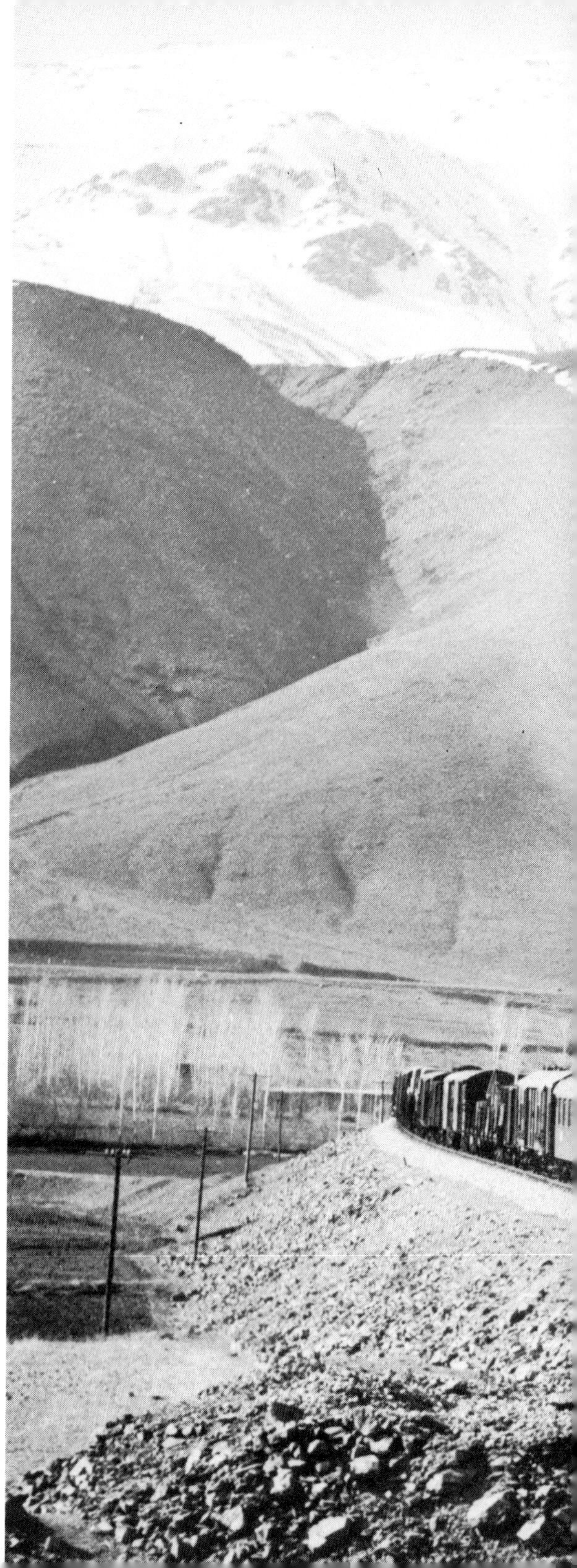

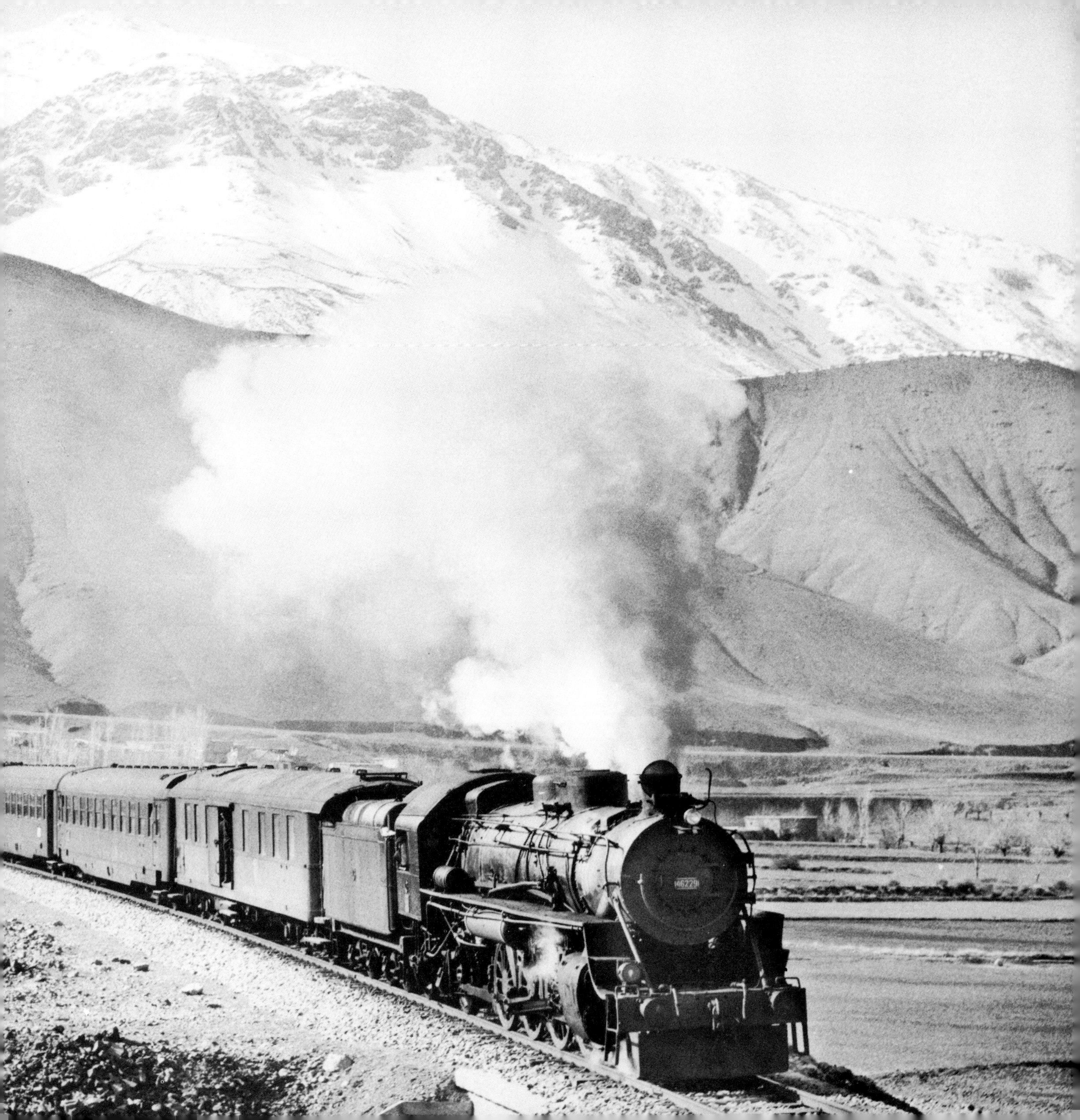

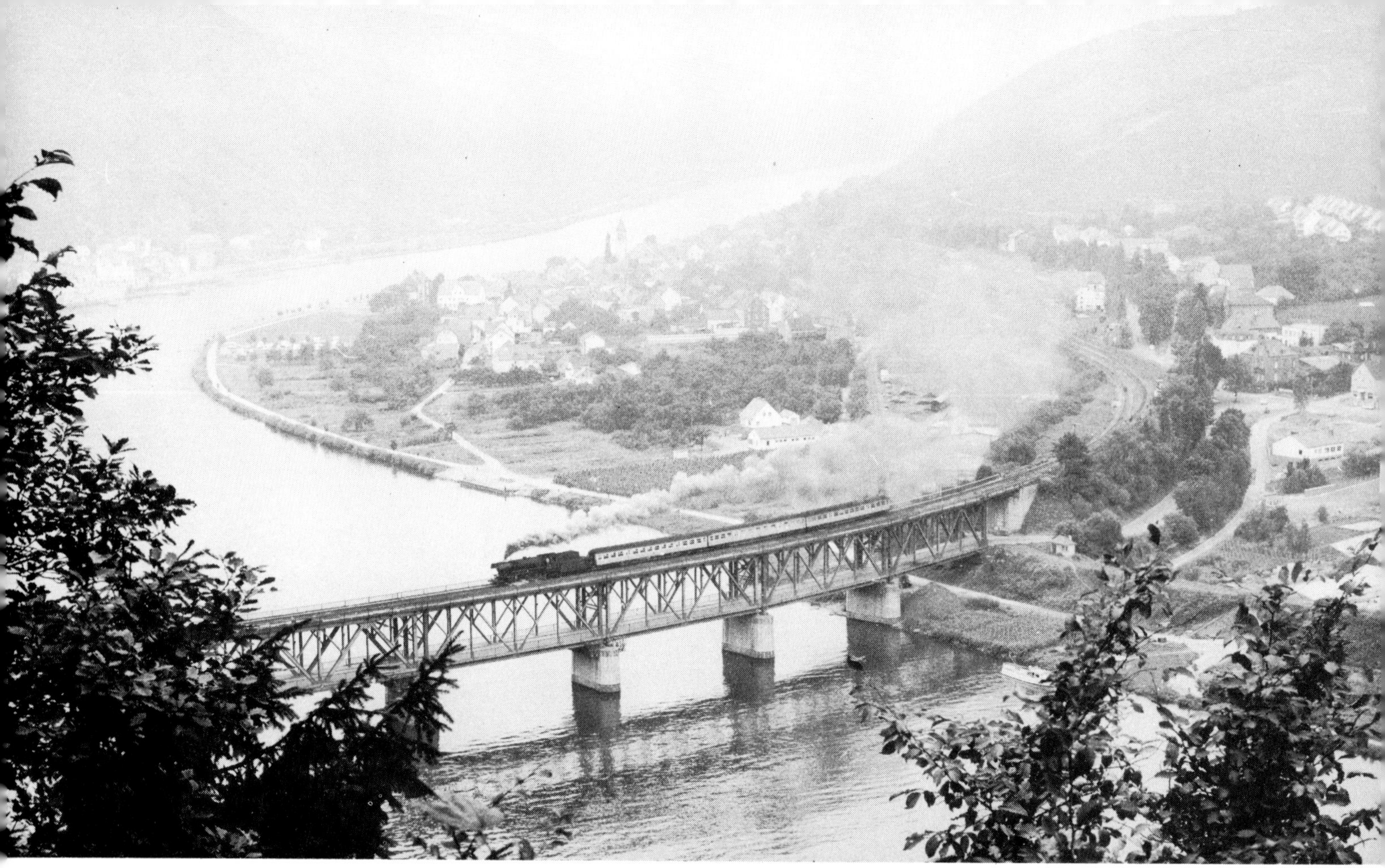

Railway photographers are naturally attracted by bridges and impressive viaducts but they can be difficult to photograph effectively. A common feature of design is the provision of extensive superstructure or a retaining parapet or metal lattice fence at the trackside which extends upwards by as much as two or three metres. Both serve to partially hide the outline of the locomotive and rolling stock if a photograph is attempted at, or below, rail level. The selection of a viewpoint overlooking the bridge is one obvious solution to the problem, as shown in this view of a West German Railways Class 23 2-6-0 crossing the River Mosselle at Bullay. It will also be noted that the train itself forms only a small part of the scene but the eye is immediately attracted by the prominent exhaust. A monochrome photograph of a diesel-hauled train at this location would not be as successful. In colour however, the eye-catching maroon livery of a DB V200 diesel-hydraulic would achieve the same effect as the exhaust from a steam locomotive.

Minolta Autocord 6 × 6 75mm Rokkor Tri-X D76 (1:1) 1/250th second f 6.3.

No reference has yet been made to the suitability of wide angle lenses for railway photography. Generally there are but few applications for a really short focal length objective; one has been resident in my equipment case for many years but the number of occasions where it has earned its keep could be counted on one hand. Wide angle lenses are however particularly valuable when photographing trains in narrow valleys set between mountains. A standard lens (defined as one which has a focal length equal to the diagonal length of the negative) was used for this photograph of a train climbing the Khyber Pass in Pakistan. It was only just possible to include the whole of the bridge and the top of the mountain in the field of view. ▶

Pakistan Railways Class SGS 0-6-0s Nos. 2487 and 2369 climb the Khyber Pass near Shaghai with the weekly Peshawar Cantonment to Landi Kotal mixed on 12 January 1979.

Pentax 6 × 7 105mm Takumar FP4 D76 (1:1) 1/250th second f 5.6.

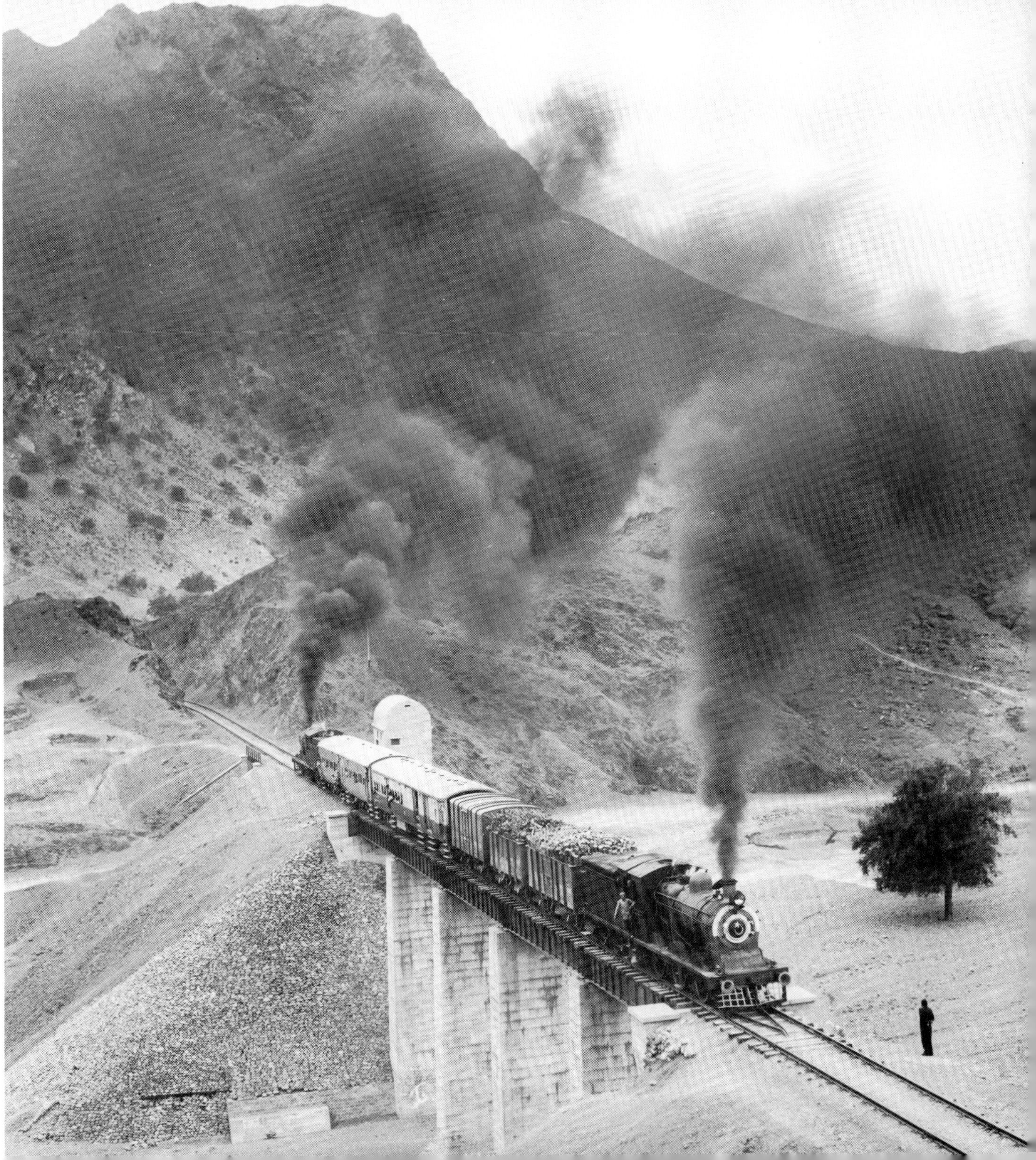

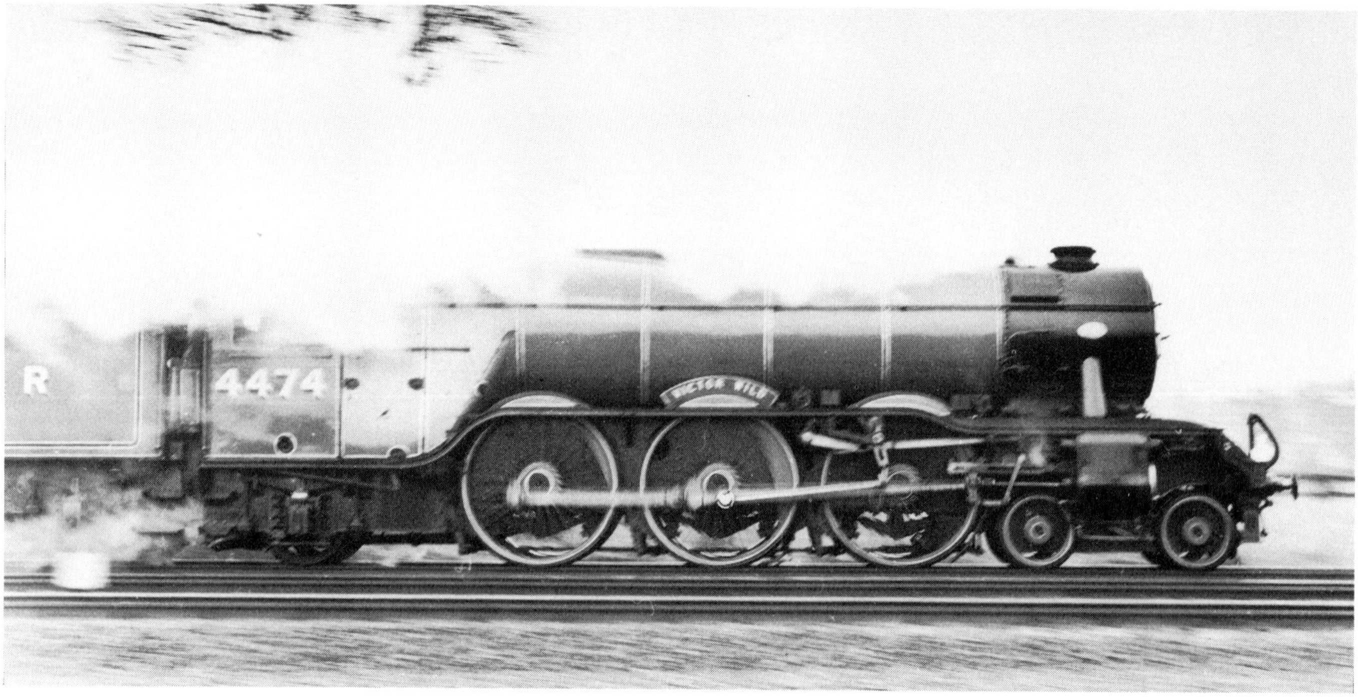
4474

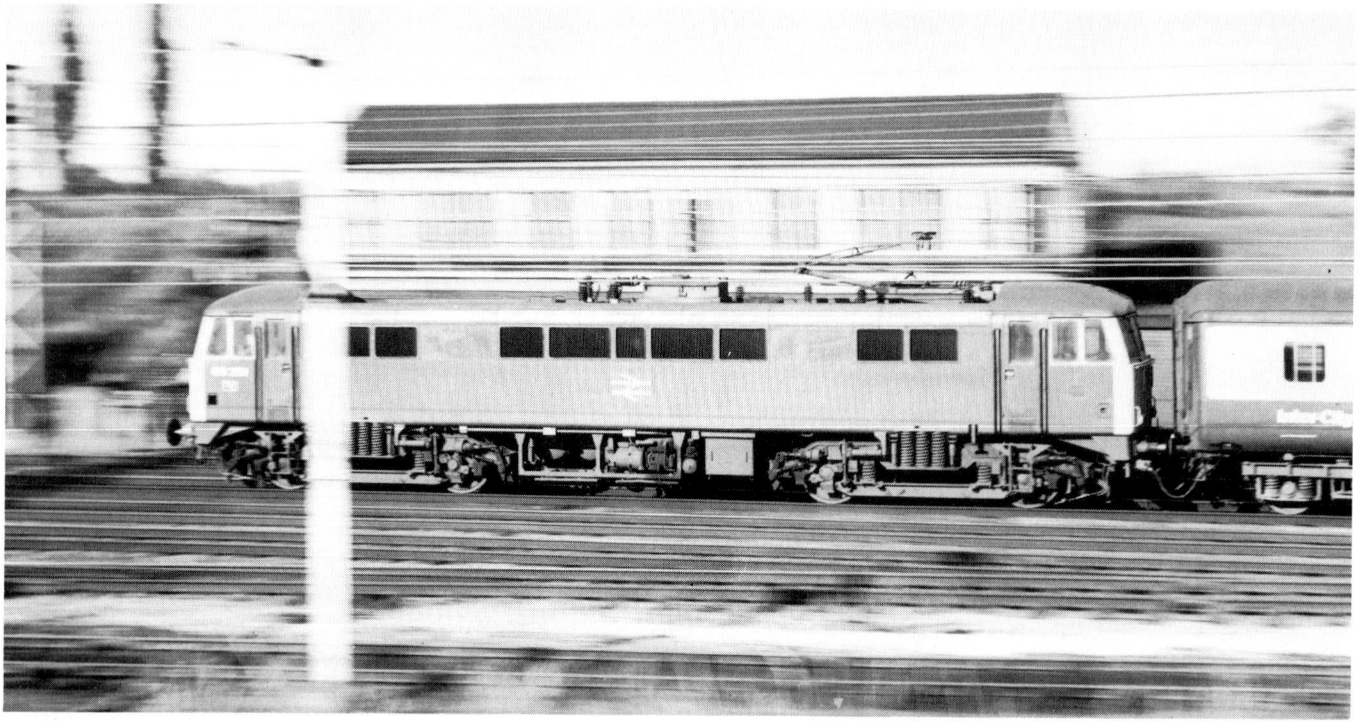

◀ Panned photographs of moving objects are, in theory, easy to obtain. A slow shutter speed. 1/30th or 1/60th second, is selected and the shutter released while the camera is moved with a swinging motion following the subject. Parallel, sympathetic movement is absolutely essential otherwise no part of the negative will be critically sharp. Inspection of the nameplate in the photograph opposite clearly shows that the optimum result was not obtained. The camera was panned such that slight effective upward or downward movement of the camera occurred while the shutter was open. Since the normal focal plane shutter travels from right to left during exposure it is rather more difficult to obtain good pan shots of subjects travelling in the opposite direction with respect to the shutter movement, because under these conditions the subject is moving sympathetically with the shutter gap.

Flying Scotsman, masquerading as No.4474 *Victor Wild,* at speed near York on 26 November 1977.

Pentax 6 × 7   105mm Takumar   Tri-X   Perceptol (1:1)   1/30th second   f 16.

The technique is almost perfect in the photograph (below left) of Class 86 No.86 251 passing Basford Hall Junction signal box but the photographer, while concentrating upon the technicalities, forgot the catenary support in the left foreground.

Pentax 6 × 7   105mm Takumar   FP4   D76 (1:1) 1/60th second   f 16.

When photographing fast-moving trains a common difficulty experienced by newcomers to the hobby is deciding exactly when to release the shutter. Many will find a tendency to fire much too early with the result that the train occupies only a very small portion of the negative. When working in black-and-white the problem may be resolved at the printing stage by selective enlargement but clearly print quality will be less than ideal. In colour, 35mm transparencies may require masking to a size approaching half frame (18 × 24mm) in order to obtain compositional satisfaction. There is no easy answer to the problem, but practice and the careful analysis of results should improve matters considerably. One dodge which may help is to place a small marker, for example a piece of card, at the position where the leading part of the train is ideally required in the photograph. Remember however that an inevitable short delay occurs between visual detection and the actual release of the shutter. This is evident in this photograph of No.4472 *Flying Scotsman* leaving Skipton for Leeds on 26 November 1977. By the time the exposure was actually made the exhaust was, unfortunately, just beginning to obscure part of the signal gantry.

Pentax 6 × 7   105mm Takumar   Tri-X   Perceptol (1:1)   1/500th second   f 5.6.

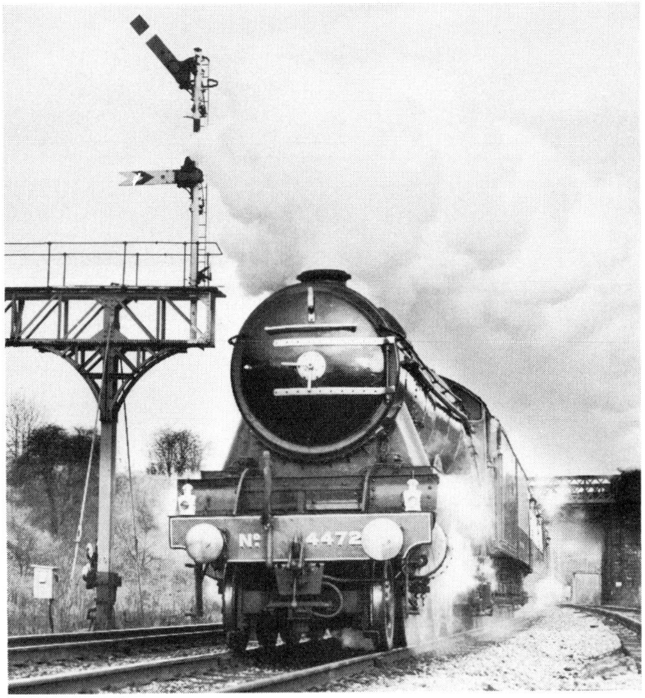

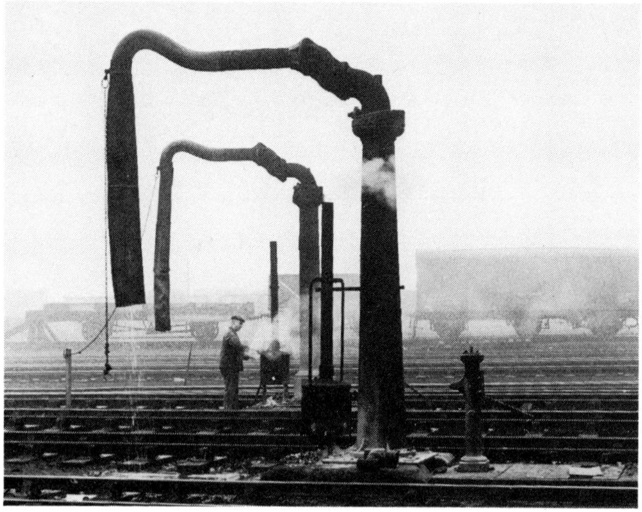

A once-familiar scene at locomotive sheds all over the country is characterised by this view in November 1966 of south end of Doncaster shed. Note how the focal point of interest is framed by the stove and the water column which, in turn, is further framed and repeated by the nearer assembly. There is, compositionally, a strong argument for presenting this photograph with a one inch trim from the right hand side but rolling stock enthusiasts would argue that all of the interesting six-wheel van should be included.

Exakta Varex IIa 50mm Pancolar FP4 Acutol
1/125th second f 4.5.

Is a locomotive or train an essential prerequisite of a ▶ railway photograph? Many photographers find much of interest in the general railway scene; complicated junctions, stations and viaducts immediately come to mind, while another speciality emerging from the recent, post-Beeching era has been the documentation of the remains of abandoned and lifted lines. Although this may be regarded as a specialised aspect of the hobby, the basic rules of composition as detailed on pages 29-30 apply, particularly where the photography of inanimate subjects is concerned. Conversely, the photographer has plenty of time to assess the relative merits of a variety of viewpoints and, if necessary, even wait for the best lighting conditions; thus there is little excuse for technical mediocrity. This view on the right, of a freight being hump shunted at Tinsley yard, was the reward of ten minutes' careful observation. The contrasting vertical and horizontal lines were immediately visually appealing, but at the same time it was realised that the composition would be improved by the presence of complementing curves. Oil tankers filled the bill admirably, and it was a case of waiting until three of them were shunted over the hump together. A minor criticism is perhaps the unfortunate way in which a pylon appears to emerge from the top of the nearer tanker. It was impossible to ensure that the three tankers were clear of all pylons at the moment of exposure.

Pentax 6 × 7 200mm Takumar Tri-X D76 (1:1)
1/500th second f 8/11.

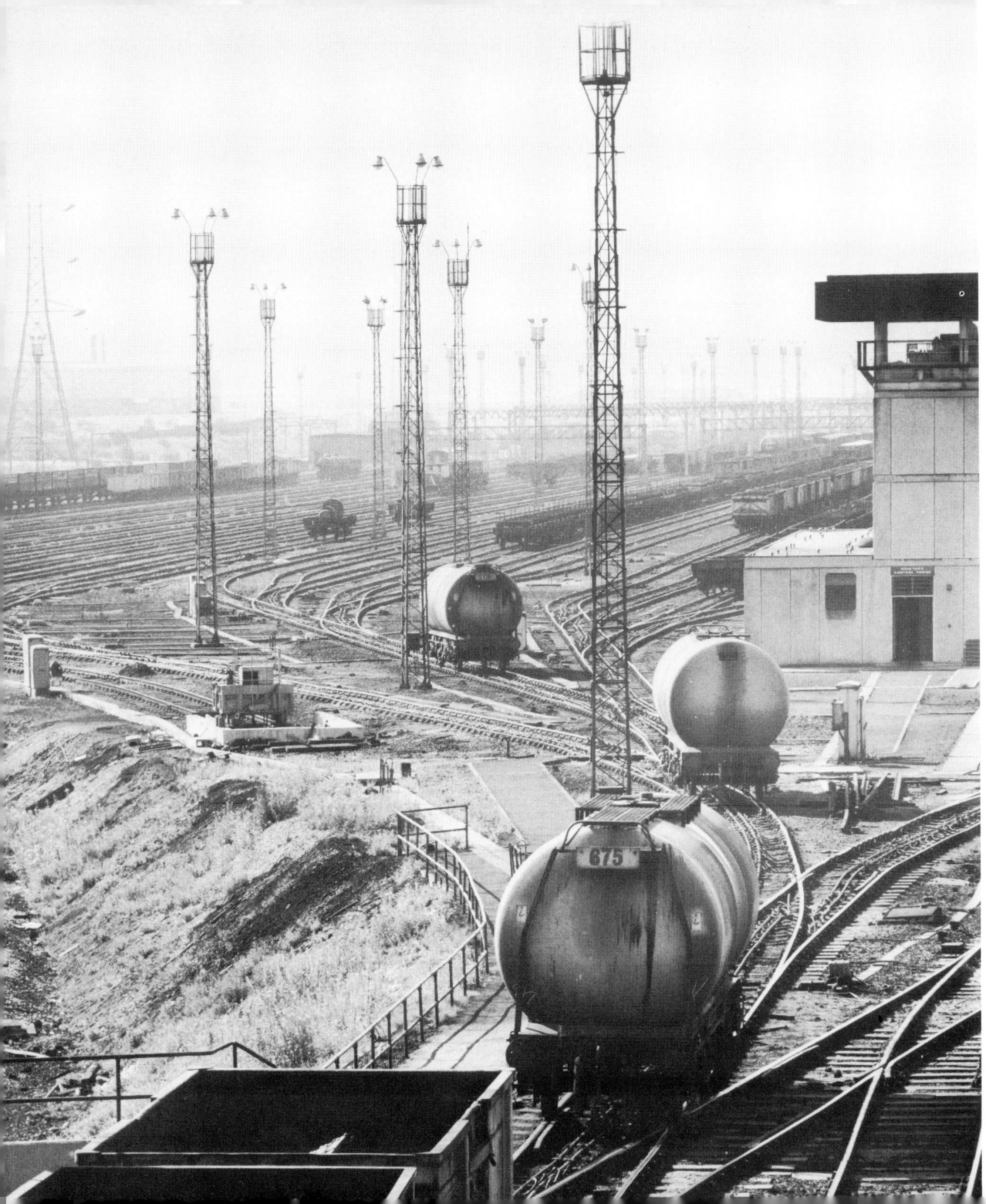
675

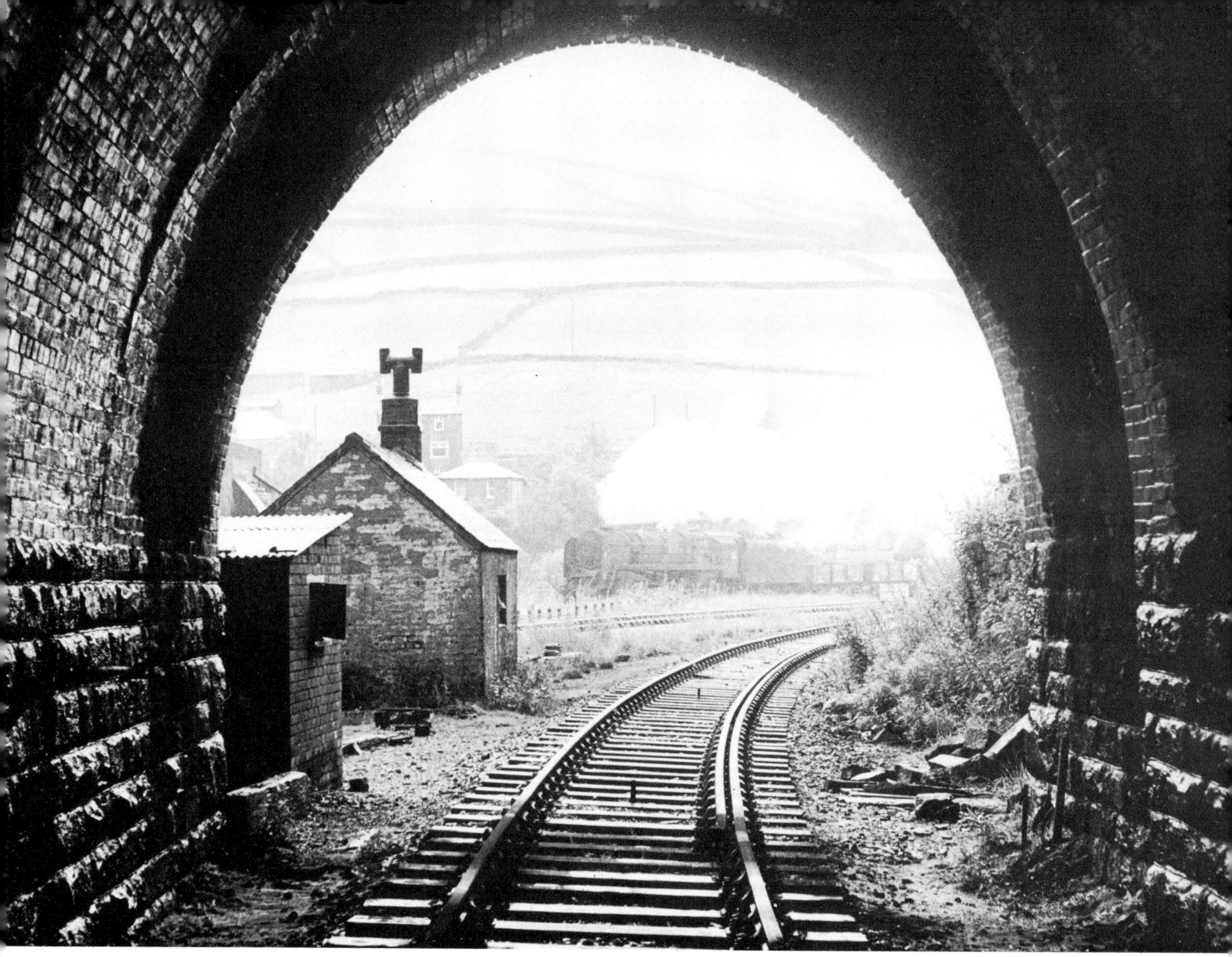

On a dull day, rain is arguably the photographer's best friend. Wet carriage roofs, track and lineside bric-à-brac reflect the available light in a multitude of ways, bringing the picture to life while conditions of high humidity will also encourage much more interesting smoke effects from steam hauled trains. Exposure is critical. The aim should be to provide for just enough light to adequately record shadow detail in the darkest part of the negative. Temptations to give just a little more for luck will often result in burnt-out highlights, particularly with slow emulsion black-and-white films. On those rare occasions when the sun shines immediately after a shower of rain the technique which will afford the optimum result is slight overexposure and a 10 per cent reduction in development. Here the most southerly of the Standedge tunnels provides shelter from the pouring rain as a Class 9F 2-10-0 climbs towards the 1894 double track bore with a freight bound for Lancashire. Incidentally, this would normally be a very dangerous, and indeed unlawful, place to wander with a camera; in fact this line had been abandoned, but not lifted, when this photograph was taken in 1966.

Exakta Varex IIa 80mm Biometer FP4 Acutol
1/125th second f 5.6.

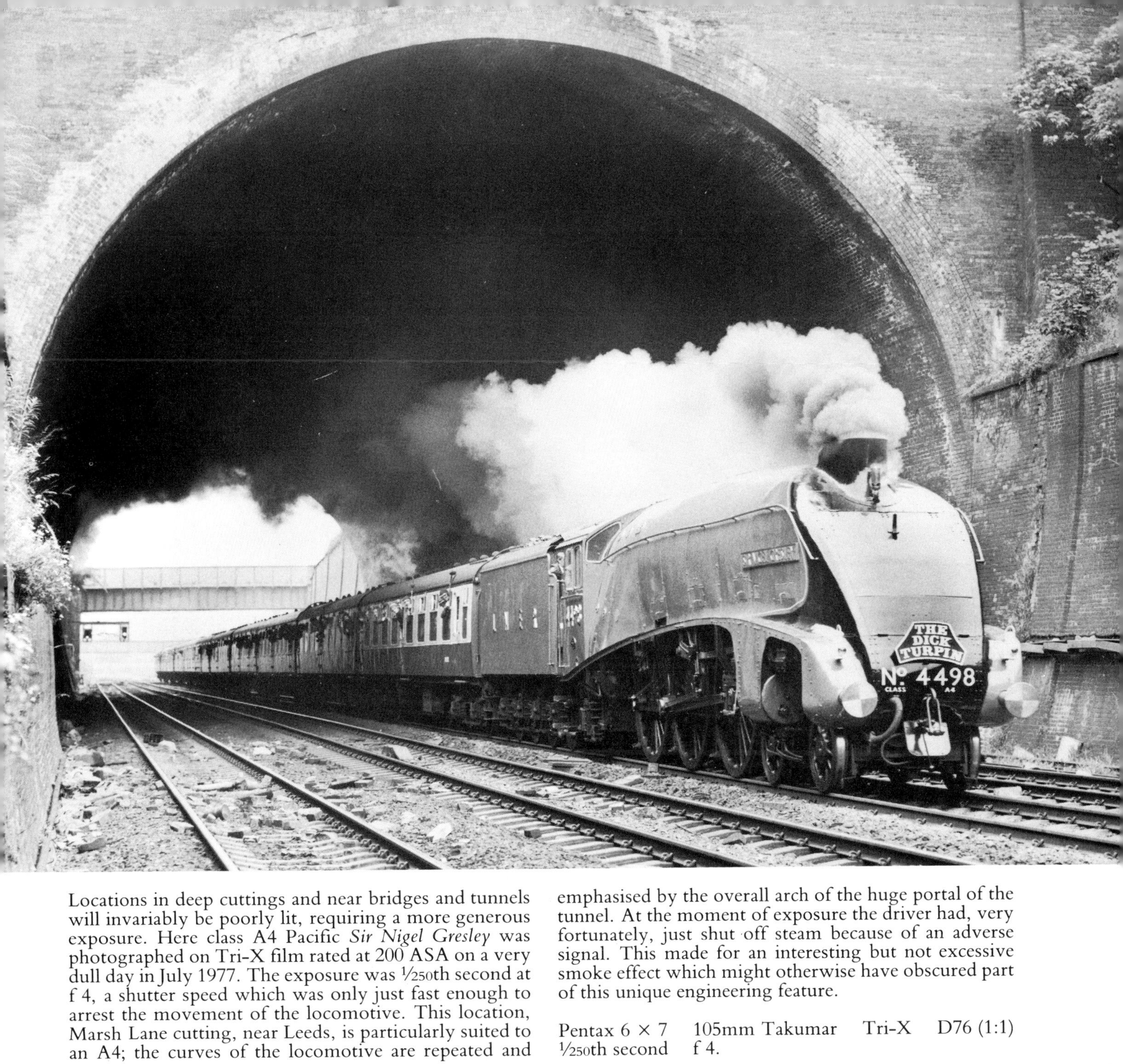

Locations in deep cuttings and near bridges and tunnels will invariably be poorly lit, requiring a more generous exposure. Here class A4 Pacific *Sir Nigel Gresley* was photographed on Tri-X film rated at 200 ASA on a very dull day in July 1977. The exposure was 1/250th second at f 4, a shutter speed which was only just fast enough to arrest the movement of the locomotive. This location, Marsh Lane cutting, near Leeds, is particularly suited to an A4; the curves of the locomotive are repeated and emphasised by the overall arch of the huge portal of the tunnel. At the moment of exposure the driver had, very fortunately, just shut off steam because of an adverse signal. This made for an interesting but not excessive smoke effect which might otherwise have obscured part of this unique engineering feature.

Pentax 6 × 7 105mm Takumar Tri-X D76 (1:1)
1/250th second f 4.

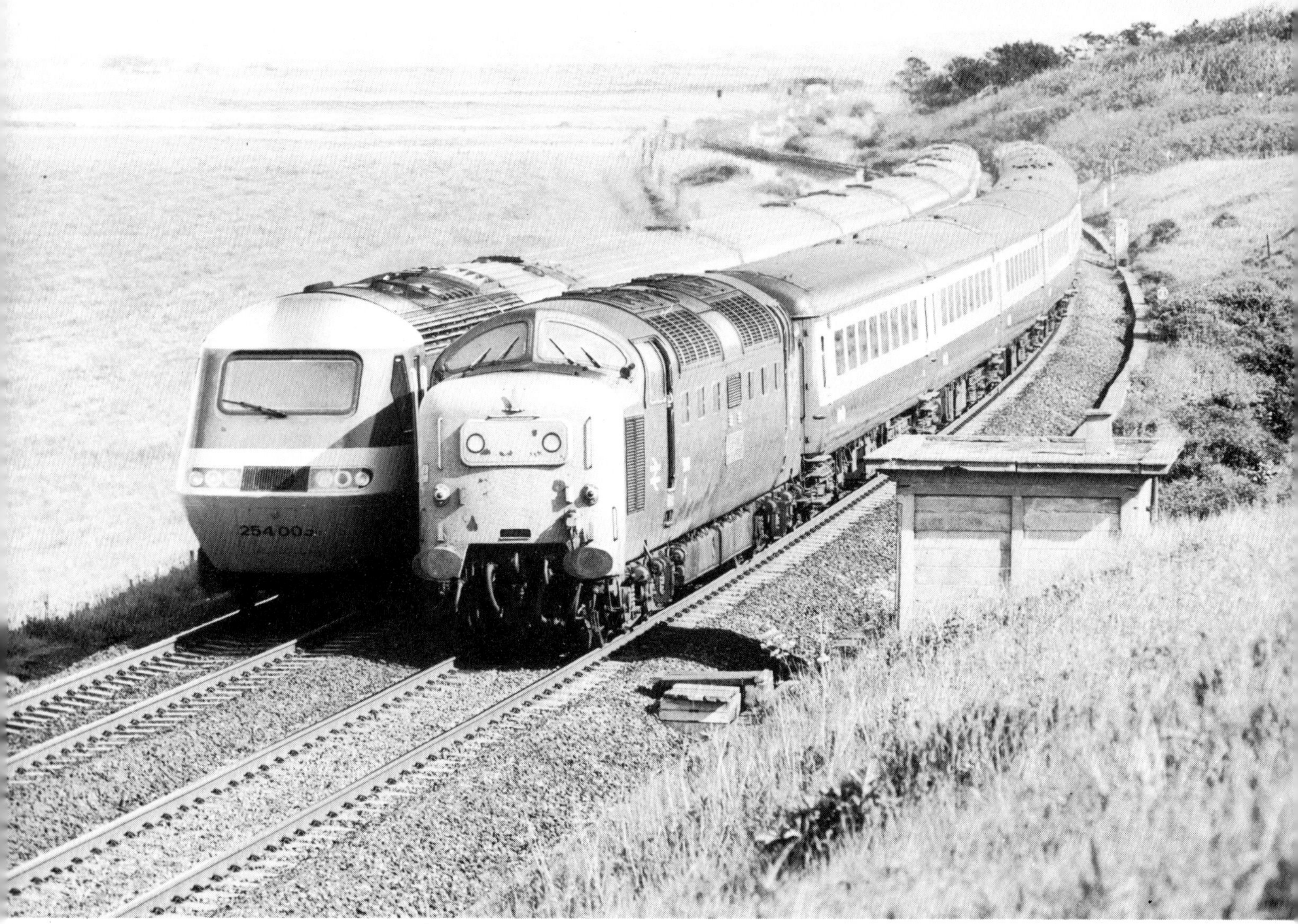

Opportunities for photographs often arise suddenly and it is essential that an automatic routine is developed so that in the short time available the photographer is free to concentrate on the subject instead of worrying about lens settings and exposures. In this photograph, the initial objective was a conventional three-quarter front view of Deltic No.55010 *Kings Own Scottish Borderer* approaching Scremeston signalbox south of Berwick with a down express. The simultaneous approach of a train in the up direction and the immediate realisation that High Speed Trains, along with diesel multiple units, photograph well in a 'going away' situation was quickly translated into a unique passing picture. At an estimated closing speed of 150 m.p.h. the two trains, relative to each other, were travelling at 220ft per second.

Pentax 6 × 7 200mm Takumar Tri-X Perceptol (1:1) 1/500th second f 8.